SATYAGRAHA IN SOUTH AFRICA

CENT PER CENT SWADESHI
THE REMOVAL OF UNTOUCHABILITY
FOOD SHORTAGE AND AGRICULTURE
HOW TO SERVE THE COW
BASIC EDUCATION
KHADI—WHY AND HOW
UNTO THIS LAST: A PARAPHRASE
TRUTH IS GOD
WOMEN AND SOCIAL INJUSTICE
KEY TO HEALTH
ECONOMIC AND INDUSTRIAL LIFE AND RELATIONS
FROM YERAVDA MANDIR: ASHRAM OBSERVANCES
ASHRAM OBSERVANCES IN ACTION
CHRISTIAN MISSIONS—THEIR PLACE IN INDIA
DISCOURSES ON THE GITA
MY RELIGION
WHAT JESUS MEANS TO ME
RAMANAMA
HINDU SWARAJ
UNTO THIS LAST
THE MORAL BASIS OF VEGETARIANISM
SATYAGRAHA
MY DIARY
CONSTRUCTIVE PROGRAMME
GO-SEVA
COMMUNISM AND COMMUNISTS
BREAD LABOUR
SELECTED WORKS OF MAHATMA GANDHI
GANDHI & INTERNATIONAL POLITICS
PATHWAY TO GOD

BY THE SAME AUTHOR

AUTOBIOGRAPHY
TRUTH IS GOD
NON-VIOLENCE IN PEACE AND WAR
SELF-RESTRAINT *V.* SELF-INDULGENCE
CENT PER CENT SWADESHI
THE REMOVAL OF UNTOUCHABILITY
FOOD SHORTAGE AND AGRICULTURE
HOW TO SERVE THE COW
BASIC EDUCATION
KHADI—WHY AND HOW
REBUILDING OUR VILLAGES
VILLAGE INDUSTRIES
WOMEN AND SOCIAL INJUSTICE
KEY TO HEALTH
ECONOMIC AND INDUSTRIAL LIFE AND RELATIONS
FROM YERAVDA MANDIR—ASHRAM OBSERVANCES
ASHRAM OBSERVANCES IN ACTION
CHRISTIAN MISSIONS—THEIR PLACE IN INDIA
DISCOURSES ON THE GITA
MY RELIGION
WHAT JESUS MEANS TO ME
RAMANAMA
HIND SWARAJ
UNTO THIS LAST
THE MORAL BASIS OF VEGETARIANISM
SATYAGRAHA
DELHI DIARY
CONSTRUCTIVE PROGRAMME
MY SOCIALISM
COMMUNISM AND COMMUNISTS
BREAD LABOUR
SELECTED WORKS OF MAHATMA GANDHI
GANDHI & INTERNATIONAL POLITICS
PATHWAY TO GOD

To
MAGANLAL K. GANDHI

SATYAGRAHA IN SOUTH AFRICA

M. K. GANDHI

TRANSLATED FROM THE GUJARATI
by
VALJI GOVINDJI DESAI

**NAVAJIVAN PUBLISHING HOUSE
AHMEDABAD 14**

Rupees Twenty

© Navajivan Trust, 1928

First Edition, 1928
Revised Second Edition, December 1950
Sixth Reprint, 2,000 Copies, April 2001

Price of this book is
subsidised by Navajivan Trust

ISBN 81-7229-041-1

Printed and Published by
Jitendra T. Desai
Navajivan Mudranalaya
Ahmedabad-380 014
INDIA

FOREWORD

Shri Valji Desai's translation has been revised by me, and I can assure the reader that the spirit of the original in Gujarati has been very faithfully kept by the translator. The original chapters were all written by me from memory. They were written partly in the Yeravda jail and partly outside after my premature release. As the translator knew of this fact, he made a diligent study of the file of *Indian Opinion* and whenever he discovered slips of memory, he has not hesitated to make the necessary corrections. The reader will share my pleasure that in no relevant or material particular has there been any slip. I need hardly mention that those who are following the weekly chapters of *My Experiments with Truth* cannot afford to miss these chapters on Satyagraha, if they would follow in all its detail the working out of the search after Truth.

M. K. GANDHI

Sabarmati
26th April, 1928

TRANSLATOR'S NOTE

(Second edition)

This is a reprint of the first edition except for some verbal alterations suggested by my friend Shri Verrier Elwin who was good enough to go through the translation at my request.

V. G. D.

St 2006 Bhadrapad krishna 6

(Third impression)

I take this opportunity to place on record my indebtedness to Shri C. F. Andrews, Shri Dattatraya Balkrishna Kalelkar and Shri Abhechand Govindji Desai who made helpful suggestions when I was doing the first few chapters.

V. G. D.

St 2017 Ashadha krishna 5

CONTENTS

CHAPTER		PAGE
	FOREWORD	vii
	TRANSLATOR'S NOTE	viii
	PREFACE	xi
I	GEOGRAPHY	3
II	HISTORY	7
III	INDIANS ENTER SOUTH AFRICA	19
IV	A REVIEW OF THE GRIEVANCES (*Natal*)	24
V	A REVIEW OF THE GRIEVANCES (*The Transvaal and other Colonies*)	29
VI	A REVIEW OF THE EARLY STRUGGLE	35
VII	A REVIEW OF THE EARLY STRUGGLE (*continued*)	45
VIII	A REVIEW OF THE EARLY STRUGGLE (*concluded*)—*The Work in England*	60
IX	THE BOER WAR	62
X	AFTER THE WAR	74
XI	THE REWARD OF GENTLENESS—THE BLACK ACT	89
XII	THE ADVENT OF SATYAGRAHA	95
XIII	SATYAGRAHA *v.* PASSIVE RESISTANCE	103
XIV	DEPUTATION TO ENGLAND	108
XV	CROOKED POLICY	115
XVI	AHMAD MUHAMMAD KACHHALIA	118
XVII	A RIFT IN THE LUTE	125
XVIII	THE FIRST SATYAGRAHI PRISONER	128
XIX	'INDIAN OPINION'	131
XX	A SERIES OF ARRESTS	134
XXI	THE FIRST SETTLEMENT	142
XXII	OPPOSITION AND ASSAULT	145
XXIII	EUROPEAN SUPPORT	160
XXIV	FURTHER INTERNAL DIFFICULTIES	169
XXV	GENERAL SMUTS' BREACH OF FAITH(?)	173
XXVI	RESUMPTION OF THE STRUGGLE	182
XXVII	A BONFIRE OF CERTIFICATES	185

XXVIII	CHARGE OF FORCING FRESH ISSUE	188
XXIX	SORABJI SHAPURJI ADAJANIA	192
XXX	SHETH DAUD MAHOMED ETC. ENTER THE STRUGGLE	197
XXXI	DEPORTATIONS	202
XXXII	A SECOND DEPUTATION	207
XXXIII	TOLSTOY FARM—I	212
XXXIV	TOLSTOY FARM—II	215
XXXV	TOLSTOY FARM—III	221
XXXVI	GOKHALE'S TOUR	236
XXXVII	GOKHALE'S TOUR (concluded)	243
XXXVIII	BREACH OF PLEDGE	247
XXXIX	WHEN MARRIAGE IS NOT A MARRIAGE	251
XL	WOMEN IN JAIL	257
XLI	A STREAM OF LABOURERS	260
XLII	THE CONFERENCE AND AFTER	265
XLIII	CROSSING THE BORDER	270
XLIV	THE GREAT MARCH	274
XLV	ALL IN PRISON	278
XLVI	THE TEST	285
XLVII	THE BEGINNING OF THE END	290
XLVIII	THE PROVISIONAL SETTLEMENT	296
XLIX	LETTERS EXCHANGED	299
L	THE END OF THE STRUGGLE	303
	CONCLUSION	306
	INDEX	308

PREFACE

The Satyagraha struggle of the Indians in South Africa lasted eight years. The term *Satyagraha* was invented and employed in connection therewith. I had long entertained a desire to write a history of that struggle myself. Some things only I could write. Only the general who conducts a campaign can know the objective of each particular move. And as this was the first attempt to apply the principle of Satyagraha to politics on a large scale, it is necessary any day that the public should have an idea of its development.

But today Satyagraha has had ample scope in India. Here there has been an inevitable series of struggles beginning with the rather local question of the Viramgam customs.

It was through the instrumentality of Bhai Motilal, the public-spirited good tailor of Vadhvan, that I became interested in the Viramgam question. I had just arrived from England and was proceeding to Saurashtra in the year 1915. I was travelling third class. At Vadhvan station Motilal came up to me with a small party. He gave me some account of the hardships inflicted on the people at Viramgam, and said:

"Please do something to end this trouble. It will be doing an immense service to Saurashtra, the land of your birth."

There was an expression of both compassion and firmness in his eyes.

"Are you ready to go to jail?" I asked.

"We are ready to march to the gallows," was the quick reply.

"Jail will do for me," I said. "But see that you do not leave me in the lurch."

"That only time can show," said Motilal.

I reached Rajkot, obtained detailed information and commenced correspondence with Government. In speeches at Bagasra and elsewhere, I dropped a hint that the people should be ready to offer Satyagraha at Viramgam if necessary. The loyal C. I. D. brought these speeches to the notice of Government. In this they served Government and unintentionally, served the people also. Finally, I had a talk with Lord Chelmsford on the matter. He promised abolition of the customs line and was as good as his word. I know others also tried for this. But I am strongly of opinion that the imminent possibility of Satyagraha was the chief factor in obtaining the desired redress.

Then came the Indian Emigration Act. Great efforts were put forth to get indenture repealed. There was a considerable public agitation. The Bombay meeting fixed May 31, 1917 as the date from which onwards indentured labour should be stopped. This is not the place for narrating how that particular date came to be selected. A deputation of ladies first waited upon the Viceroy in connection with this. I cannot help mentioning here the name of the high-souled sister, Mrs Jaiji Petit. It was she who may be said to have organized this deputation. Here, too, success came merely through preparedness for Satyagraha. But it is important to remember the distinction that in this case public agitation was also necessary. The stopping of indentured labour was very much more important than the abolition of the Viramgam customs. Lord Chelmsford committed a series of blunders beginning with the passing of the Rowlatt Act. Still, I think, he was a wise ruler. But what Viceroy can escape for long the influence of the permanent officials of the Civil Service ?

The third in order came the Champaran struggle, of which Rajendra Babu has written a detailed history. Here Satyagraha had actually to be offered. Mere preparedness for it did not suffice, as powerful vested interests were arrayed in opposition. The peace maintained by the people of Champaran deserves to be placed on record. I can bear witness to the perfect non-violence of the leaders in thought, word and deed. Hence it was that this age-long abuse came to an end in six months.

The fourth struggle was that of the mill-hands of Ahmedabad. Gujarat is perfectly familiar with its history. How peaceful the labourers were! As for the leaders, there can hardly be anything for me to say. Still I hold the victory in this case was not quite pure, as the fast I had to observe in order to sustain the labourers in their determination exercised indirect pressure upon the mill-owners. The fast was bound to influence them, as I enjoyed friendly relations with them. Still the moral of the fight is clear. If the labourers carry on their struggle peacefully, they must succeed and also win the hearts of their masters. They have not won their masters' hearts, as they were not innocent in thought, word and deed. They were non-violent in deed, which is certainly to their credit.

The fifth was the Kheda struggle. I cannot say that in this case all the local leaders of Satyagraha parties adhered to the pure truth. Peace was certainly maintained. The non-violence of the peasantry, however, was only superficial, like that of the mill-hands. So we came out of the struggle with bare honour. However there was a great awakening among the people. But Kheda had not fully grasped the lesson of non-violence; the mill-hands had not understood the true meaning of peace. The people had therefore to suffer. At the time of the Rowlatt Act Satyagraha, I had to confess my Himalayan blunder, to fast myself and invite others to do so.

The sixth was in connection with the Rowlatt Act. Therein our inherent shortcomings came to the surface. But the original foundation was well and truly laid. We admitted all our shortcomings and did penance for them. The Rowlatt Act was a dead letter even when it was promulgated, and that black act was finally even repealed. This struggle taught us a great lesson.

The seventh was the struggle to right the Khilafat and the Punjab wrongs and to win Swaraj. It is still going on. And my confidence is unshaken, that if a single Satyagrahi holds out to the end, victory is absolutely certain.

But the present fight is epic in character. I have already described our course of unconscious preparation for it. When I took up the Viramgam question, little did I know that other fights were in store. And even about Viramgam I knew nothing when I was in South Africa. That is the beauty of Satyagraha. It comes up to oneself; one has not to go out in search for it. This is a virtue inherent in the principle itself. A *dharma-yuddha*, in which there are no secrets to be guarded, no scope for cunning and no place for untruth, comes unsought; and a man of religion is ever ready for it. A struggle which has to be previously planned is not a righteous struggle. In a righteous struggle God Himself plans campaigns and conducts battles. A *dharma-yuddha* can be waged only in the name of God, and it is only when the Satyagrahi feels quite helpless, is apparently on his last legs and finds utter darkness all around him, that God comes to the rescue. God helps when one feels oneself humbler than the very dust under one's feet. Only to the weak and helpless is divine succour vouchsafed.

We are yet to realize this truth, and so I think the history of Satyagraha in South Africa will be helpful to us.

The reader will note South African parallels for all our experiences in the present struggle to date. He will also see from this history that there is so far no ground whatever for despair in the fight that is going on. The only condition of victory is a tenacious adherence to our programme.

I am writing this preface at Juhu. I wrote the first thirty chapters of the history in Yeravda jail. Shri Indulal Yajnik was good enough to write to my dictation. The subsequent chapters I hope to write hereafter. I had no books of reference in jail. Nor do I propose to get them here. I have neither the time nor the inclination to write a regular detailed history. My only object in writing this book is that it may be helpful in our present struggle, and serve as a guide to any regular historian who may arise in the future. Although I am writing without books of reference at hand, I must ask the reader not to imagine that any single item in this volume is inaccurate or that there is the least exaggeration at any point.

M. K. GANDHI

Juhu
St 1980 Phalgun vadi 13
2nd April, 1924

SATYAGRAHA IN SOUTH AFRICA

CHAPTER I
GEOGRAPHY

Africa is one of the biggest continents in the world. India is said to be not a country but a continent, but considering area alone, four or five Indias could be carved out of Africa. Africa is a peninsula like India; South Africa is thus mainly surrounded by the sea. There is a general impression that Africa is the hottest part of the earth, and in a sense this is true. The equator passes through the middle of Africa, and people in India cannot have any idea of the heat in countries situated along this line. The heat which we feel in the extreme south of India gives us some notion of it. But in South Africa there is nothing of that kind, as it is far away from the equator. The climate of many parts is so healthy and temperate that Europeans can settle there in comfort, while it is nearly impossible for them to settle in India. Moreover, there are lands of great elevation in South Africa like Tibet or Kashmir, but these do not attain a height of ten to fourteen thousand feet as in Tibet. Consequently, the climate is dry and cold enough to be endured, and some places in South Africa are highly recommended as sanatoria for consumptives. One of these is Johannesburg, the golden city of South Africa. Only fifty years ago, the site on which it now stands was desolate and covered with dry grass. But when gold mines were discovered, houses began to be built one after another, as if by magic, and today there are many handsome and substantial buildings. The wealthy people of the place have got trees from the more fertile tracts of South Africa and from Europe, paying as much as a guinea for a tree, and have planted them there. A traveller ignorant of this previous history would imagine that these trees had been there for all time.

I do not propose to describe all the parts of South Africa, but will confine myself only to those which are connected with our subject-matter. One part of South Africa is under the Portuguese, and the rest under the British. The territory under the Portuguese is called Delagoa Bay, and this is the first South African port for steamers from India. As we proceed further south, we come to Natal, the first British Colony. Its chief sea-port is called Port Natal, but we know it as Durban, under which name it is generally known all over South Africa. Durban is the largest city in Natal. The capital is Pietermaritzburg, situated inland at a distance of about sixty miles from Durban and at a height of about two thousand feet above sea-level. The climate of Durban is somewhat like that of Bombay, although rather colder. If we proceed further inland beyond Natal we reach the Transvaal, whose mines supply the world with the largest amount of gold. Some years ago diamond mines were also discovered in one of which was the world's largest diamond. The *Cullinan*, so called after the name of the proprietor of the mine, weighed over 3,000 carats, or over $1\frac{1}{3}$ lb. avoirdupois, while the *Kohinoor* now weighs about 100 carats and the *Orloff*, one of the Russian crown jewels, about 200 carats.

But though Johannesburg is the centre of the gold-mining industry and has diamond mines in the neighbourhood, it is not the official capital of the Transvaal. The capital is Pretoria, at a distance of about thirty-six miles from Johannesburg. In Pretoria one chiefly finds officials and politicians and the population drawn by them. It is therefore a comparatively quiet place, while Johannesburg is full of bustle. As a visitor from a quiet village, or for the matter of that a small town in India, to Bombay, would be confounded with the din and roar of the city, even so would a visitor from Pretoria be affected with Johannesburg. It would be no exaggeration to say that the citizens of Johannesburg do not walk but seem as if they ran. No one has the leisure to look at any one else, and every one is apparently engrossed in thinking how to amass the maximum wealth in the minimum of time! If leaving the Transvaal we travel further inland towards the West, we come to Orange Free State or Orangia. Its capital is Bloemfontein, a very quiet and small town.

There are no mines in Orangia like those in the Transvaal. A few hours' railway journey from here takes us to the boundary of the Cape Colony, the biggest of all the South African colonies. Its capital, which is also its largest sea-port, is known as Cape Town and is situated on the Cape of Good Hope, so called by King John of Portugal, as after its discovery he hoped his people would be able to find a new and easier way of reaching India, the supreme object of the maritime expeditions of that age.

Over and above these four principal British colonies, there are several territories under British 'protection,' inhabited by races which had migrated there before the appearance of Europeans on the scene.

The chief industry of South Africa is agriculture and for this it is pre-eminently fitted. Some parts of it are delightful and fertile. The principal grain is maize, which is grown without much labour and forms the staple food of the Negro inhabitants of South Africa. Wheat also is grown in some parts. South Africa is famous for its fruits. Natal cultivates many varieties of excellent bananas, pawpaws and pineapples, and that too in such abundance that they are available to the poorest of the poor. In Natal as well as other colonies, oranges, peaches and apricots grow in such plenty that thousands get them in the country for the labour of gathering them. The Cape Colony is the land of grapes and plums. Hardly any other place grows such fine grapes, and during the season they can be had so cheap that even a poor man can have his fill. It is impossible that there should be no mangoes in places inhabited by Indians. Indians planted mango trees in South Africa and consequently mangoes also are available in considerable quantities. Some varieties of these can certainly compete with the best mangoes of Bombay. Vegetables also are extensively grown in that fertile country, and it may be said that almost all the vegetables of India are grown there by Indians with a palate for home delicacies.

Cattle also are bred in considerable numbers. Cows and oxen are better built and stronger than in India. I have been ashamed, and my heart has often bled, to find many cows and oxen in India, which claims to protect the cow, as emaciated as the people themselves. Although I have moved about over all parts of South Africa with open eyes, I do not remember to have seen a single emaciated cow or bull.

Not only has Nature showered her other gifts upon this country, but she has not been stingy in beautifying it with a fine landscape.

The scenery of Durban is considered very beautiful, but that of Cape Town surpasses it. Cape Town is situated at the foot of the Table Mountain which is neither too high nor too low. A gifted lady who dotes on South Africa says in her poem about this mountain that no other gave her such a sense of the unique. There may be exaggeration in this. I think there is. But one of her points struck me as true. She says the Table Mountain stands in the position of a friend to the citizens of Cape Town. Not being too high, it does not inspire awe. People are not compelled to worship it from afar, but build their houses upon it and live there. And as it is just on the seashore, the sea always washes its foot with its clear waters. Young and old, men and women, fearlessly move about the whole mountain, which resounds every day with the voices of thousands. Its tall trees and flowers of fine fragrance and variegated hues impart such a charm to the mountain that one can never see too much of it, or move too much about it.

South Africa cannot boast of such mighty rivers as the Ganga or the Indus. The few that are there are comparatively small. The water of rivers cannot reach many places. No canals can be taken to the highlands. And how can there be canals in the absence of large rivers? Wherever there is a deficiency of surface water in South Africa, artesian wells are sunk, and water needed for irrigating fields is pumped up by windmills and steam-engines. Agriculture receives much encouragement from Government. Government sends out agricultural experts to advise the cultivators, maintains model farms where experiments are carried on for their benefit, provides them with good cattle and seed, bores artesian wells for them at very little cost and permits them to repay this amount by instalments.

Similarly Government erects barbed wire fences to protect their fields.

As South Africa is to the south, and India to the north, of the equator, climatic conditions there are just the reverse of what they are here. The seasons occur in a reverse order. For example, while we have summer here, South Africa is passing through winter. Rainfall is uncertain and capricious. It may occur any time. The average annual rainfall rarely exceeds twenty inches.

CHAPTER II
HISTORY

The geographical divisions briefly noticed in the first chapter are not at all ancient. It has not been possible definitely to ascertain who were the inhabitants of South Africa in remote times. When the Europeans settled in South Africa, they found the Negroes there. These Negroes are supposed to have been the descendants of some of the slaves in America who managed to escape from their cruel bondage and migrated to Africa. They are divided into various tribes such as the Zulus, the Swazis, the Basutos, the Bechuanas, etc. They have a number of different languages. These Negroes must be regarded as the original inhabitants of South Africa. But South Africa is such a vast country that it can easily support twenty or thirty times its present population of Negroes. The distance between Cape Town and Durban is about eighteen hundred miles by rail; the distance by sea also is not less than one thousand miles. The combined area of these four colonies is 473,000 square miles. In 1914 the Negro population in this vast region was about five millions, while the Europeans numbered about a million and a quarter.

Among the Negroes, the tallest and the most handsome are the Zulus. I have deliberately used the epithet 'handsome' in connection with Negroes. A fair complexion and a pointed nose represent our ideal of beauty. If we discard this superstition for a moment, we feel that the Creator did not spare Himself in fashioning the Zulu to perfection. Men and women are both tall and broad-chested in proportion to their height. Their muscles are strong and well set. The calves of the legs and the arms are muscular and always well rounded. You will rarely find a man or woman walking with a stoop or with a hump back. The lips are certainly large and thick, but as they are in perfect symmetry with the entire physique, I for one would not say that they are unshapely. The eyes are round and bright. The nose is flat and large, such as becomes a large face, and the curled hair on the head sets off to advantage the Zulu's skin which is black and shining like ebony. If we ask a Zulu to which of the various races inhabiting South Africa he will award the palm for beauty, he will unhesitatingly decide in favour of his own people, and in this I would not see any want of judgment on his part. The physique of the Zulu is powerfully built and finely shaped by nature without any such effort as is made by Sandow and others in Europe in order to develop the muscles. It is a law of nature that the skin of races living near the equator should be black. And if we believe that there must be beauty in everything fashioned by nature, we would not only steer clear of all narrow and one-sided conceptions of beauty, but we in India would be free from the improper sense of shame and dislike which we feel for our own complexion if it is anything but fair.

The Negroes live in round huts built of wattle and daub. The huts have a single round wall and are thatched with hay. A pillar inside supports the roof. A low entrance through which one can pass only by bending oneself is the only aperture for the passage of air. The entrance is rarely provided with a door. Like ourselves, the Negroes plaster the walls and the floor with earth and animal dung. It is said the Negroes cannot make anything square in shape. They have trained their eyes to see and make only round things. We never find nature drawing straight lines or rectilineal figures, and these innocent children of nature derive all their knowledge from their experience of her.

The furniture in the hut is in keeping with the simplicity of the place. There would be no room for tables, chairs, boxes and such other things, and even now these things are rarely seen in a hut.

Before the advent of European civilization, the Negroes used to wear animal skins, which also served them as carpets, bedsheets and quilts. Now-a-days they use blankets. Before British rule men as well as women moved about almost in a state of nudity. Even now many do the same in the country. They cover the private parts with a piece of skin. Some dispense even with this. But let not anyone infer from this that these people cannot control their senses. Where a large society follows a particular custom, it is quite possible that the custom is harmless even if it seems highly improper to the members of another society. These Negroes have no time to be staring at one another. When Shukadeva passed by the side of women bathing in a state of nudity, so the author of the *Bhagavata* tells us, his own mind was quite unruffled; nor were the women at all agitated or affected by a sense of shame. I do not think there is anything supernatural in this account. If in India today, there should be none who would be equally pure on a similar occasion, that does not set a limit to our striving after purity, but only argues our own degradation. It is only vanity which makes us look upon the Negroes as savages. They are not the barbarians we imagine them to be.

The law requires Negro women to cover themselves from the chest to the knees when they go to a town. They are thus obliged to wrap a piece of cloth round their body. Consequently pieces of that size command a large sale in South Africa, and thousands of such blankets or sheets are imported from Europe every year. The men are similarly required to cover themselves from the waist to the knees. Many, therefore, have taken to the practice of wearing second-hand clothing from Europe. Others wear a sort of knickers with a fastening tape. All these clothes are imported from Europe.

The staple food of the Negroes is maize, and meat when available. Fortunately, they know nothing about spices or condiments. If they find spices in their food or even if it is coloured by turmeric, they turn up their noses at it, and those among them who are looked upon as quite uncivilized will not so much as touch it. It is no uncommon thing for a Zulu to take at a time one pound of boiled maize with a little salt. He is quite content to live upon porridge made from crushed mealies boiled in water. Whenever he can get meat, he eats it, raw or cooked, boiled or roasted, with only salt. He does not mind taking the flesh of any animal.

The Negro languages are named after the various tribes. The art of writing was recently introduced by Europeans. There is nothing like a Negro alphabet. The Bible and other books have now been printed in the Negro languages in Roman character. The Zulu language is very sweet. Most words end with the sound of broad 'a'; so the language sounds soft and pleasing to the ear. I have heard and read that there is both meaning and poetry in the words. Judging from the few words which I happened to pick up, I think this statement is just. There are for most of the places sweet and poetical Negro names whose European equivalents I have mentioned. I am sorry I do not remember them and so cannot present them here to the reader.

According to the Christian missionaries, the Negroes previously had not, and have not now, any religion at all. But taking the word religion in a wide sense, we can say that the Negroes do believe in and worship a supreme Being beyond human comprehension. They fear this power too. They are dimly conscious of the fact that the dissolution of the body does not mean the utter annihilation of a person. If we acknowledge morality as the basis of religion, the Negroes being moral may be held even to be religious. They have a perfect grasp of the distinction between truth and falsehood. It is doubtful whether Europeans or ourselves practise truthfulness to the same extent as the Negroes in their primitive state do. They have no temples or anything else of that kind. There are many superstitions among them as among other races.

The reader will be surprised to learn, that this race, which is second to none in the world in point of physical strength, is so timid that a Negro is afraid at the sight even of a European child. If some one aims a revolver at him, he will either flee or will be too stupefied to have the power even to move. There is certainly reason for this. The notion is firmly impressed on the Negro mind, that it is only by some magic that a handful of Europeans have been able to subdue such a numerous and savage race as themselves. The Negro was well acquainted with the use of the spear, and the bow and arrows. Of these he has been deprived. He had never seen, never fired, a gun. No match is needed, nothing more has to be done beyond moving a finger and yet a small tube all at once emits a sound, a flash is seen, and a bullet wounds and causes the death of a person in an instant. This is something the Negro cannot understand. So he stands in mortal terror of those who wield such a weapon. He and his forefathers before him have seen that such bullets have taken the lives of many helpless and innocent Negroes. Many do not know even now how this happens.

'Civilization' is gradually making headway among the Negroes. Pious missionaries deliver to them the message of Christ as they have understood it, open schools for them, and teach them how to read and write. But many who, being illiterate and therefore strangers to civilization, were so far free from many vices, have now become corrupt. Hardly any Negro who has come in contact with civilization has escaped the evil of drink. And when his powerful physique is under the influence of liquor, he becomes perfectly insane and commits all manner of crimes. That civilization must lead to the multiplication of wants is as certain as that two and two make four. In order to increase the Negro's wants or to teach him the value of labour, a poll-tax and a hut tax have been imposed upon him. If these imposts were not levied, this race of agriculturists living on their farms would not enter mines hundreds of feet deep in order to extract gold or diamonds, and if their labour were not available for the mines, gold as well as diamonds would remain in the bowels of the earth. Likewise, the Europeans would find it difficult to get any servants, if no such tax was imposed. The result has been that thousands of Negro miners suffer, along with other diseases, from a kind of phthisis called 'miners' phthisis.' This is a fatal disease. Hardly any of those who fall in its clutches recover. The reader can easily imagine what self-restraint thousands of men living in mines away from their families can possibly exercise. They consequently fall easy victims to venereal disease. Not that thoughtful Europeans of South Africa are not alive to this serious question. Some of them definitely hold it can hardly be claimed that civilization has, all things considered, exercised a wholesome influence on this race. As for the evil effects, he who runs may read them.

About four hundred years ago the Dutch founded a settlement in this great country, then inhabited by such a simple and unsophisticated race. They kept slaves. Some Dutchmen from Java with their Malay slaves entered the country which we now know as Cape Colony. These Malays are Musalmans. They have Dutch blood in their veins and inherit some of the qualities of the Dutch. They are found scattered throughout South Africa, but Cape Town is their stronghold. Some of them today are in the service of Europeans, while others follow independent avocations. Malay women are very industrious and intelligent. They are generally cleanly in their ways of living. They are experts in laundry work and sewing. The men carry on some petty trade. Many drive hackney carriages. Some have received higher English education. One of them is the well known Doctor Abdul Rahman of Cape Town. He was a member of the old Colonial legislature at Cape Town. Under the new constitution this right of entering the Parliament has been taken away.

While giving a description of the Dutch, I incidentally said something about the Malays. But let us now see how the Dutch progressed. The Dutch have been as skilful cultivators as they have been brave soldiers. They saw that the country around them was highly suited for agriculture. They also saw that the 'natives' easily maintained themselves by working for only a short time during the year. Why should they not force these people to labour for them? The Dutch had guns. They were clever strategists. They knew how to tame human beings like other animals and they believed that their religion did not object to their doing so. In this way they commenced agriculture with the labour of the South African 'natives' with not a single doubt as to the morality of their action.

As the Dutch were in search of good lands for their own expansion, so were the English who also gradually arrived on the scene. The English and the Dutch were of course cousins. Their characters and ambitions were similar. Pots from the same pottery are often likely to clash against each other. So these two nations, while gradually advancing their respective interests and subduing the Negroes, came into collision. There were disputes and then battles between them. The English suffered a defeat at Majuba Hill. Majuba left a soreness which assumed a serious form and came to a head in the Boer War which lasted from 1899 to 1902. And when General Cronje surrendered, Lord Roberts was able to cable to Queen Victoria that Majuba had been avenged. But when this first collision occurred between the two nations previous to the Boer War, many of the Dutch were unwilling to remain under even the nominal authority of the British and 'trekked' into the unknown interior of South Africa. This was the genesis of the Transvaal and the Orange Free State.

These Dutch came to be known in South Africa as Boers. They have preserved their language by clinging to it as a child clings to its mother. They have an intense realization of the close relation between their language and their liberty. In spite of many attacks, they have preserved their mother tongue intact. The language assumed a new form suited to their genius. As they could not maintain very close relations with Holland, they began to speak a patois derived from the Dutch as the Prakrits are derived from Sanskrit. And not wishing to impose an unnecessary burden upon their children, they have given a permanent shape to this patois. It is called Taal. Their books are written in Taal, their children are educated through it, and Boer members of the Union Parliament make it a point to deliver their speeches in it. Since the formation of the Union, Taal or Dutch and English have been officially treated on a footing of equality throughout South Africa, so much so that the Government Gazettes and records of Parliament must be in both languages.

The Boers are simple, frank and religious. They settle in the midst of extensive farms. We can have no idea of the extent of these farms. A farm with us means generally an acre or two, and sometimes even less. In South Africa a single farmer has hundreds or thousands of acres of land in his possession. He is not anxious to put all this under cultivation at once, and if any one argues with him, he will say, 'Let it lie fallow. Lands which now lie fallow will be cultivated by our children.'

Every Boer is a good fighter. However much the Boers may quarrel among themselves, their liberty is so dear to them that when it is in danger, all get ready and fight as one man. They do not need elaborate drilling, for fighting is a characteristic of the whole nation. General Smuts, General De Wet, and General Hertzog are all of them great lawyers, great farmers and equally great soldiers. General Botha had one farm of nine thousand acres. He was familiar with all the intricacies of agriculture. When he went to Europe in connection with negotiations for peace, it was said of him that there was hardly any one in Europe who was as good a judge of sheep as he was. General Botha had succeeded the late President Kruger. His knowledge of English was excellent; yet when he met the King and ministers in England, he always preferred to talk in his own mother tongue. Who can say that this was not the proper thing to do? Why should he run the risk of committing a mistake in order to display his knowledge of English? Why should he allow his train of thought to be disturbed in the search for the right word? The British ministers might quite unintentionally employ some unfamiliar English idiom, he might not understand what they meant, be led into giving the wrong reply and get confused; and thus his cause would suffer. Why should he commit such a serious blunder?

Boer women are as brave and simple as the men. If the Boers shed their blood in the Boer war, they were able to offer this sacrifice owing to the courage of their womenfolk and the inspiration they received from them. The women were not afraid of widowhood and refused to waste a thought upon the future.

I have stated above that the Boers are religiously minded Christians. But it cannot be said that they believe in the New Testament. As a matter of fact Europe does not believe in it; in Europe, however, they do claim to respect it, although only a few know and observe Christ's religion of peace. But as to the Boers it may be said that they know the New Testament only by name. They read the Old Testament with devotion and know by heart the descriptions of battles it contains. They fully accept Moses' doctrine of 'an eye for an eye and a tooth for a tooth.' And they act accordingly.

Boer women understood that their religion required them to suffer in order to preserve their independence, and therefore patiently and cheerfully endured all hardships. Lord Kitchener left no stone unturned in order to break their spirit. He confined them in separate concentration camps, where they underwent indescribable sufferings. They starved, they suffered biting cold and scorching heat. Sometimes a soldier intoxicated with liquor or maddened by passion might even assault these unprotected women. Still the brave Boer women did not flinch. And at last King Edward wrote to Lord Kitchener, saying that he could not tolerate it, and that if it was the only means of reducing the Boers to submission, he would prefer any sort of peace to continuing the war in that fashion, and asking the General to bring the war to a speedy end.

When this cry of anguish reached England, the English people were deeply pained. They were full of admiration for the bravery of the Boers. The fact that such a small nationality should sustain a conflict with their worldwide empire was rankling in their minds. But when the cry of agony raised by the women in the concentration camps reached England not through themselves, not through their men,— they were fighting valiantly on the battlefield,— but through a few high-souled Englishmen and women who were then in South Africa, the English people began to relent. The late Sir Henry Campbell-Bannerman read the mind of the English nation and raised his voice against the war. The late Mr Stead publicly prayed and invited others to pray, that God might decree the English a defeat in the war. This was a wonderful sight. Real suffering bravely borne melts even a heart of stone. Such is the potency of suffering or *tapas*. And there lies the key to Satyagraha.

The result was that the peace of Vereeniging was concluded, and eventually all the four Colonies of South Africa were united under one Government. Although every Indian who reads newspapers knows about this peace, there are a few facts connected with it, which perhaps are not within the knowledge of many. The Union did not immediately follow the peace, but each Colony had its own legislature. The ministry was not fully responsible to the legislature. The Transvaal and the Free State were governed on Crown Colony lines. Generals Botha and Smuts were not the men to be satisfied with such restricted freedom. They kept aloof from the Legislative Council. They non-co-operated. They flatly refused to have anything to do with the Government. Lord Milner made a pungent speech, in the course of which he said that General Botha need not have attached so much importance to himself. The country's Government could well be carried on without him. Lord Milner thus decided to stage Hamlet without the Prince of Denmark.

I have written in unstinted praise of the bravery, the love of liberty and the self-sacrifice of the Boers. But I did not intend to convey the impression that there were no differences of opinion among them during their days of trial, or that there were no weak-kneed persons among them. Lord Milner succeeded in setting up a party among the Boers who were easy to satisfy, and persuaded himself to believe that he could make a success of the legislature with their assistance. Even a stage play cannot be managed without the hero: and an administrator in this matter-of-fact world who ignores the central figure in the situation he has to deal with and still expects to succeed can only be described as insane. Such indeed was the case of Lord Milner. It was said that though he indulged in bluff, he found it so difficult to govern the Transvaal and the Free State without the assistance of General Botha, that he was often seen in his garden in an anxious and excited state of mind. General Botha distinctly stated that by the treaty of Vereeniging, as he understood it, the Boers were immediately entitled to complete internal autonomy. He added that, had that not been the case, he would never have signed the treaty. Lord Kitchener declared in reply that he had given no such pledge to General Botha. The Boers, he said, would be gradually granted full self-government as they proved their loyalty! Now who was to judge between these two? How could one expect General Botha to agree if arbitration was suggested? The decision arrived at in the matter by the Imperial Government of the time was very creditable to them. They conceded that the stronger party should accept the interpretation of the agreement put upon it by the other and weaker party. According to the principles of justice and truth, that is the correct canon of interpretation. I may have meant to say anything, but I must concede that my speech or writing was intended to convey the meaning ascribed to it by my hearer or reader in so far as he is concerned. We often break this golden rule in our lives. Hence arise many of our disputes, and half-truth, which is worse than untruth, is made to do duty for truth.

Thus when truth—in the present case General Botha—fully triumphed, he set to work. All the colonies were eventually united, and South Africa obtained full self-government. Its flag is the Union Jack, it is shown in red on maps, and yet it is no exaggeration to say that South Africa is completely independent. The British Empire cannot receive a single farthing from South Africa without the consent of its Government. Not only that, but British ministers have conceded that if South Africa wishes to remove the Union Jack and to be independent even in name, there is nothing to prevent it from doing so. And if the Boers have so far not taken this step, there are strong reasons for it. For one thing, the Boer leaders are shrewd and sagacious men. They see nothing improper in maintaining with the British Empire a partnership in which they have nothing to lose. But there is another practical reason. In Natal the English preponderate, in Cape Colony there is a large population of Englishmen though they do not outnumber the Boers; in Johannesburg the English element is predominant. This being the case, if the Boers seek to establish an independent republic in South Africa, the result would be internecine strife and possibly a civil war. South Africa, therefore, continues to rank as a dominion of the British Empire.

The way in which the Constitution of the Union was framed is worthy of note. A National Convention, composed of delegates representative of all parties appointed by the Colonial legislatures, unanimously prepared a draft Constitution and the British Parliament had to approve it in its entirety. A member of the House of Commons drew the attention of the House to a grammatical mistake and suggested that it should be rectified. The late Sir Henry Campbell-Bannerman, while rejecting the suggestion, observed that faultless grammar was not essential to carrying on a government, that the Constitution was framed as a result of negotiations between the British Cabinet and the ministers of South Africa and that they did not reserve even the right of correcting a grammatical error to the British Parliament. Consequently, the Constitution recast in the form of an Imperial bill passed through both Houses of Parliament, just as it was, without the slightest alteration.

There is one more circumstance worthy of notice in this connection. There are some provisions in the Act of Union which may appear meaningless to the lay reader. They have led to a great increase in expenditure. This had not escaped the notice of the framers of the Constitution; but their object was not to attain perfection, but by compromise to arrive at an understanding and to make the Constitution a success. That is why the Union has four capitals, no colony being prepared to part with its own capital. Similarly, although the old colonial legislatures were abolished, provincial councils with subordinate and delegated functions were set up. And though Governorships were abolished, officers corresponding to the rank of Governor and styled Provincial Administrators were appointed. Every one knows that four local legislatures, four capitals and four Governors are unnecessary and serve for mere show. But the shrewd statesmen of South Africa did not object. The arrangement is showy and entails additional expenditure, but union was desirable and therefore the statesmen did what they thought fit, regardless of outside criticism and got their policy approved by the British Parliament.

I have endeavoured to sketch very briefly the history of South Africa, as without it, it appeared to me difficult to explain the inner meaning of the great Satyagraha struggle. It now remains to be seen how the Indians came to this country and struggled against their adversities before the inauguration of Satyagraha.

CHAPTER III

INDIANS ENTER SOUTH AFRICA

We saw in the preceding chapter how the English arrived. They settled in Natal, where they obtained some concessions from the Zulus. They observed that excellent sugarcane, tea and coffee could be grown in Natal. Thousands of labourers would be needed in order to grow such crops on a large scale, which was clearly beyond the capacity of a handful of colonists. They offered inducements and then threats to the Negroes in order to make them work but in vain, as slavery had been then abolished. The Negro is not used to hard work. He can easily maintain himself by working for six months in the year. Why then should he bind himself to an employer for a long term? The English settlers could make no progress at all with their plantations in the absence of a stable labour force. They therefore opened negotiations with the Government of India and requested their help for the supply of labour. That Government complied with their request, and the first batch of indentured labourers from India reached

Natal on November 16, 1860, truly a fateful date for this history; had it not been for this, there would have been no Indians and therefore no Satyagraha in South Africa, and this book would have remained unwritten.

In my opinion, the Government of India were not well advised in taking the action they did. The British officials in India consciously or unconsciously were partial to their brethren in Natal. It is true that as many terms as possible, purporting to safeguard the labourers' interests, were entered in the indentures. Fairly good arrangements were made for their board. But adequate consideration was not given to the question as to how these illiterate labourers who had gone to a distant land were to seek redress if they had any grievances. No thought was given to their religious needs or to the preservation of their morality. The British officials in India did not consider that although slavery had been abolished by law, employers could not be free from a desire to make slaves of their employees. They did not realize, as they ought to have realized, that the labourers who had gone to Natal would in fact become temporary slaves. The late Sir W. W. Hunter, who had deeply studied these labour conditions, used a remarkable phrase about them. Writing about the Indian labourers in Natal, he said that theirs was a state of semi-slavery. On another occasion, in the course of a letter, he described their condition as bordering on slavery. And tendering evidence before a commission in Natal, the most prominent European in that Colony, the late Mr. Harry Escombe, admitted as much. Testimony to the same effect can be readily gathered from the statements of leading Europeans in Natal. Most of these were incorporated in the memorials on the subject submitted to the Government of India. But the fates would have their course. And the steamer which carried those labourers to Natal carried with them the seed of the great Satyagraha movement.

I have not the space here in the present volume to narrate how the labourers were deluded by Indian recruiting agents connected with Natal; how under the influence of such delusion they left the mother country; how their eyes were opened on reaching Natal; how still they continued to stay there; how others followed them; how they broke through all the restraints which religion or morality imposes, or to be more accurate, how these restraints gave way, and how the very distinction between a married woman and a concubine ceased to exist among these unfortunate people.

When the news that indentured labourers had gone to Natal reached Mauritius, Indian traders having connection with such labourers were induced to follow them there. Thousands of Indians, labourers as well as traders, have settled in Mauritius which is on the way to Natal from India. An Indian trader in Mauritius, the late Sheth Abubakar Amad, thought of opening a shop in Natal. The English in Natal had then no idea of what Indian traders were capable of, nor did they care. They had been able to raise very profitable crops of sugarcane, tea and coffee, with the assistance of indentured labour. They manufactured sugar, and in a surprisingly short time supplied South Africa with a modest quantity of sugar, tea and coffee. They made so much money that they built palatial mansions for themselves and turned a wilderness into a veritable garden. In such circumstances they naturally did not mind an honest and plucky trader like Abubakar Sheth settling in their midst. Add to this that an Englishman actually joined him as partner. Abubakar Sheth carried on trade and purchased land, and the story of his prosperity reached Porbandar, his native place, and the country around. Other Memans consequently reached Natal. Borahs from Surat followed them. These traders needed accountants, and Hindu accountants from Gujarat and Saurashtra accompanied them.

Two classes of Indians thus settled in Natal, first free traders and their free servants, and secondly indentured labourers. In course of time the indentured labourers had children. Although not bound to labour, these children were affected by several stringent provisions of the colonial law. How can the children of slaves escape the brand of slavery? The labourers went to Natal under indenture for a period of five years. They were under no obligation to labour after the expiry of that period, and were entitled to work as free labourers or trade in Natal, and settle there if they wished. Some elected to do so while others returned home. Those who remained in Natal came to be known as 'Free Indians.' It is necessary to understand the peculiar position of this class. They were not admitted to all the rights enjoyed by the entirely free Indians of whom I have first spoken. For instance, they were required to obtain a pass if they wanted to go from one place to another, and if they married and desired the marriage to be recognized as valid in law, they were required to register it with an official known as Protector of Indian Immigrants. They were also subject to other severe restrictions.

The Indian traders saw that they could trade not only with indentured labourers and 'Free Indians,' but with the Negroes as well. Indian merchants were a source of great convenience to the Negroes, who very much feared the European traders. The European trader wanted to trade with the Negro, but it would be too much for Negro customers to expect courtesy at his hands. They might think it a great good fortune if he gave them full consideration for their money. Some of them had bitter experiences. A man might purchase an article worth four shillings, place a sovereign on the counter, and receive four shillings as balance instead of sixteen, and sometimes even nothing whatever. If the poor Negro asked for the balance or showed how the amount paid him was less than his due, the reply would be gross abuse. He might thank his stars if things stopped there; otherwise the abuse would be reinforced by a blow or a kick. I do not mean to suggest that all English traders behaved like this. But it can safely be asserted that the number of such cases was fairly large. On the other hand, Indian traders had a good word for the Negroes and even joked with them. The simple Negro would like to enter the shop and handle and examine the goods he wanted to purchase. Indian traders permitted all this. It is true that in this they were not actuated by altruistic motives, it may have had something to do with their self-interest. The Indian

INDIANS ENTER SOUTH AFRICA

might not miss the opportunity, if it offered, of cheating his Negro customer, but his courtesy made him popular with the Negroes. Moreover, the Negro never feared the Indian traders. On the other hand, cases have occurred in which an Indian tried to cheat Negroes, but on being detected, was roughly handled by them. And more often Negro customers have been heard to abuse Indian traders. Thus, so far as Indians and Negroes were concerned, it is the former who feared the latter. The result was that trade with Negroes proved very profitable to Indian traders. And the Negroes were to be found throughout South Africa.

There were Boer republics in the Transvaal and the Orange Free State during the eighties of the last century. I need scarcely say that in these republics the Negro had no power, it was all a white men's affair. Indian traders had heard that they could also trade with the Boers, who, being simple, frank and unassuming, would not think it below their dignity to deal with Indian traders. Several Indian traders therefore proceeded to the Transvaal and the Free State and opened shops there. As there were no railways there at the time, they earned large profits. The expectations of the Indian traders were fulfilled and they carried on considerable trade with the Boers and the Negroes as customers. Similarly several Indian traders went to the Cape Colony and began to earn fairly well. The Indians were thus distributed in small numbers in all the four colonies.

Absolutely free Indians now number between forty to fifty thousands, while the 'Free Indians' so called, that is, the labourers who are freed from their indentures and their descendants, number about a hundred thousand.

CHAPTER IV
A REVIEW OF THE GRIEVANCES
Natal

The European planters of Natal wanted only slaves. They could not afford to have labourers who, after serving their term, would be free to compete with them to however small an extent. No doubt the indentured labourers had gone to Natal, as they had not been very successful in agriculture or other pursuits in India. But it is not to be supposed that they had no knowledge of agriculture or that they did not understand the value of land. They found that if they grew only vegetables in Natal, they could earn good incomes, and that their earnings would be still better if they owned a small piece of land. Many, therefore, on the termination of their indentures, began to pursue some trade or other on a small scale. This was, on the whole, advantageous to the settlers in Natal. Various kinds of vegetables, which had not been grown before for want of a competent class of cultivators, now became available. Other kinds, which had been grown in small quantities, could now be had in abundance. The result was a fall in the price of vegetables. But the European planters did not relish this new development. They felt they now had competitors in a field in which they believed they had a monopoly. A movement was, therefore, set on foot against these poor time-expired labourers. The reader will be surprised to learn, that while on the one hand the Europeans demanded more and more labourers and easily took in as many of them as went from India, on the other hand they started an agitation to harass ex-indenture labourers in a variety of ways. This was the reward for their skill and hard toil!

The movement assumed many forms. One set of agitators demanded that the labourers who completed their indentures should be sent back to India, and that therefore fresh labourers arriving in Natal from that time forward should have a new clause entered in their indentures, providing for their compulsory return to India at the expiration of their term of service unless they renewed their indentures. A second set advocated the imposition of a heavy annual capitation tax on the labourers who did not re-indenture themselves at the end of the first period of five years. Both, however, had the same object in view, namely, by hook or crook to make it impossible for ex-indentured labourers to live as free men in Natal in any circumstances. This agitation attained such serious dimensions, that the Government of Natal appointed a commission. As the demands of both these classes of agitators were quite unfair, and as the presence of the ex-indentured labourers was clearly beneficial to the entire population from an economic standpoint, the independent evidence recorded by the commission was against the agitators, who thus failed to achieve any tangible result for the time being. But as fire, although extinguished, leaves a trail behind it, the agitation created some impression on the Government of Natal. How could it be otherwise? The Government of Natal was friendly to the planters. It therefore communicated with the Government of India and laid before it the proposals of both the sets of agitators. But the Government of India could not all at once accept proposals which would reduce indentured labourers to perpetual slavery. One justification or excuse for sending labourers to such a far-off land under indenture was that the labourers, after completing the indentures, would become free to develop their powers fully and consequently improve their economic condition. As Natal then was still a Crown Colony, the Colonial Office was fully responsible for its government. Natal, therefore, could not look for help from that quarter too in satisfying its unjust demands. For this and similar reasons a movement was set on foot to attain responsible government, which was eventually conferred on Natal in 1893. Natal now began to feel its strength. The Colonial Office too did not any longer find it difficult to accept whatever demands Natal might choose to make. Delegates from the new responsible Government of Natal came to India to confer with the Government of India. They proposed the imposition of an annual poll-tax of twenty-five pounds, or three hundred and seventy-five rupees, on every Indian who had been freed from indenture. It was evident that no Indian labourer could pay such an exorbitant tax and live in Natal as a free man. Lord Elgin, the Governor-General of India, considered that the amount was excessive, and ultimately he accepted an annual poll-tax of three pounds. This was equivalent to nearly six months' earnings on the indenture scale. The tax was levied, not only on the labourer himself, but also upon his wife, his daughters aged thirteen years or upwards, and his sons aged sixteen years or upwards. There was hardly any labourer who had not a wife and a couple of children. Thus, as a general rule, every labourer was required to pay an annual tax of twelve pounds. It is impossible to describe the hardships that this tax entailed. Only those, who actually underwent the hardships, could realize them, and only those who witnessed their sufferings could have some idea of them. The Indians carried on a powerful agitation against this action of the Government of Natal. Memorials were submitted to the Imperial Government and the Government of India, but to no purpose except for the reduction in the amount of the tax. What could the poor labourers do or understand in this matter? The agitation on their behalf was carried on by the Indian traders, actuated by motives of patriotism or of philanthropy.

Free Indians fared no better. The European traders of Natal carried on a similar agitation against them for mainly the same reasons. Indian traders were well established. They acquired lands in good localities. As the number of freed labourers began to increase, there was a larger and larger demand for the class of goods required by them. Bags of rice were imported from India in their thousands and sold at a good profit. Naturally this trade was largely in the hands of Indians who had besides a fair share of the trade with Zulus. They thus became an eyesore to petty European traders. Again, some Englishmen pointed out to the Indian traders, that according to law they were entitled to vote in the elections for the Legislative Assembly of Natal, and to stand as candidates for the same. Some Indians therefore got their names entered on the electoral roll. This made the European politicians of Natal join the ranks of anti-Indians. They doubted whether the Europeans could stand in competition with Indians if the Indians' prestige increased, and if their position was consolidated, in Natal. The first step, therefore, taken by the responsible Government of Natal in connection with free Indians was that they decided to enact a law, disfranchising all Asiatics save those who were then rightly contained in any voters' list. A bill to that effect was first introduced into the Legislative Assembly of Natal in 1894. This was based on the principle of excluding Indians as Indians from the franchise, and was in Natal the first piece of legislation affecting them in which racial distinction was made. Indians resisted this measure. A memorial was prepared during one night and four hundred signatures were appended to it. When the memorial was submitted to the Legislative Assembly of Natal, that body was startled. But the bill was passed all the same. A memorial bearing ten thousand signatures was submitted to Lord Ripon who was then Secretary of State for the Colonies. Ten thousand signatures meant almost the total population at the time of free Indians in Natal. Lord Ripon disallowed the bill and declared that the British Empire could not agree to the establishment of a colour bar in legislation. The reader will be in a position later on to appreciate how great was this victory for Indians. The Natal Government, therefore, brought forward another bill, removing racial distinction but indirectly disqualifying Indians. Indians protested against this as well but without success. This new bill was ambiguous in meaning. Indians were in a position to carry it finally to the Judicial Committee of the Privy Council with a view to its interpretation; but they did not think it advisable to do so. I still think that they did the right thing in avoiding this endless litigation. It was no small thing that the colour bar was not allowed to be set up.

But the planters and the Government of Natal were not likely to stop there. To nip the political power of Indians in the bud was for them the indispensable first step; but the real point of their attack was Indian trade and free Indian immigration. They were uneasy at the thought of the Europeans in Natal being swamped if India with its teeming millions invaded Natal. The approximate population of Natal at the time was 400,000 Zulus and 40,000 Europeans as against 60,000 indentured, 10,000 ex-indentured and 10,000 free Indians. The Europeans had no solid grounds for their apprehensions, but it is impossible to convince by argument men who have been seized with vague terrors. As they were ignorant of the helpless condition of India and of the manners and customs of the Indian people, they were under the impression that the Indians were as adventurous and resourceful as themselves. They could scarcely be blamed if they thus created a bugbear of the vast population of India in comparison with their own small numbers. However that may be, the result of the successful opposition to the disfranchising bill was, that in two other laws passed by the Natal Legislature it had to avoid racial distinction and to attain its end in an indirect manner. The position, therefore, was not as bad as it might have been. On this occasion too Indians offered a strenuous resistance, but in spite of this the laws were enacted. One of these imposed severe restrictions on Indian trade and the other on Indian immigration in Natal. The substance of the first Act was that no one could trade without a licence issued by an official appointed in accordance with its provisions. In practice any European could get a licence while the Indian had to face no end of difficulty in the matter. He had to engage a lawyer and incur other expenditure. Those who could not afford it had to go without a licence. The chief provision of the other Act was that only such immigrants as were able to pass the education test in a European language could enter the Colony. This closed the doors of Natal against crores of Indians. Lest I should inadvertently do the Government of Natal an injustice, I must state that the Act further provided that an Indian resident in Natal for three years before the passing of that Act might obtain a certificate of domicile enabling him to leave the Colony and return at any time with his wife and minor children without being required to pass the education test.

The indentured and free Indians in Natal were and still are subject to other disabilities, both legal and extra-legal, in addition to those described above. But I do not think it necessary to tax the reader with a recital of them. I propose to give such details only as are essential to a clear understanding of the subject. A history of the condition of Indians in different parts of South Africa would take up much space. But that is beyond the scope of the present volume.

CHAPTER V

A REVIEW OF THE GRIEVANCES

The Transvaal and other Colonies

As in Natal, so in the other Colonies anti-Indian prejudice had more or less begun to grow even before 1880. Except in the Cape Colony, the general opinion held was that as labourers the Indians were all right, but it had become an axiom with many Europeans that the immigration of free Indians was purely a disadvantage to South Africa. The Transvaal was a republic. For Indians to declare their British citizenship before its President was only to invite ridicule. If they had any grievance, all they could do was to bring it to the notice of the British Agent at Pretoria. Still the wonder is that when the Transvaal came under the British flag, there was none from whom Indians could expect even such assistance as the Agent rendered when the Transvaal was independent. When during Lord Morley's tenure of the office of the Secretary of State for India, a deputation on behalf of the Indians waited upon him, he declared in so many words that as the members of the deputation were aware, the Imperial Government could exercise but little control over self-governing dominions. They could not dictate to them;

they could plead, they could argue, they could press for the application of their principles. Indeed in some instances they could more effectively remonstrate with foreign Powers, as they remonstrated with the Boer Republic, than with their own people in the Colonies. The relations of the mother country with the colonies were in the nature of a silken tie which would snap with the slightest tension. As force was out of the question, he assured the deputation that he would do all he could by negotiations. When war was declared on the Transvaal, Lord Landsdowne, Lord Selborne and other British statesmen declared that the scandalous treatment accorded to the Indians by the South African Republic was one of the causes of the war.

Let us now see what sort of treatment this was. Indians first entered the Transvaal in 1881. The late Sheth Abubakar opened a shop in Pretoria and purchased land in one of its principal streets. Other traders followed in his wake. Their great success excited the jealousy of European traders who commenced an anti-Indian campaign in the newspapers, and submitted petitions to the Volksraad or Parliament, praying that Indians should be expelled and their trade stopped. The Europeans in this newly opened up country had a boundless hunger for riches. They were almost strangers to the dictates of morality. Here are some statements they made in their petitions: "These Indians have no sense of human decency. They suffer from loathsome diseases. They consider every woman as their prey. They believe that women have no souls." These four sentences contain four lies. It would be easy to multiply such specimens. As were the Europeans, so were their representatives. Little did the Indian traders know what a sinister and unjust movement was being carried on against them. They did not read newspapers. The newspaper campaign and the petitions had the desired effect, and a bill was introduced into the Volksraad. The leading Indians were taken aback when they came to know how events had shaped themselves. They went to see President Kruger who did not so much as admit them into his house but made them stand in the courtyard. After hearing them for a while, he said, "You are the descendants of Ishmael and therefore from your very birth bound to slave for the descendants of Esau. As the descendants of Esau we cannot admit you to rights placing you on an equality with ourselves. You must rest content with what rights we grant to you." It cannot be said, that this reply from the President was inspired by malice or anger. President Kruger had been taught from his childhood the stories of the Old Testament, and he believed them to be true. How can we blame a man who gives candid expression to his opinions such as they are? Ignorance, however, is bound to do harm even when associated with candour, and the result was that in 1885 a very drastic law was rushed through the Volksraad, as if thousands of Indians were on the point of flooding the Transvaal. The British Agent was obliged to move in the matter at the instance of Indian leaders. The question was finally carried to the Secretary of State for the Colonies. In the terms of this Law 3 of 1885 every Indian settling in the Republic for the purpose of carrying on trade was required to register at a cost of twenty-five pounds subject to heavy penalties, and no Indian could hold an inch of land or enjoy the rights of citizenship. All this was so manifestly unjust that the Transvaal Government could not defend it in argument. There was a treaty subsisting between the Boers and the British known as the London Convention, Article XIV of which secured the rights of British subjects. The British Government objected to the Law as being in contravention of that Article. The Boers urged in reply that the British Government had previously given their consent, whether express or implied, to the law in question.

A dispute thus arose between the British and the Boer Governments, and the matter was referred to arbitration. The arbitrator's award was unsatisfactory. He tried to please both parties. The Indians were therefore the losers. The only advantage they reaped, if advantage it can be called, was that they did not lose as much as they might have done otherwise. The Law was amended in 1886 in accordance with the arbitrator's award. The registration fee was reduced from twenty-five to three pounds. The clause, which completely debarred Indians from holding landed property, was removed, and it was provided instead, that the Indians could own fixed property in such locations, wards and streets as were specially set apart for their residence by the Transvaal Government. This Government did not honestly carry out the terms of the amended clause, and withheld from Indians the right to purchase freehold land even in the locations. In all towns inhabited by Indians, these locations were selected in dirty places situated far away from the towns where there was no water supply, no lighting arrangement and no sanitary convenience to speak of. Thus the Indians became the Panchamas of the Transvaal. It can be truly said that there is no difference between these locations and the untouchables' quarters in India. Just as the Hindus believe that touching Dhedhs or residence in their neighbourhood would lead to pollution, so did the Europeans in the Transvaal believe for all practical purposes that physical contact with the Indians or living near them would defile them. Again the Transvaal Government interpreted Law 3 of 1885 to mean that the Indians could trade, too, exclusively in the locations. The arbitrator had decided that the interpretation of the law rested with the ordinary tribunals of the Transvaal. The Indian traders were therefore in a very awkward condition. Still they managed to maintain their position fairly well by carrying on negotiations in one place, by having recourse to law courts in another, and by exerting what little influence they possessed in a third. Such was the miserable and precarious position of Indians in the Transvaal at the outbreak of the Boer War.

We shall now turn to examine the position in the Free State. Hardly a dozen Indians had opened shops there when the Europeans started a powerful agitation. The Volksraad passed a stringent law and expelled all Indian traders from the Free State, awarding them nominal compensation. That law provided that no Indian could on any account hold fixed property or carry on mercantile or farming business or enjoy franchise rights in the Free

State. With special permission an Indian could settle as a labourer or as a hotel waiter. But the authorities were not obliged to grant even this precious permission in every case. The result was that a respectable Indian could not live in the Free State even for a couple of days without great difficulty. At the time of the Boer War there were no Indians in the Free State except a few waiters.

In the Cape Colony, too, there was some newspaper agitation against Indians, and the treatment to which they were subjected was not free from humiliating features. For example Indian children could not attend public schools, etc., and Indian travellers could hardly secure accommodation in hotels. But there were no restrictions as to trade and the purchase of land for a long time.

There were reasons for this state of things. As we have already seen, there was a fair proportion of the Malays in the population of the Cape Colony in general and of Cape Town in particular. As the Malays are Musalmans, they soon came in contact with their Indian co-religionists, and consequently with other Indians later on. Moreover, some Indian Musalmans married Malay women. How could the Government of the Cape Colony legislate against the Malays? The Cape was their motherland, Dutch was their mother tongue, they had been living with the Dutch from the very first and therefore largely imitated them in their ways of life. The Cape Colony, therefore, has been the least affected by colour prejudice.

Again as the Cape Colony was the oldest settlement and the chief centre of culture in South Africa, it produced sober, gentlemanly and large-hearted Europeans. In my opinion, there is no place on earth and no race, which is not capable of producing the finest types of humanity, given suitable opportunities and education. It has been my good fortune to come across this class of people in all parts of South Africa. In the Cape Colony, however, the proportion of such persons was very much the larger. Perhaps the best known and the most learned among them is Mr Merriman who was a member of the first and subsequent ministries that came in power after the grant of responsible government to the Cape Colony in 1872, was again the Premier in the last ministry when the Union was established in 1910, and was known as the Gladstone of South Africa. Then there are the Moltenos and the Schreiners. Sir John Molteno was the first Premier of the Colony in 1872. Mr W. P. Schreiner was a well-known advocate, for some time Attorney-General, and later on Premier. His sister, Olive Schreiner, was a gifted lady popular in South Africa and well known wherever the English language is spoken. Ever since she wrote the book, she became famous as the authoress of *Dreams*. Her love for all mankind was unbounded. Love was written in her eyes. Although she belonged to such a distinguished family and was a learned lady, she was so simple in habits that she cleaned utensils in her house herself. Mr Merriman, the Moltenos and the Schreiners, had always espoused the cause of the Negroes. Whenever the rights of the Negroes were in danger, they stoutly stood up in their defence. They had kindly feelings for the Indians as well, though they made a distinction between Negroes and Indians. Their argument was that as the Negroes had been the inhabitants of South Africa long before the European settlers, the latter could not deprive them of their natural rights. But as for the Indians it would not be unfair if laws calculated to remove the danger of their undue competition were enacted. All the same they had a warm corner in their hearts for Indians. When Gokhale went to South Africa, Mr Schreiner presided over the Townhall meeting in Cape Town, where he was accorded his first public reception in that country. Mr Merriman also treated him with great courtesy and expressed his sympathy with the Indian cause. There were other Europeans of the type of Mr Merriman. I have mentioned these well-known names as typical of their class.

The newspapers in Cape Town, too, were less hostile to Indians than in other parts of South Africa.

While it is true that for these reasons there has always been less race hatred in the Cape Colony than in other parts, it is but natural that the anti-Indian feeling which constantly found expression in the other colonies also found its way to the Cape. There too two laws copied from Natal were passed, namely, the Immigration Restriction Act and the Dealers' Licences Act.

It can be said that the door in South Africa, which was formerly wide open, had thus been almost closed against Indians at the time of the Boer War. In the Transvaal there was no restriction on immigration except the registration fee of three pounds. When Natal and the Cape Colony closed their ports to Indians, they had difficulty in landing on their way to the Transvaal which was in the interior. They could reach it via Delagoa Bay, a Portuguese port. But the Portuguese also more or less imitated the British. It must be mentioned that some stray Indians were able to find their way to the Transvaal via Natal or Delagoa Bay by suffering great hardships or by bribing port officers.

CHAPTER VI
A REVIEW OF THE EARLY STRUGGLE

While considering the position of Indians in the previous chapters, we have seen to some extent how they withstood the attacks made upon them. In order, however, to give an adequate idea of the origin of Satyagraha, it is necessary to devote special space to the endeavours made with a view to defend Indian interests in the pre-Satyagraha days.

Up till 1893 there were hardly any free and well-educated Indians in South Africa capable of espousing the Indian cause. English-knowing Indians were mostly clerks whose knowledge of English was only commensurate with the needs of their occupation and not adequate to drafting representations, and who, again, must give all their time to their employers. A second group of English-educated Indians was composed of such of them as were born in South Africa. They were mostly the descendants of indentured labourers, and if at all qualified for the work, were in Government service as interpreters in law courts. Thus they were not in a position to help the Indian cause beyond expressing their fellow-feeling.

Again, indentured and ex-indentured labourers hailed mainly from Uttar Pradesh and Madras State, while, as we have already seen, the Musalmans mostly traders and the Hindus mostly clerks, who chiefly represented the class of free Indians, belonged to Gujarat. Besides there were a few Parsi traders and clerks, but the total population of Parsis in South Africa did not probably exceed thirty or forty souls. A fourth group among free Indians was composed of Sindhi traders. There were two hundred or more Sindhis in South Africa. Wherever the Sindhi has settled outside India he deals in 'fancy goods,' namely, silks and brocades, carved boxes and other furniture made of ebony, sandalwood and ivory and similar goods. His customers are mainly Europeans.

Indentured labourers were called 'coolies' by the Europeans. A 'coolie' means a porter. The expression was used so extensively that the indentured labourers began to describe themselves as 'coolies.' Hundreds of Europeans called Indian lawyers and Indian traders 'coolie' lawyers and 'coolie' traders. There were some Europeans who were unable to perceive or believe that the name implied an insult, but many used it as a term of deliberate contempt. Free Indians, therefore, tried to differentiate themselves from the indentured labourers. For this and other reasons peculiar to conditions in India, a distinction was sought to be drawn in South Africa between indentured and freed labourers on the one hand and free Indians on the other.

Free Indians and especially the Musalman traders undertook to resist the wrongs detailed above, but no direct attempt was made to seek the co-operation of the indentured and ex-indentured labourers. Probably it did not occur to any one to enlist their support; if the idea did suggest itself to some, there was in their opinion the risk of making matters worse by allowing them to join the movement. And as it was considered that the free traders were the chief target of attack, the measures for defence were limited to that class. It can be truly said that free Indians fought well against difficulties, seeing that they were thus seriously handicapped, that they were ignorant of English, and that they had had no experience of public work in India. They sought the help of European barristers, had petitions prepared, waited upon the authorities on some occasions in deputations, and did what they could to mend matters. This was the state of things up till 1893.

It will be helpful to the reader to bear some important dates in mind. Before 1893 Indians had been hounded out of the Orange Free State. In the Transvaal, Law 3 of 1885 was in force. In Natal, measures, calculated to enable only indentured labourers to live in the colony and to turn out the rest, were under contemplation, and responsible government had been achieved to that end.

I left India for South Africa in April, 1893. I had no idea of the previous history of the Indian emigrants. I went there on a purely professional visit. A well-known firm of Porbandar Memans then carried on trade in Durban under the name and style of Dada Abdulla. An equally well-known and rival firm traded at Pretoria under the designation of Taib Haji Khanmamad. Unfortunately, an important law-suit was pending between the rivals. A partner of the firm of Dada Abdulla who was in Porbandar thought that it would help their case if they engaged me and sent me to South Africa. I had been just called to the bar and was quite a novice in the profession, but he had no fear of my mishandling their case, as he did not want me to conduct the case in the court but only to instruct the able South African lawyers they had retained. I was fond of novel experiences. I loved to see fresh fields and pastures new. It was disgusting to have to give commission to those who brought me work. The atmosphere of intrigue in Saurashtra was choking to me. The engagement was only for one year. I did not see any objection to my accepting it. I had nothing to lose as Messrs Dada Abdulla expressed their willingness to pay my travelling expenses as well as the expenses that would be incurred in South Africa and a fee of one hundred and five pounds. This arrangement had been made through my elder brother, now deceased, who was as father to me. For me his will was a command. He liked the idea of my going to South Africa. So I reached Durban in May 1893.

Being a barrister-at-law, I was well dressed according to my lights and landed at Durban with a due sense of my importance. But I was soon disillusioned. The partner of Dada Abdulla who had engaged me had given me an account of what things were like in Natal. But what I saw there with my own eyes absolutely belied his misleading picture. My informant was, however, not to blame. He was a frank, simple man, ignorant of the real state of affairs. He had no idea of the hardships to which Indians were subjected in Natal. Conditions which implied grave insult had not appeared to him in that light. I observed on the very first day that the Europeans meted out most insulting treatment to Indians.

I will not describe my bitter experience in the courts within a fortnight of my arrival, the hardships I encountered on railway trains, the thrashings I received on the way and the difficulty in and the practical impossibility of securing accommodation in hotels. Suffice it to say, that all these experiences sank in me. I had gone there only for a single case prompted by self-interest and curiosity. During the first year, therefore, I was merely the witness and the victim of these wrongs. I then awoke to a sense of my duty. I saw that from the standpoint of self-interest South Africa was no good to me. Not only did I not desire but I had a positive aversion to earning money or sojourning in a country where I was insulted. I was on the horns of a dilemma. Two courses were open to me. I might either free myself from the contract with Messrs Dada Abdulla on the ground that circumstances had come to my knowledge which had not been disclosed to me before, and run back to India. Or I might bear all hardships and fulfil my engagement. I was pushed out of the train by a police constable at Maritzburg, and the train having left, was sitting in the waiting room, shivering in the bitter cold. I did not know where my luggage was, nor did I dare to inquire of anybody, lest I might be insulted and assaulted once again. Sleep was out of the question. Doubt took possession of my mind. Late at night, I came to the conclusion that to run back to India would be cowardly. I must accomplish what I had undertaken. I must reach Pretoria, without minding insults and even assaults. Pretoria was my goal. The case was being fought out there. I made up my mind to take some steps, if that was possible, side by side with my work. This resolution somewhat pacified and strengthened me but I did not get any sleep.

Next morning I wired to the firm of Dada Abdulla and to the General Manager of the Railway. Replies were received from both. Dada Abdulla and his partner Sheth Abdulla Haji Adam Jhaveri who was then in Natal took strong measures. They wired to their Indian agents in various places to look after me. They likewise saw the General Manager. The Indian traders of Maritzburg came to see me in response to the telegram received by the local agent. They tried to comfort me and told me that all of them had had the same bitter experiences as myself, but they did not mind such things, being habituated to them. Trade and sensitiveness could ill go together. They had therefore made it a principle to pocket insults as they might pocket cash. They told me how Indians could not enter the railway station by the main gate and how difficult it was for them to purchase tickets. I left for Pretoria the same night. The Almighty Searcher of all hearts put my determination to a full test. I suffered further insults and received more beatings on my way to Pretoria. But all this only confirmed me in my determination.

Thus in 1893, I obtained full experience of the condition of Indians in South Africa. But I did nothing beyond occasionally talking with the Indians in Pretoria on the subject. It appeared to me that to look after the firm's case and to take up the question of the Indian grievances in South Africa at the same time was impossible. I could see that trying to do both would be to ruin both. 1894 was thus already upon us. I returned to Durban and prepared to return to India. At the farewell entertainment held by Dada Abdulla, some one put a copy of the *Natal*

Mercury in my hands. I read it and found that the detailed report of the proceedings of the Natal Legislative Assembly contained a few lines under the caption 'Indian Franchise.' The local Government was about to introduce a Bill to disfranchise Indians, which could only be the beginning of the end of what little rights they were then enjoying. The speeches made at the time left no doubt about the intention of the Government. I read the report to the traders and others present and explained the situation to them as best I could. I was not in possession of all the facts. I suggested that the Indians should strenuously resist this attack on their rights. They agreed but declared their inability to fight the battle themselves and urged me to stay on. I consented to stay a month or so longer by which time the struggle would be fought out. The same night I drew up a petition to be presented to the Legislative Assembly. A telegram was sent to the Government requesting a delay of proceedings. A committee was appointed at once with Sheth Haji Adam as chairman and the telegram was sent in his name. The further reading of the Bill was postponed for two days. That petition was the first ever sent by the Indians to a South African legislature. It did create an impression although it failed to defeat the Bill, the later history of which I have narrated in chapter Four. This was the South African Indians' first experience of such agitation, and a new thrill of enthusiasm passed through the community. Meetings were held every day and more and more persons attended them. The requisite funds were over-subscribed. Many volunteers helped in preparing copies, securing signatures and similar work without any remuneration. There were others who both worked and subscribed to the funds. The descendants of the ex-indentured Indians joined the movement with alacrity. They knew English and wrote a fine hand. They did copying and other work ungrudgingly day and night. Within a month a memorial with ten thousand signatures was forwarded to Lord Ripon, and the immediate task I had set before myself was done.

I asked for leave to return home. But the agitation had aroused such keen interest among the Indians that they would not let me go. They said: "You yourself have explained to us that this is the first step taken with a view to our ultimate extinction. Who knows whether the Colonial Secretary will return a favourable reply to our memorial? You have witnessed our enthusiasm. We are willing and ready to work. We have funds too. But for want of a guide, what little has been done will go for nothing. We therefore think it is your duty to stay on." I also felt that it would be well if a permanent organization was formed to watch Indian interests. But where was I to live and how? They offered me a regular salary, but I expressly declined. One may not receive a large salary for public work. Besides I was a pioneer. According to my notions at the time, I thought I should live in a style usual for barristers and reflecting credit on the community, and that would mean great expense. It would be improper to depend for my maintenance upon a body whose activities would necessitate a public appeal for funds, and my power of work would be thereby crippled. For this and similar reasons I flatly refused to accept remuneration for public work. But I suggested that I was prepared to stay if the principal traders among them could see their way to give me legal work and give me retainers for it beforehand. The retainers might be for a year. We might deal with each other for that period, examine the results, and then continue the arrangement if both parties were agreeable. This suggestion was cordially accepted by all.

I applied for admission as an advocate of the Supreme Court of Natal. The Natal Law Society opposed my application on the sole ground that the law did not contemplate that coloured barristers should be placed on the roll. The late Mr Escombe, the famous advocate, who was Attorney-General and afterwards also Premier of Natal, was my counsel. The prevailing practice for a long time was that the leading barrister should present such applications without any fees, and Mr Escombe advocated my cause accordingly. He was also Senior Counsel for my employers. The Senior Court over-ruled the Law Society's objection, and granted my application. Thus the Law Society's opposition brought me into further prominence without their wishing it. The newspapers of South Africa ridiculed the Law Society and some of them even congratulated me.

The temporary committee was placed on a permanent footing. I had never attended a session of the Indian National Congress, but had read about it. I had seen Dadabhai, the Grand Old Man of India and admired him. I was therefore a Congress devotee, and wished to popularize the name. Inexperienced as I was, I did not try to find out a new name. I was also afraid of committing a mistake. So I advised the Indians to call their organization the Natal Indian Congress. I laid before them very imperfectly what meagre knowledge I had of the Indian National Congress. Anyhow the Natal Indian Congress was founded about May 1894. There was this difference between the Indian and the Natal Congress, that the latter organization worked throughout the year and those who paid an annual subscription of at least three pounds were admitted to membership. Amounts exceeding that sum were gratefully received. Endeavours were made to obtain the maximum amount from each member. There were about half a dozen members who paid twenty-four pounds a year. There was a considerable number of those paying twelve pounds. About three hundred members were enrolled in a month. They included Hindus, Musalmans, Parsis and Christians, and came from all Indian States that were represented in Natal. The work proceeded with great vigour throughout the first year. The well-to-do traders went about far off villages in their own conveyances, enrolling new members and collecting subscriptions. Everybody did not pay for the mere asking. Some required to be persuaded. This persuasion was a sort of political training, and made people acquainted with the facts of the situation. Again, a meeting of the Congress was held at least once a month, when detailed accounts were presented and adopted. Current events were explained and recorded in the minute-book. Members asked various questions. Fresh subjects were considered. The advantage of all this was that those who never spoke at such meetings got accustomed to do so. The speeches again must be in proper form. All this was a novel experience. The community was deeply interested. In the meanwhile the welcome news came that Lord Ripon had disallowed the Disfranchising Bill, and this redoubled their zeal and self-confidence.

Side by side with external agitation, the question of internal improvement was also taken up. The Europeans throughout South Africa had been agitating against Indians on the ground of their ways of life. They always argued that the Indians were very dirty and close-fisted. They lived in the same place where they traded. Their houses were mere shanties. They would not spend money even on their own comforts. How could cleanly open-handed Europeans with their multifarious wants compete in trade with such parsimonious and dirty people? Lectures were therefore delivered, debates held, and suggestions made at Congress meetings on subjects such as domestic sanitation, personal hygiene, the necessity of having separate buildings for houses and shops and for well-to-do traders of living in a style befitting their position. The proceedings were conducted in Gujarati.

The reader can see what an amount of practical and political education the Indians thus received. Under the auspices of the Congress, the Natal Indian Educational Association was formed for the benefit of the young Indians, who, being the children of ex-indentured labourers, were born in Natal and spoke English. Its members paid a nominal fee. The chief objects of the Association were to provide a meeting place for those youths, to create in them a love for the mother country and to give them general information about it. It was also intended to impress upon them that free Indians considered them as their own kith and kin, and to create respect for the latter in the minds of the former. The funds of the Congress were large enough to leave a surplus after defraying its expenses. This was devoted to the purchase of land which yields an income to the present day.

I have deliberately entered into all these details, for without them the reader cannot realize how Satyagraha spontaneously sprang into existence and how the Indians went through a natural course of preparation for it. I am compelled to omit the remarkable subsequent history of the Congress, how it was confronted with difficulties, how Government officials attacked it and how it escaped scatheless from their attacks. But one fact must be placed on record. Steps were taken to save the community from the habit of exaggeration. Attempts were always made to draw their attention to their own shortcomings. Whatever force there was in the arguments of the Europeans was duly acknowledged. Every occasion, when it was possible to co-operate with the Europeans on terms of equality and consistent with self-respect, was heartily availed of. The newspapers were supplied with as much information about the Indian movement as they could publish, and whenever Indians were unfairly attacked in the Press replies were sent to the newspapers concerned.

There was an organization in the Transvaal similar to the Natal Indian Congress but quite independent of it. There were likewise differences in the constitutions of the two bodies into which we need not enter. There was a similar body in Cape Town as well with a constitution different from that of the Natal Congress and the Transvaal Association. Still the activities of all the three bodies were nearly identical.

The Natal Congress completed its first year in the middle of 1895. My work as an advocate met with the approval of my clients, and my stay in Natal was prolonged. In 1896 I went to India for six months with the leave of the community. I had hardly completed that period in India, when I received a cablegram from Natal asking me to return at once, and so did I. The events of 1896-97 demand a fresh chapter for their treatment.

CHAPTER VII

A REVIEW OF THE EARLY STRUGGLE

Continued

Thus the Natal Indian Congress was placed on a permanent footing. I spent nearly two years and a half in Natal, mostly doing political work. I then saw that if I was still to prolong my stay in South Africa, I must bring over my family from India. I likewise thought of making a brief sojourn in the homeland and of acquainting Indian leaders with the condition of Indian settlers in Natal and other parts of South Africa. The Congress allowed me leave of absence for six months and the late Mr Adamji Miyankhan, the well-known merchant of Natal, was appointed Secretary in my stead. He discharged his duties with great ability. He had a fair knowledge of English, which had been greatly supplemented by use. He had studied Gujarati in the ordinary course. As he had mercantile dealings chiefly with the Zulus, he had acquired an intimate knowledge of the Zulu language and was well conversant with Zulu manners and customs. He was a man of very quiet and amiable disposition. He was not given to much speech. I have entered into these details in order to show, that to the holding of responsible positions, truthfulness, patience, tolerance, firmness, presence of mind, courage and commonsense are far more essential qualifications than a knowledge of English or mere learning. Where these fine qualities are absent, the best literary attainments are of little use in public work.

I returned to India in the middle of the year 1896. As steamers from Natal were then more easily available for Calcutta than for Bombay, I went on board one bound for that city. For the indentured labourers were embarked from Calcutta or Madras. While proceeding to Bombay from Calcutta, I missed my train on the way and had to stop in Allahabad for a day. My work commenced there. I saw Mr Chesney of the *Pioneer*. He talked with me courteously, but told me frankly that his sympathies were with the Colonials. He, however, promised that if I wrote anything, he would read it and notice it in his paper. This was good enough for me.

While in India, I wrote a pamphlet on the condition of Indians in South Africa. It was noticed by almost all newspapers and it passed through two editions. Five thousand copies were distributed in various places in India. It was during this visit that I had the privilege of seeing Indian leaders, Sir Pherozeshah Mehta, Justices Badruddin Tyebji and Mahadev Govind Ranade and others in Bombay, and Lokamanya Tilak and his circle, Prof. Bhandarkar and Gopal Krishna Gokhale and his circle in Poona. I delivered speeches in Bombay, Poona and Madras. I do not propose to deal with these events in detail.

I cannot, however, resist the temptation of describing here a sacred reminiscence of Poona, although it is not strictly relevant to our subject. The Sarvajanik Sabha was controlled by the Lokamanya, while Shri Gokhale was connected with the Deccan Sabha. I first saw Tilak Maharaj. When I spoke to him about my intention to hold a meeting in Poona, he asked me if I had seen Gopalrao. I did not understand whom he meant. He therefore asked me again if I had seen Shri Gokhale and if I knew him.

"I have not yet seen him. I know him by name and mean to see him," I replied.

"You do not seem to be familiar with Indian politics," said the Lokamanya.

"I stayed in India only for a short time after my return from England, and had not then applied myself to political questions, as I thought it beyond my capacity," I said.

Lokamanya then said: "In that case I must give you some information. There are two parties in Poona, one represented by the Sarvajanik Sabha and the other by the Deccan Sabha."

I replied: "I know something about this matter."

Lokamanya: "It is easy to hold a meeting here. But it seems to me that you wish to lay your case before all the parties here and seek to enlist the support of all. I like your idea. But if a member of the Sarvajanik Sabha is selected to preside over your meeting, no member of the Deccan Sabha will attend it. Similarly, if a member of the Deccan Sabh were to preside, members of the Sarvajanik Sabha would absent themselves. You should therefore find out a non-partisan as chairman. I can only offer suggestions in the matter, and shall not be able to render any other assistance. Do you know Prof. Bhandarkar? Even if you do not know him, you should see him. He is considered a neutral. He does not take part in politics, but perhaps you can induce him to preside over your meeting. Speak to Shri Gokhale about this, and seek his advice too. In all probability he will give you the same advice. If a man of the position of Prof. Bhandarkar consents to preside, I am certain that both the parties will see to it that a good meeting is held. At any rate you can count upon our fullest help in the matter."

I then saw Gokhale. I have written elsewhere how I fell in love with him at this very first sight. The curious may look up the files of *Young India** or *Navajivan*† for it. Gokhale liked the advice which Lokamanya had given me. Accordingly I paid my respects to the venerable Professor. He heard attentively the story of the Indian wrongs in Natal and said, "You see I rarely take part in public life. Then again, I am getting old. But what you have told me has stirred me deeply. I like your idea of seeking the co-operation of all parties. You are young and ignorant of political conditions in India. Tell the members of both the parties that I have agreed to your request. On an intimation from any of them that the meeting is to be held, I will certainly come and preside." A successful meeting was held in Poona. The leaders of both the parties attended and spoke in support of my cause.

---

* Issue of July 13, 1921.

† Issue of July 28, 1921.

I then went to Madras. There I saw Sir (then Mr Justice) Subrahmanya Aiyar, Shri P. Anandacharlu, Shri G. Subrahmanyam, the then editor of the *Hindu,* Shri Parameshvaran Pillai, editor of the *Madras Standard,* Shri Bhashyam Iyengar, the famous advocate, Mr Norton and others. A great meeting too was held. From Madras I went to Calcutta, where I saw Surendranath Banerji, Maharaja Jyotindra Mohan Tagore, the late Mr Saunders, the editor of the *Englishman,* and others. While a meeting was being arranged in Calcutta, I received a cablegram from Natal asking me to return at once. This was in November 1896. I concluded that some movement hostile to the Indians must be on foot. I therefore left my work at Calcutta incomplete and went to Bombay, where I took the first available steamer with my family. S. S. *Courland* had been purchased by Messrs Dada Abdulla and represented one more enterprise of that very adventurous firm, namely, to run a steamer between Porbandar and Natal. The *Naderi,* a steamer of the Persian Steam Navigation Company, left Bombay for Natal immediately after. The total number of passengers on the two steamers was about 800.

The agitation in India attained enough importance for the principal Indian newspapers to notice it in their columns and for Reuter to send cablegrams about it to England. This I came to know on reaching Natal. Reuter's representative in England had sent a brief cablegram to South Africa, containing an exaggerated summary of my speeches in India. This is not an unusual experience. Such exaggeration is not always intentional. Very busy people with prejudices and prepossessions of their own read something superficially and then prepare a summary which is sometimes partly a product of imagination. This summary, again, is differently interpreted in different places. Distortion thus takes place without any one intending it. This is the risk attending public activities and this is also their limitation. While in India I had criticized the Europeans of Natal. I had spoken very strongly against the £ 3 tax on indentured labourers. I had given a vivid account of the sufferings of an indentured labourer named Subrahmanyam who had been assaulted by his master, whose wounds I had seen and whose case was in my hands. When the Europeans in Natal read the distorted summary of my speeches, they were greatly exasperated against me. The remarkable fact, however, was that what I had written in Natal was more severe and detailed than what I wrote and spoke in India. My speeches in India were free from the slightest exaggeration. On the other hand, as I knew from experience that if we describe an event to a stranger, he sees more in it than what we intend to convey, I had deliberately described the South African situation in India less forcibly than the facts warranted. But very few Europeans would read what I wrote in Natal, and still fewer would care for it. The case, however, was obviously different with my speeches and writings in India. Thousands of Europeans would read Reuter's summaries. Moreover, a subject which is considered worthy of being communicated by cablegram becomes invested with an importance it does not intrinsically possess. The Europeans of Natal thought that my work in India carried the weight attributed to it by them and that therefore the system of indentured labour would perhaps come to an end, and hundreds of European planters would suffer in consequence. Besides, they felt blackened before India.

While the Europeans of Natal were thus in an excited state of mind, they heard that I was returning to Natal with my family per S. S. *Courland*, that it carried from 300 to 400 Indian passengers, and that S. S. *Naderi* was also arriving at the same time with an equal number of Indians. This inflamed them all the more, and there was a great explosion of feeling. The Europeans of Natal held large meetings, which were attended by almost all the prominent members of their community. The Indian passengers in general and myself in particular came in for a great deal of severe criticism. The expected arrival of the *Courland* and the *Naderi* was represented as an 'invasion' of Natal. The speakers said that I had brought those 800 passengers to Natal and that this was my first step towards flooding Natal with free Indians. A unanimous resolution was passed that the passengers of both the steamers including myself should be prevented from landing in Natal. If the Government of Natal would not or could not prevent the passengers from landing, the Committee appointed at the meeting was to take the law into their own hands and to prevent the Indians from landing by main force. Both the steamers reached Durban on the same day.

The reader will remember that bubonic plague made its first appearance in India in 1896. In their effort to prevent our landing the Government of Natal were hampered by legal difficulties as the Immigration Restriction Act had not yet come into being. Otherwise their sympathies were entirely with the Committee of Europeans referred to above. The late Mr Escombe, a member of the Government, took a prominent part in the proceedings of that Committee. It was he who instigated them. There is a rule in force at all ports that if a case of contagious disease occurs on board a steamer, or if a steamer is coming from an infected port, it is detained in quarantine for a certain period. This restriction can be imposed only on sanitary grounds, and under orders from the Health Officer of the port. The Government of Natal abused their power by enforcing the above rule for political purposes. Although there was no contagious disease on board, both the steamers were detained far beyond the usual time-limit, for as many as twenty-three days. Meanwhile, the Committee of Europeans continued their activities. Messrs Dada Abdulla, who were the owners of the *Courland* and the agents for the *Naderi*, were subjected to a severe hectoring by them. Inducements were offered to them if they agreed to take back the passengers, and they were threatened with loss of business if they refused to do so. But the partners of the firm were no cowards. They said they did not care if they were ruined; they would fight to the bitter end but would not be coerced into committing the crime of sending away those helpless but innocent passengers; they were no strangers to patriotism. The old advocate of the firm, Mr F. A. Laughton, K.C., was also a brave man.

A REVIEW OF THE EARLY STRUGGLE

As luck would have it, the late Shri Mansukhlal Hiralal Nazar, a Kayastha gentleman from Surat and a nephew of the late Mr Justice Nanabhai Haridas, reached Africa about the same time. I did not know him, nor was I aware of his going. I need scarcely say that I had no hand in bringing the passengers who arrived by the *Naderi* and the *Courland*. Most of them were old residents of South Africa. Many again were bound for the Transvaal. Threatening notices were served by the Committee of Europeans even upon these passengers. The captains of the steamers read them out to the passengers. The notices expressly stated that the Europeans of Natal were in a dangerous temper, and said in effect that if in spite of the warning the Indian passengers attempted to land, the members of the Committee would attend at the port and push every Indian into the sea. I interpreted this notice to the passengers on the *Courland*. An English-knowing passenger on board the *Naderi* did the same for his fellow-passengers. The passengers on both the steamers flatly declined to go back and added that many of them were proceeding to the Transvaal, that some of the rest were old residents of Natal, that in any case every one of them was legally entitled to land and that the threats of the Committee notwithstanding, they were determined to land in order to test their right to do so.

The Government of Natal was at its wits' end. How long could an unjust restriction be enforced? Twenty-three days had passed already. Dada Abdulla did not flinch, nor did the passengers. The quarantine was thus lifted after 23 days and the steamers were permitted to steam into harbour. Meanwhile, Mr Escombe pacified the excited Committee of Europeans. At a meeting which was held, he said, "The Europeans in Durban have displayed commendable unity and courage. You have done all you could. Government has also helped you. The Indians were detained for 23 days. You have given sufficient expression to your sentiments and your public spirit. That will make a profound impression on the Imperial Government. Your action has made the path of the Government of Natal easy. If you now prevent by force a single Indian passenger from landing, you will injure your own interests and place the Government in an awkward position. And even then you will not succeed in preventing the Indians from landing. The passengers are not at all to blame. There are women and children among them. When they embarked at Bombay, they had no idea of your feelings. I would therefore advise you to disperse and not to obstruct these people. I assure you, however, that the Government of Natal will obtain from the Legislative Council the requisite powers in order to restrict future immigration." This is only a summary of Mr Escombe's speech. His audience was disappointed, but he had great influence over the Europeans of Natal. They dispersed in consequence of his advice and both the steamers came into port.

A message reached me from Mr Escombe advising me not to land with the others but to wait until evening when he would send the Superintendent of Water Police to escort me home, and adding that my family were free to land at any time. This was not an order according to law, but was by way of advice to the captain not to allow me to land and of warning to me of the danger that was hanging over my head. The captain had not the power forcibly to prevent me from landing. But I came to the conclusion that I should accept this suggestion. I sent my family to the residence of my old friend and client, Parsi Rustomji, instead of to my own place, and told them that I would meet them there. When the passengers had disembarked, Mr Laughton, counsel for Dada Abdulla and a personal friend of mine, came up and met me. He asked me why I had not yet landed. I told him about Mr Escombe's letter. He said that he did not like the idea of my waiting till evening and then entering the city like a thief or offender, that if I was not afraid, I should accompany him there and then, and that we would walk to the town as if nothing had happened. I replied: "I do not think I am afraid. It is only a question of propriety whether or not I should accept Mr Escombe's suggestion. And we should also consider whether the captain of the steamer is responsible in the matter." Mr Laughton smiled and said: "What has Mr Escombe done for you that you must needs heed his suggestion? And what reason have you to believe that he is actuated by kindliness and not by some ulterior motive? I know more than you what has happened in the town, and what hand Mr Escombe had in the happenings there." I interrupted him with a shaking of the head. "We might assume," continued Mr Laughton, "that he is actuated by the best of motives. But I am positively of opinion that if you comply with his suggestion, you will stand humiliated. I would, therefore, advise you, if you are ready, to accompany me just now. The captain is our man, and his responsibility is our responsibility. He is accountable only to Dada Abdulla. I know what they will think of the matter, as they have displayed great courage in the present struggle." I replied: "Let us then go. I have no preparations to make. All I have to do is to put on my turban. Let us inform the captain and start." We took the captain's leave.

Mr Laughton was an old and well-known advocate of Durban. I had come in intimate contact with him before I returned to India. I used to consult him in difficult cases and often to engage him as my senior. He was a brave and powerfully built man.

Our road lay through the principal street of Durban. It was about half past four in the evening when we started. The sky was slightly overcast and the sun was not to be seen. It would take a pedestrian at least one hour to reach Rustomji Sheth's place. The number of persons present about the wharf was not larger than what is to be usually seen there. As soon as we landed, some boys saw us. As I was the only Indian who put on a turban of a particular type, they at once reconized me, began to shout 'Gandhi,' 'Gandhi,' 'thrash him,' 'surround him,' and came up towards us. Some began to throw pebbles at us. A few elderly Europeans joined the boys. Gradually the party of rioters began to grow. Mr Laughton thought that there was danger in our going on foot. He therefore hailed a rickshaw. I had never sat in a rickshaw before, as it was thoroughly disgusting to me to sit in a vehicle pulled by human beings. But I then felt that it was my duty to use that vehicle. I have experienced five or seven times in my life that one, whom God wishes to save, cannot fall even if he will. If I did not fall I cannot take any credit for it to myself. These rickshaws are pulled by Zulus. The elderly Europeans and the boys threatened the rickshaw puller that if he allowed me to sit in his rickshaw, they would beat him and smash his rickshaw to pieces. The rickshaw boy, therefore, said 'Kha' (meaning 'no') and went away. I was thus spared the shame of a rickshaw ride.

We had no alternative now but to proceed to our destination on foot. A mob followed us. With every step we advanced, it grew larger and larger. The gathering was enormous when we reached West Street. A man of powerful build took hold of Mr Laughton and tore him away from me. He was not therefore in a position to come up with me. The crowd began to abuse me and shower upon me stones and whatever else they could lay their hands on. They threw down my turban. Meanwhile a burly fellow came up to me, slapped me in the face and then kicked me. I was about to fall down unconscious when I held on to the railings of a house near by. I took breath for a while and when the fainting was over, proceeded on my way. I had almost given up the hope of reaching home alive. But I remember well that even then my heart did not arraign my assailants.

While I was thus wending my way, the wife of the Superintendent of Police at Durban was coming from the opposite direction. We knew each other well. She was a brave lady. Although the sky was cloudy and the sun about to set, she opened her sunshade for my protection and began to walk at my side. The Europeans would not insult a lady, especially the wife of the old and popular Superintendent of Police, nor would they hurt her. They must avoid injuring her while aiming blows at me. The injuries, therefore, which I received after she joined me, were not serious. Meanwhile the Superintendent of Police came to know of the attack upon me and sent a party of constables for my protection. The police surrounded me.

The Police Station was on our way. When we reached there I saw that the Superintendent of Police was waiting for us. He offered me asylum in the Police Station, but I declined the offer with thanks and said, "I must reach my destination. I have faith in the fair play of the citizens of Durban and in the righteousness of my own cause. I am thankful to you for sending the police party for my protection. Mrs Alexander too has contributed to my safety."

I reached Rustomji's house without further trouble. It was nearly evening when I reached there. Dr Dadibarjor, the medical officer of the *Courland*, who was with Rustomji Sheth, began to treat me. He examined my wounds. There were not many of them. One blind wound in particular was very painful. But I was not yet privileged to rest in peace. Thousands of Europeans gathered before Rustomji Sheth's house. After nightfall, hooligans also joined the crowd. The crowd sent word to Rustomji Sheth that if he did not hand me over to them, they would burn him and his house along with me. Rustomji Sheth was too good an Indian to be daunted. When Superintendent Alexander came to know how matters stood, he quietly joined the crowd with a number of detectives. He sent for a bench and stood upon it. Thus under the pretence of talking to the crowd, he took possession of the entrance to Rustomji's house so that none could break and enter it. He had already posted detectives at proper places. Immediately on arrival, he had instructed a subordinate to disguise himself as an Indian trader by putting on Indian dress and painting his face to see me and deliver to me the following message: "If you wish to save your friend, his guests and property, and your own family, I advise you to disguise yourself as an Indian constable, come out through Rustomji's godown, steal through the crowd with my man and reach the Police Station. A carriage is awaiting you at the corner of the street. This is the only way in which I can save you and others. The crowd is so excited that I am not in a position to control it. If you are not prompt in following my directions, I am afraid the crowd will raze Rustomji's house to the ground and it is impossible for me to imagine how many lives will be lost and how much property destroyed."

I gauged the situation at once. I quickly disguised myself as a constable and left Rustomji's house. The Police Officer and I reached the Police Station in safety. In the meantime Mr Alexander was humouring the crowd by singing topical songs and talking to them. When he knew that I had reached the Police Station, he became serious and asked:

"What do you want?"

"We want Gandhi."

"What will you do with him?"

"We will burn him."

"What harm has he done to you?"

"He has vilified us in India and wants to flood Natal with Indians."

"What if he does not come out?"

"We will then burn this house."

"His wife and children are also there. There are other men and women besides. Would you not be ashamed of burning women and children?"

"The responsibility for that will rest with you. What can we do when you make us helpless in the matter? We do not wish to hurt any one else. It would be enough if you hand over Gandhi to us. If you do not surrender the culprit, and if others are injured in our endeavour to capture him, would it be fair on your part to blame us?"

The Superintendent gently smiled and informed the crowd that I had left Rustomji's house, passed through their midst, and reached another place already. The crowd laughed loudly and shouted, "It is a lie, it is a lie."

The Superintendent said: "If you will not believe your old Superintendent of Police, please appoint a committee of three or four men from amongst you. Let others promise that they will not enter the house, and that if the committee fail to find Gandhi in the house, you will peacefully return to your homes. You got excited today and did not obey the police. That reflects discredit on you, not on the police. The police therefore played a trick with you; it removed your prey from your midst and you have lost the game. You certainly cannot blame the police for this. The police, whom you yourselves have appointed, have simply done their duty."

The Superintendent addressed the crowd with such suavity and determination, that they gave him the promise he had asked for. A committee was appointed. It searched Rustomji's house through and through, and reported to the crowd that the Superintendent was right and had beaten them in the game. The crowd was disappointed. But they kept their word and dispersed without committing any mischief. This happened on January 13, 1897.

The same morning after the quarantine on the steamers had been removed, the reporter of a Durban newspaper had seen me on the steamer. He had asked me everything. It was quite easy to dispose of the charges against me to his satisfaction. I showed to him in detail that I had not indulged in the least exaggeration. What I had done was only my duty. If I had failed to discharge it, I would be unworthy of the name of man. All this appeared in the newspapers the next day. Sensible people among the Europeans admitted their mistake. The newspapers expressed their sympathy with the standpoint of the Europeans in Natal, but at the same time fully defended my action. This enhanced my reputation as well as the prestige of the Indian community. It was proved that the Indians, poor as they were, were no cowards, and that the Indian traders were prepared to fight for their self-respect and for their country regardless of loss.

Thus though the Indian community had to suffer hardship and though Dada Abdulla incurred big losses, the ultimate result, I believe, was entirely beneficial. The community had an opportunity of measuring their own strength and their self-confidence increased in consequence. I had a most valuable experience, and whenever I think of that day, I feel that God was preparing me for the practice of Satyagraha.

The events in Natal had their repercussion in England. Mr Chamberlain, Secretary of State for the Colonies, cabled to the Government of Natal asking them to prosecute my assailants and to see that justice was done to me.

Mr Escombe, who was Attorney-General with the Government of Natal, called me. He told me about Mr Chamberlain's cable. He expressed his regret for the injuries I had sustained, and his pleasure that the consequences of the assault were not more serious. He added, "I can assure you that I did not at all intend that you or any other member of your communtiy should be injured. As I feared that you might possibly be hurt, I sent you word to say that you should land at night. You did not like my suggestion. I do not wish to blame you in the least that you accepted Mr Laughton's advice. You were perfectly entitled to do what you thought fit. The Government of Natal fully accepts Mr Chamberlain's demand. We desire that the offenders should be brought to book. Can you identify any of your assailants?"

I replied: "I might perhaps be able to identify one or two of them. But I must say at once before this conversation proceeds that I have already made up my mind not to prosecute my assailants. I cannot see that they are at fault. What information they had, they had obtained from their leaders. It is too much to expect them to judge whether it was correct or otherwise. If all that they heard about me was true, it was natural for them to be excited and do something wrong in a fit of indignation. I would not blame them for it. Excited crowds have always tried to deal out justice in that manner. If any one is to blame it is the Committee of Europeans, you yourself and therefore, the Government of Natal. Reuter might have cabled any distorted account. But when you knew that I was coming to Natal, it was your duty and duty of the Committee to question me about the suspicions you entertained with regard to my activities in India, to hear what I had to say and then do what might appear proper in the circumstances. Now I cannot prosecute you or the Committee for the assault. And even if I could, I would not seek redress in a court of law. You took such steps as seemed advisable to you for safeguarding the interests of the Europeans of Natal. That is a political matter, and it remains for me to fight with you in the political field and to convince you and the other Europeans that the Indians who constitute a large proportion of the population of the British Empire wish to preserve their self-respect and safeguard their rights without injuring the Europeans in the least."

Mr Escombe said, "I quite understand what you say, and I appreciate it. I was not prepared to hear that you were not willing to prosecute your assailants. I would not have been displeased in the least had you prosecuted them. But since you have signified your determination not to prosecute, I do not hesitate to say not only that you have come to a right decision in the matter, but you will render further service to your community by your self-restraint. I must at the same time admit that your refusal to prosecute your assailants will save the Government of Natal from a most awkward position. If you so desire, the Government will see that your assailants are arrested, but it is scarcely necessary to tell you that it would irritate the Europeans and give rise to all manner of criticism, which no Government would relish. But if you have finally made up your mind not to prosecute, you should write to me a note signifying your intention to that effect. I cannot defend my Government merely by sending Mr Chamberlain a summary of our conversation. I should cable to him a summary of your note. I am not, however, asking you to let me have the note just now. You had better consult your friends. Consult Mr Laughton also. And if after such consultations you still adhere to your resolution not to prosecute, write to me. But your note should clearly state that you, on your own responsibility, refuse to prosecute your assailants. Then only can I make use of it."

I said: "I had no idea that you had sent for me in this connection. I have not consulted any one on the subject, nor do I wish to consult any one now. When I decided to land and proceed with Mr Laughton, I had made up my mind that I should not feel aggrieved in case I was injured. Prosecuting my assailants is therefore out of the question. This is a religious question with me, and I believe with you that I shall serve my community as well as myself by this act of self-restraint. I propose, therefore, to take all the responsibility on my shoulders and to give you the note you ask for here and now."

I then obtained some blank paper from him, wrote out the desired note and handed it over to him.

CHAPTER VIII

A REVIEW OF THE EARLY STRUGGLE
Concluded

The Work in England

The reader has seen in the previous chapters how the Indians tried to ameliorate their condition and enhanced their prestige. Side by side with the effort to develop strength from within they sought such assistance as they could from India and England. I have dealt to some extent with the activities in India. It now remains to note what steps were taken to enlist support from England. It was essential, in the first place, to establish relations with the British Committee of the Indian National Congress; weekly letters with full particulars were therefore written to Dadabhai, the Grand Old Man of India, and to Sir William Wedderburn, the Chairman of the Committee and whenever there was an occasion to send copies of representations, a sum of at least 10 pounds was remitted as a contribution towards postal charges and the general expenditure of the Committee.

I shall here place on record a sacred reminiscence of Dadabhai Naoroji. He was not the Chairman of the Committee. It seemed to us, however, that the proper course for us was to send money to him in the first instance which he might then forward to the Chairman on our behalf. But Dadabhai returned the very first instalment sent to him and suggested that we should remit money, and address communications, intended for the Committee directly to Sir William Wedderburn. He himself would certainly render all possible assistance. But the prestige of the Committee would increase only if we approached the Committee through Sir William. I also observed that Dadabhai, though far advanced in age, was very regular in his correspondence. Even when he had nothing particular to write about he would acknowledge receipt of letters by return of post with a word of encouragement thrown in. Even such letters he used to write personally, and kept copies of them in his tissue paper book.

I have shown in a previous chapter that although we had called our organization the 'Congress,' we never intended to make our grievances a party question. We therefore corresponded with gentlemen belonging to other parties as well, with the full knowledge of Dadabhai. The most prominent among them were Sir Muncherjee Bhownuggree and Sir W. W. Hunter. Sir Muncherjee was then a member of Parliament. His assistance was valuable, and he always used to favour us with important suggestions. But if there was any one who had realized the importance of the Indian question in South Africa before the Indians themselves and accorded them valuable support, it was Sir William Wilson Hunter. He was editor of the Indian section of the *Times*, wherein he discussed our question in its true perspective, ever since we first addressed him in connection with it. He wrote personal letters to several gentlemen in support of our cause. He used to write to us almost every week when some important question was on the anvil. This is the purport of his very first letter: "I am sorry to read of the situation there. You have been conducting your struggle courteously, peacefully and without exaggeration. My sympathies are entirely with you on this question. I will do my best publicly as well as in private to see that justice is done to you. I am certain that we cannot yield even an inch of ground in this matter. Your demand being so reasonable, no impartial person would even suggest that you should moderate it." He reproduced the letter almost word for word in the first article he wrote for the *Times* on the question. His attitude remained the same throughout, and Lady Hunter wrote in the course of a letter that shortly before his death he had prepared an outline of a series of articles which he had planned on the Indian question.

I have mentioned the name of Shri Mansukhlal Nazar in the last chapter. This gentleman was deputed to England on behalf of the Indian community to explain the situation in detail. He was instructed to work with members of all parties, and during his stay in England he kept in touch with Sir W. W. Hunter, Sir Muncherjee Bhownuggree and the British Committee of the Indian National Congress. He was likewise in touch with several retired officers of the Indian Civil Service, with the India Office and with the Colonial Office. Thus our endeavours were directed in all possible quarters. The result of all this evidently was that the condition of Indians overseas became a question of first-rate importance in the eyes of the Imperial Government. This fact reacted for good as well as for evil on the other colonies. That is to say, in all the colonies where Indians had settled, they awoke to the importance of their own position and the Europeans awoke to the danger which they thought the Indians were to their predominance.

CHAPTER IX

THE BOER WAR

The reader has seen in the previous chapters what was the condition of the Indians in South Africa at the outbreak of the Boer War and what were the steps taken so far in order to ameliorate it.

In 1899 Dr Jameson carried out his raid on Johannesburg in pursuance of the conspiracy which he had entered into with the owners of the gold mines. The conspirators had expected that the Boer Government would come to know of the raid only after they captured Johannesburg. Dr Jameson and his associates badly blundered in this calculation of theirs. They fell into another error when they imagined that even in case of the plot being discovered, untrained Boer farmers could do nothing against sharpshooters trained in Rhodesia. The raiders had likewise expected that a large majority of the population of Johannesburg would receive them with open arms. Here too the good

Doctor was reckoning without his host. President Kruger had full information beforehand. With great deliberation, skill and secrecy he made preparations to meet Dr Jameson and simultaneously arranged to arrest his fellow conspirators. Dr Jameson, therefore, was greeted by the Boers with gunfire before he had reached anywhere near Johannesburg. The Doctor's party was in no position to try conclusions with the army which faced them. Arrangements were similarly complete for preventing a rising in Johannesburg. None dared raise their heads and the millionaires of Johannesburg were dumbfounded in consequence of President Kruger's action. The result of his excellent preparations was that the raid was disposed of with a minimum of loss in men as well as money.

Dr Jameson and his friends, the owners of gold mines, were arrested and placed on their trial without delay. Some were sentenced to be hanged. Most of these convicts were millionaires; but the Imperial Government could do nothing for them, as they were guilty of a raid in broad daylight. President Kruger became an important man all at once. Mr Chamberlain, the Secretary of State for the Colonies, sent a humble cablegram to him, and appealed to his sense of mercy on behalf of the convicted magnates. President Kruger was perfect master of his own game. He had no apprehension of his independence being challenged by any power in South Africa. The conspiracy of Dr Jameson and his friends was a well-planned affair in their own eyes, but to President Kruger it seemed to be an act of insensate folly. He therefore complied with Mr Chamberlain's humble request and not only did not enforce the sentence of death against any of the convicts but granted them all full pardon and set them free.

But things could not go on like this for any length of time. President Kruger knew that the Jameson raid was only a minor symptom of a serious malady. It was impossible that the millionaires of Johannesburg should not endeavour to wipe out their disgrace by all means in their power. Again, nothing had been done to carry out the reforms for which the Jameson raid purported to have been organized. The millionaires, therefore, were not likely to hold their peace. Lord Milner, the British High Commissioner in South Africa, had full sympathy with their demands. Mr Chamberlain, too, while expressing his appreciation of President Kruger's magnanimity towards the Jameson raiders, had drawn his attention to the necessity for reforms. Every one believed that an appeal to the sword was inevitable. The demands of the Uitlanders were calculated in the end to extinguish Boer domination in the Transvaal. Both the parties were aware that the ultimate result would be war, and both were therefore preparing for it. The war of words which ensued was worthy of note. When President Kruger ordered out arms and ammunition, the British Agent warned him that the British would be compelled to bring troops into South Africa in self-defence. When British troops arrived in South Africa President Kruger taunted the British and pushed forward his preparations for war. Thus each side was protesting against the other's activities and strengthening its own preparations.

When President Kruger had completed his preparations, he saw that to delay any longer was to play into the hands of his enemies. The British had an inexhaustible supply of men and money. They could, therefore, afford to bide their time, gradually preparing for war and in the meantime ask President Kruger to redress the grievances of Uitlanders, and thus show to the world that they could not help waging war as he refused to grant redress. Then they would enter the war with such grand preparations that the Boers could not stand the shock and would have to accept British demands in a spirit of humiliation. Every Boer man between eighteen and sixty years in age was a skilled fighter. Boer women, too, were capable for fighting if they chose. National independence had with the Boers all the force of a religious principle. Such a brave people would not suffer humiliation even at the hands of a world empire.

President Kruger had already arrived at an understanding with the Orange Free State. Both the Boer republics followed an identical policy. President Kruger had not the slightest intention of accepting the British demands whether in full or even to the extent of satisfying

THE BOER WAR

the Uitlanders. Both the republics, therefore, thought that war being inevitable, for them to give any more time to the British was only to give them a chance of advancing their preparations. President Kruger thereupon delivered an ultimatum to Lord Milner, and at the same time mobilized troops on the frontiers of the Transvaal as well as the Free State. The result of such action was a foregone conclusion. A world empire like the British would not take a threat lying down. The time limit laid down in the ultimatum expired and the Boers, advancing with lightning speed, laid siege to Ladysmith, Kimberley and Mafeking. This great war thus broke out in 1899. The reader will remember that one of the causes of the war alleged by the British was the treatment accorded to the Indians by the Boers.

The great question, as to what the Indians in South Africa should do on this occasion, now presented itself for solution. Among the Boers, the entire male population joined the war. Lawyers gave up their practice, farmers their farms, traders their trade, and servants left their service. The British in South Africa did not join the war in anything like the same proportion as the Boers. However, a large number of civilians in Cape Colony, Natal and Rhodesia enrolled themselves as volunteers. Many distinguished English traders and lawyers followed suit. I now found very few lawyers in the court where I was practising as an advocate. Most of the senior members of the bar were engaged in war work. One of the charges laid against the Indians was, that they went to South Africa only for money-grabbing and were merely a dead-weight upon the British. Like worms which settle inside wood and eat it up hollow, the Indians were in South Africa only to fatten themselves upon them. The Indians would not render them the slightest aid if the country was invaded or if their homes were raided. The British in such a case would have not only to defend themselves against the enemy but at the same time to protect the Indians. We Indians carefully considered this charge. All of us felt that this was a golden opportunity for us to prove that it was baseless. But on the other hand the following considerations were also urged by some:

"The British oppress us equally with the Boers. If we are subjected to hardships in the Transvaal, we are not very much better off in Natal or the Cape Colony. The difference, if any, is only one of degree. Again we are more or less a community of slaves; knowing as we do that a small nation like the Boers is fighting for its very existence, why should we be instrumental in their destruction? Finally, from a practical point of view, no one will take it upon himself to predict a defeat for the Boers. And if they win, they will never fail to wreak vengeance upon us."

There was a powerful party among us which strongly advanced the above argument. I could understand it and allowed it due weight. However, it did not commend itself to me, and I refuted it to myself and to the community as follows :

"Our existence in South Africa is only in our capacity as British subjects. In every memorial we have presented, we have asserted our rights as such. We have been proud of our British citizenship, or have given our rulers and the world to believe that we are so proud. Our rulers profess to safeguard our rights because we are British subjects, and what little rights we still retain, we retain because we are British subjects. It would be unbecoming to our dignity as a nation to look on with folded hands at a time when ruin stared the British in the face as well as ourselves, simply because they ill-treat us here. And such criminal inaction could only aggravate our difficulties. If we missed this opportunity, which had come to us unsought, of proving the falsity of a charge which we believed to be false, we should stand self-condemned, and it would be no matter for surprise if then the English treated us worse than before and sneered at us more than ever. The fault in such a case would lie entirely at our door. To say, that the charges preferred against ourselves had no foundation in fact and were absolutely untenable, would only be to deceive ourselves. It is true that we are helots in the Empire, but so far we have tried to better our condition, continuing the while to remain in the Empire. That has been the policy of all our leaders in

India, and ours too. And if we desire to win our freedom and achieve our welfare as members of the British Empire, here is a golden opportunity for us to do so by helping the British in the war by all the means at our disposal. It must largely be conceded that justice is on the side of the Boers. But every single subject of a state must not hope to enforce his private opinion in all cases. The authorities may not always be right, but so long as the subjects own allegiance to a state, it is their clear duty generally to accommodate themselves, and to accord their support, to acts of the state.

"Again, if any class among the subjects considers that the action of a government is immoral from a religious standpoint, before they help or hinder it, they must endeavour fully and even at the risk of their lives to dissuade the government from pursuing such a course. We have done nothing of the kind. Such a moral crisis is not present before us, and no one says that we wish to hold aloof from this war for any such universal and comprehensive reason. Our ordinary duty as subjects, therefore, is not to enter into the merits of the war, but when war has actually broken out, to render such assistance as we possibly can. Finally, to suggest that in case the Boers won, — and a Boer victory was well within the range of possibility, — our last state would be worse than our first, and the Boers would exact frightful revenge, would be doing injustice to the chivalrous Boers as well as to ourselves. To waste the slightest thought upon such a contingency would only be a sign of our effeminacy and a reflection on our loyalty. Would an Englishman think for a moment what would happen to himself if the English lost the war? A man about to join a war cannot advance such an argument without forfeiting his manhood."

I advanced these arguments in 1899, and even today I do not see any reason for modifying them. That is to say, if I had today the faith in the British Empire which I then entertained, and if I now cherished the hope, which I did at that time, of achieving our freedom under its aegis, I would advance the same arguments, word for word, in South Africa, and, in similar circumstances, even in India. I heard many attempted refutations of these arguments in South Africa and subsequently in England. But I discovered no ground for changing my views. I know that my present opinions have no bearing on the subject of this volume, but there are two valid reasons why I have adverted to the matter here. I have, in the first place, no right to expect that the reader who takes up this book in a hurry will give it a patient and attentive perusal, and such a reader will find it difficult to reconcile the above views with my present activities. Secondly, the underlying principle in the above arguments is Satyagraha, insistence on truth. That one should appear to be as one really is and should act accordingly, is not the last, but the first step to practical religion. The building up of a religious life is impossible without such a foundation.

To return to our narrative.

My arguments commended themselves to many. The reader must not suppose that I was the only one to advance them. Moreover, even before these views were set forth, there were many Indians who held that we should do our bit in the war. But now the practical question arose: Who would lend an ear to the weak voice of the Indians when there was raging this terrible whirlwind of war? What weight would this offer of help carry? None of us had ever wielded a weapon of war. Even the work performed by non-combatants in a war required training. None of us knew even how to march in step. It was no easy task to perform long marches with one's baggage on one's own shoulders. Again, the whites would treat us all as 'coolies,' insult us and look down upon us. How was all this to be borne? And if we volunteered for service, how could we induce the Government to accept our offer? Finally, we came to the conclusion, that we should make earnest endeavours to get our offer accepted, that the experience of work would teach us to do more work, that if we had the will, God would grant us the ability to serve, that we need not worry how we could do the work entrusted but should train ourselves for it as best we might, and that having once decided to serve, we

THE BOER WAR

should cease to think of discriminating between dignified work and other and serve, putting up even with insults if it came to that.

We encountered formidable difficulties in getting our offer favourably entertained. The story is interesting but this is not the place to detail it. Suffice it to say that the leaders among us received training in nursing the wounded and the sick, obtained medical certificates of physical fitness and sent a formal letter to the Government. This letter and the eagerness we evinced to serve in whatever capacity the Government would accept us created a very good impression. The Government thanked us in reply but rejected our offer for the time. Meanwhile the Boers continued to advance like a great flood, and it was feared that they might reach Durban. There were heaps of wounded and dead everywhere. We were continually renewing our offer, and sanction was given at last for the formation of an Indian Ambulance Corps. We had expressed our willingness even to do sweepers' or scavengers' work in hospitals. No wonder, therefore, that the idea of an Ambulance Corps was perfectly welcome to us. Our offer had been made, in the first instance, in respect of free and ex-indentured Indians, but we had suggested the desirability of permitting the indentured Indians too to join the rest. As Government was then in need of as many men as they could get, they approached the employers of indentured labourers to allow their men to volunteer. Thus a large and splendid Corps composed of nearly eleven hundred Indians left Durban for the front. At the time of our departure, we received the congratulations and the blessings of Mr Escombe, whose name is already familiar to the reader and who was the head of the European volunteers in Natal.

All this was a complete revelation to the English newspapers. No one expected that the Indians would take any part in the war. An Englishman wrote in a leading newspaper a poem eulogistic of the Indians with the following line as a refrain: 'We are sons of the Empire after all.'

There were between three and four hundred ex-indentured Indians in the Corps, who had been recruited by the efforts of the free Indians. Of these, thirty-seven were looked upon as leaders, as the offer to Government had been sent under their signatures and as they had brought the others together. Among the leaders there were barristers and accountants, while the rest were either artisans such as masons or carpenters, or ordinary labourers. Hindus and Musalmans, Madrasis and upcountry men, all classes and creeds were well represented. There was hardly any trader in the Corps, but the traders subscribed considerable sums of money. The Corps had needs which were not adequately met by the military rations, and which, if satisfied, might provide them with some amenities in their hard camp life. The traders undertook to supply such comforts, and likewise rendered good assistance in entertaining the wounded in our charge with sweets, cigarettes and such other things. Whenever we camped near towns, the local traders did their best to look after us.

The indentured labourers, who joined this Corps were under the charge of English overseers from their respective factories. But the work for them was the same as for ourselves and as we were all to live together, they were highly pleased at the prospect, and the management of the entire Corps naturally passed into our hands. Thus the whole Corps was described as the Indian Corps, and the community received the credit for its work. As a matter of fact the Indians were not entitled to the credit for the inclusion of indentured labourers in the Corps, which should rightly have gone to the planters. But there is no doubt that the free Indians, that is to say, the Indian community, deserved credit for the excellent management of the Corps when once it was formed and this was acknowledged by General Buller in his despatches.

Doctor Booth, under whom we had placed ourselves for training in first aid, joined the Corps in the capacity of Medical Superintendent. He was a pious clergyman, and though his work chiefly lay among the Indian Christians, he freely mixed with Indians of all denominations. Most of the thirty-seven leaders mentioned above had received their training at his hands.

There was a European Ambulance Corps as well as the Indian, and both worked side by side in the same place.

Our offer to Government was absolutely unconditional, but the letter by which they accepted it granted us immunity from service within the firing line. This meant that the permanent Ambulance Corps attached to the army was to bear far away the soldiers as they got wounded and leave them behind the army outside the line of fire. The temporary Ambulance Corps of Europeans as well as Indians were formed in view of the great effort which General Buller was to put forth for the relief of General White in Ladysmith and in which, it was apprehended, there might be more wounded than could be dealt with by the permanent Corps. In the country where the armies were operating there were no made roads between the battlefield and the base-hospital and it was therefore impossible to carry the wounded by means of ordinary transport. The base-hospital was always situated near a railway station and at a distance of between seven and twenty-five miles from the battlefield.

We soon got work and that too harder than we had expected. To carry the wounded seven or eight miles was part of our ordinary routine. But sometimes we had to carry badly wounded soldiers and officers over a distance of twenty-five miles. The march would commence at eight in the morning, medicines must be administered on the way, and we were required to reach the base-hospital at five. This was very hard work indeed. It was only once that we had to carry the wounded twenty-five miles in a single day. Again the British army met with reverse after reverse in the beginning of the war and large numbers were wounded. The officers therefore were compelled to give up their idea of not taking us within the firing line. But it must be stated that when such an emergency arose we were told that as the terms of our contract included immunity from such service, General Buller had no intention of forcing us to work under fire if we were not prepared to accept such risk, but if we undertook it voluntarily, it would be greatly appreciated. We were only too willing to enter the danger zone and had never liked to remain outside. We therefore welcomed this opportunity. But none of us received a bullet wound or any other injury.

The Corps had many pleasant experiences into which I may not enter here. It must however be placed on record, that although our Corps, including the indentured labourers who might be supposed to be rather uncouth, often came in contact with the members of the temporary Ambulance Corps composed of Europeans as well as with the European soldiers, none of us felt that Europeans treated us with contempt or even with discourtesy. The temporary Corps was composed of South African Europeans, who had taken part in the anti-Indian agitation before the war. But the knowledge that the Indians, forgetful of their wrongs, were out to help them in the hour of their need, had melted their hearts for the time being. I have stated already that our work was mentioned by General Buller in his despatches. War medals too were conferred on the thirty-seven leaders.

When General Buller's operations in connection with the relief of Ladysmith were over, that is in about two months' time, our Corps was disbanded as well as the European. The war continued long after this. We were always prepared to rejoin, and it was stated in the order disbanding our Corps that Government would certainly utilize our services if operations on a large scale were again necessary.

This contribution of the Indians in South Africa to the war was comparatively insignificant. They suffered hardly any loss of life. Yet even a sincere desire to be of help is bound to impress the other party, and is doubly appreciated when it is quite unexpected. Such fine feeling for the Indians lasted during the continuance of the war.

Before closing this chapter, I must place a noteworthy incident on record. Among those who were in Ladysmith when it was invested by the Boers, there were besides Englishmen a few stray Indian settlers. Some of these were traders, while the rest were indentured labourers, working on the railways or as servants to English gentlemen, one of whom was Parbhusingh. The officer in command at Ladysmith assigned various duties to every resident of the place. The most dangerous and most responsible work was assigned to Parbhusingh who was a 'coolie.' On a hill near Ladysmith the Boers had stationed a pom-pom, whose operations destroyed many buildings and even occasioned some loss of life. An interval of a minute or two must pass before a shell which had been fired from the gun reached a distant objective. If the besieged got even such a short notice, they could take cover before the shell dropped in the town and thus save themselves. Parbhusingh was to sit perched up in a tree, all the time that the gun was working, with his eyes fixed on the hill and to ring a bell the moment he observed a flash. On hearing the bell, the residents of Ladysmith instantly took cover and saved themselves from the deadly cannon ball whose approach was thus announced.

The officer in charge of Ladysmith, in eulogizing the invaluable services rendered by Parbhusingh, stated that he worked so zealously that not once had he failed to ring the bell. It need hardly be said that his own life was constantly in peril. The story of his bravery came to be known in Natal and at last reached the ears of Lord Curzon, then Viceroy of India, who sent a Kashmir robe for presentation to Parbhusingh and wrote to the Natal Government, asking them to carry out the presentation ceremony with all possible publicity. This duty was assigned to the Mayor of Durban who held a public meeting in the Town Hall for the purpose. This incident has a twofold lesson for us. First, we should not despise any man, however humble or insignificant-looking he may be. Secondly, no matter how timid a man is, he is capable of the loftiest heroism when he is put to the test.

CHAPTER X
AFTER THE WAR

The most important phase of the war was over in 1900. Ladysmith, Kimberley and Mafeking had been relieved. General Cronje had surrendered at Paardeburg. Parts of the British colonies occupied by the Boers had been wrested from their hands and Lord Kitchener had conquered the Transvaal and the Orange Free State. Only guerilla warfare was left.

I thought that my work in South Africa was now over. I had stayed there six years instead of one month as originally intended. The outlines of the work before us were fairly fixed. Still I could not leave South Africa without the willing consent of the Indian community. I informed my colleagues that I intended taking up public work in India. I had learnt in South Africa the lesson of service instead of self-interest, and was longing for opportunities of such work. Shri Mansukhlal Nazar was there and so was Mr Khan. Some Indian youths born and bred in South Africa had returned from England as barristers. In these circumstances it would not be improper if I returned to India. When I had urged all these arguments, I was permitted to return only on the condition that if an unexpected situation arose in South Africa requiring my presence there, the community might recall me any day and I should at once go back. They undertook in such a case to bear my travelling expenses and the expenses incurred during my stay in South Africa. I agreed to this arrangement and returned to India.

I decided to practise in Bombay as a barrister, primarily with a view to public work under the advice and guidance of Gokhale and secondarily in order to make a living for myself side by side with public work. I rented chambers accordingly and began to get some work. Thanks to my close connection with South Africa, clients who had returned from that country alone gave me work which more than sufficed for my necessities. But peace was never to be my portion in this life. I had been in Bombay hardly three or four months when I received an urgent cablegram from South Africa stating that the situation there was serious, that Mr Chamberlain was expected shortly, and that my presence was necessary.

I wound up my Bombay office and house and started for South Africa by the first available steamer. This was near the end of 1902. I had returned to India towards the close of 1901 and had opened my office at Bombay about March 1902. The cablegram did not contain full details. I guessed that there was trouble in the Transvaal. But I went to South Africa without my family as I thought I would be able to return to India in four or six months, I was however simply amazed when I reached Durban and heard everything. Many of us had hoped that the position of Indians throughout South Africa would improve after the war. We did not anticipate trouble in the Transvaal and the Free State at any rate, as Lord Landsdowne, Lord Selborne and other high functionaries had declared when the war broke out that the treatment accorded to the Indians by the Boers was one of the causes of the war. The British Agent at Pretoria had often told me that if the Transvaal became a British Colony, all the grievances under which the Indians laboured would be instantly redressed. The Europeans too believed that as the Transvaal was now under the British flag, the old laws of the Boer republic directed against the Indians could not be enforced. This principle was so widely accepted that the auctioneers who before the war did not accept bids from Indians for the purchase of land now openly accepted such bids. Many Indians thus purchased lands at public auctions, but when they tendered the deeds of transfer to the revenue officer for registration, the officer in charge refused to register the deeds quoting Act 3 of 1885 ! All this I learnt on landing at Durban. The leaders said that Mr Chamberlain would first come to Durban and we must first acquaint him with the situation in Natal. This done, I was to follow him to the Transvaal.

A deputation waited upon Mr Chamberlain in Natal. He gave it a courteous hearing and promised to confer with the Natal Government on the subject of its representations. Personally I did not expect that the laws which had been promulgated in Natal before the war would be modified very soon. These laws have already been described in a previous chapter.

As the reader is aware, any Indian could at any time enter the Transvaal before the war. I observed that this was not the case now any longer. The restrictions however, equally applied to all — Europeans as well as Indians. The condition of the country was still such, that if a large number of people entered the Transvaal all at once, there would not be sufficient food and clothing to go round, as all the shops had not reopened after the war. The goods stocked in the shops had been unceremoniously appropriated by the late Boer Government. I therefore thought, that if the restrictions were only temporary, there was no reason for apprehension. But then there was a difference in the procedure by which a European and an Indian could obtain a permit, and this afforded ground for misgiving and alarm. Permit offices were opened in the various ports of South Africa. For all practical purposes a European could obtain permit for the mere asking, while an Asiatic Department was created in the Transvaal for dealing with Indians. The creation of this special department was a new departure. Indians were required to apply to the head of that department in the first instance. After he had granted their applications, they could generally obtain permits at Durban or any other port.

If I had to go through all these formalities there was no hope of my getting a permit before Mr Chamberlain left the Transvaal. The Indians in the Transvaal could not procure a permit for me. It was more than they could do. They had therefore relied upon my connections in Durban for obtaining a permit for me. I did not know the permit officer, but as I knew the Police Superintendent of Durban, I asked him to accompany me to the permit office. He consented and gave the necessary assurances. I obtained a permit on the strength of the fact that I had stayed in the Transvaal for a year in 1893 and thus reached Pretoria.

The atmosphere in Pretoria was decidedly ominous. I could see that the Asiatic Department was merely a frightful engine of oppression for the Indians. The officers in charge were some of the adventurers who had accompanied the army from India to South Africa during the war and had settled there in order to try their luck. Some of them were corrupt. Two officers were even prosecuted for bribery. The jury declared them not guilty, but as really there was no doubt entertained as to their guilt, they were subsequently dismissed from service. Partiality was the order of the day. When a separate department is thus created and when restricting existing rights is the sole reason for its existence, officers are naturally inclined to devise fresh restriction from time to time in order to justify their existence and in order to show that they are efficient in the discharge of their duties. This is exactly what happened in the present case.

I saw that I had to begin my work from the very beginning. The Asiatic Department could not at once make out how I had managed to enter the Transvaal. They did not venture to ask me directly. I imagine they thought me above smuggling myself into the country. They indirectly obtained information as to how I had secured a permit. A deputation from Pretoria prepared to wait upon Mr Chamberlain. I drafted the memorial for submission to him but the Asiatic Department excluded me from the deputation. It appeared to the Indian leaders that they should not see Mr Chamberlain if I was prevented from going with them. But I did not countenance this idea. I said that I should not mind the insult to me and advised them to ignore it too. The memorial was there and it was essential that it should be presented to Mr Chamberlain. Mr George Godfrey, an Indian barrister, who was present at the time, was charged with the task of reading the memorial. The deputation waited upon Mr Chamberlain. My name being mentioned in course of the interview, he said, "I have already seen Mr Gandhi in Durban. I therefore refused to see him here, in order that I might learn about the situation in the Transvaal at first hand from local residents." In my view this remark only added fuel to the fire. Mr Chamberlain spoke out as he had been tutored by the Asiatic Department, which thus tried to import into the Transvaal the atmosphere which pervades India. Every one knows how British officers consider Bombay men as foreigners, in, say, Champaran. At that rate how could I who lived in Durban know anything about the situation in the Transvaal? Thus did the Asiatic Department coach Mr Chamberlain. Little did he know that I had lived in the Transvaal, and that even if I had not, I was fully conversant with the Indian situation there. There was only one pertinent question in the present case: Who possessed the best knowledge of the situation in the Transvaal? The Indians had already answered it for themselves by asking me to go there all the way from India. But it is no new experience to find that arguments based on reason do not always appeal to men in authority. Mr Chamberlain was then so much under the influence of the men on the spot and so anxious was he to humour the Europeans that there was little or no hope of his doing us justice. Still the deputation waited upon him, only in order that no legitimate step for obtaining redress might be omitted whether by oversight or through a sense of wounded self-respect.

I was now confronted by a dilemma even more difficult than the one which faced me in 1894. From one standpoint, it seemed I could return to India as soon as Mr Chamberlain left South Africa. On the other hand I could clearly see that if I returned with the vain fancy of serving on a larger field in India while I was fully aware of the great danger which stared the South African Indians in the face, the spirit of service which I had acquired would be stultified. I thought that even if that meant living in South Africa all my life, I must remain there until the gathering clouds were dispersed or until they broke upon and swept us all away, all our counteracting efforts notwithstanding. This is how I spoke to the Indian leaders. Now, as in 1894, I declared my intention to maintain myself by legal practice. As for the community, this was precisely what they wanted.

I soon applied for admission to practise in the Transvaal. There was some apprehension that the Law Society here too would oppose my application, but it proved groundless. I was enrolled as an attorney of the Supreme Court, and opened an office in Johannesburg. Of all places in the Transvaal, Johannesburg had the largest population of Indians and was therefore well suited for me to settle in, from the standpoint of public work as well as of my own maintenance. I was daily gaining bitter experience of the corruptness of the Asiatic Department, and the best efforts of the Transvaal British Indian Association were directed to finding a remedy for this disease. The repeal of Act 3 of 1885 now receded in the background as a distant objective. The immediate aim was limited to saving ourselves from the on-rushing flood in the shape of this Asiatic Department. Indian deputations waited upon Lord Milner, upon Lord Selborne who had come there, upon Sir Arthur Lawley who was Lieutenant Governor of the Transvaal and who subsequently became Governor of Madras, and upon officers of lesser dignity. I often used to see Government officers. We obtained some slight relief here and there, but it was all patchwork. We used to receive some such satisfaction as is experienced by a man who has been deprived of his all by robbers and who by beseeching the robbers induces them to return something of very small value. It was in consequence of this agitation that the officers whose dismissal I have referred to above were prosecuted. Our misgivings as regards the restrictions on Indian immigration proved correct. Permits were no longer required from Europeans, while they continued to be demanded from Indians. The late Boer Government never strictly enforced their drastic anti-Asiatic legislation, not because they were generous but because their administration was lax. A good officer has not under the British Government as much scope for the exercise of his goodness as he had under the Boer regime. The British Constitution is old and stereotyped, and officers under it have to work like machines. Their liberty of action is restricted by a system of progressive checks. Under the British Constitution, therefore, if the policy of the Government is liberal, the subjects receive the utmost advantage of its liberality. On the other hand if their policy is oppressive or niggardly, the subjects feel the maximum weight of their heavy hand. The reverse is the case under constitutions such as that of the late Boer republic. Whether or not the subjects reap full advantage from a liberal law largely depends upon the officers who are charged with its administration. Thus, when British power was established in the Transvaal, all laws adversely affecting the Indians began to be more and more strictly enforced day by day. Loopholes, wherever they existed, were carefully closed. We have already seen that the Asiatic Department was bound to be harsh in its operations. The repeal of the old laws was therefore out of the question. It only remained for the Indians to try and see how their rigours might be mitigated in practice.

One principle must be discussed sooner or later, and if we discuss it at this stage, it will perhaps facilitate an understanding of the Indian point of view and of the situation as it developed hereafter. Soon after the establishment of British rule in the Transvaal and the Free State, Lord Milner appointed a committee whose terms of reference were to prepare a list of such of the old laws of both the republics as placed restrictions on the liberty of the subject or were opposed to the spirit of the British Constitution. The anti-Indian laws could clearly have been included in this description. But Lord Milner's object in appointing the committee was not to redress the grievances of Indians but those of Britishers. He wanted to repeal at the earliest opportunity those laws which indirectly pressed hard upon Britishers. The committee submitted their report in a very short time, and many acts, large and small, which affected Britishers prejudicially, were, it can be said, repealed by a stroke of the pen.

The same committee prepared a list of anti-Indian acts. These were published in the form of a book which served as a handy manual easily used or from our standpoint abused by the Asiatic Department.

Now, if the anti-Indian laws did not mention the Indians by name and were not thus made expressly applicable to them alone but to all subjects, and if their enforcement had been left to the discretion of administrators; or had the laws imposed general restrictions which could have been enforced against Indians in a specially rigorous manner, the object of the legislators would all the same have been achieved by such laws, and yet the laws would have been general laws. None would have felt insulted by their enactment, and when the existing bitterness was softened by time, there would be no need to modify the laws, but only a more liberal administration of the laws would have sufficed to relieve the aggrieved community. Just as I have called laws of the second kind general laws, those of the first kind can be described as particular or racial, and establish what is known as the 'colour bar,' as on the specific ground of colour they impose greater restrictions on members of the dark or brown races than on Europeans.

To take one instance from the laws which were already in force. The reader will remember that the first disfranchising Act which was enacted in Natal but was subsequently disallowed by the Imperial Government provided for the disqualification as voters of all Asiatics as such. Now if such a law were to be altered public opinion should be so far educated that the majority be not only not hostile but actually friendly to Asiatics. The colour bar it set up could only be removed when such cordial feelings were established. This is an illustration of racial or class legislation. The Act referred to was withdrawn and a second Act was enacted in its place which nearly achieved an identical object yet was of a general nature, the sting of racial distinction being removed. The substance of one of its clauses is as follows: 'No person can be placed on the voters' roll in Natal who is a native of countries which have not hitherto possessed elective representative institutions based on the parliamentary franchise.' No reference is made here to Indians or Asiatics. The opinions of counsels could differ as to whether or not India possesses representative institutions based on the parliamentary franchise. But assuming for the sake of argument that India did not in 1894 and does not even now enjoy the parliamentary franchise, no one can say offhand that the officer in charge of voters' lists in Natal has done an illegal act if he includes the names of Indians in the lists. There is always a general presumption in favour of the right of the subject. So long therefore as the government of the day does not become positively hostile, the names of Indians and others could be included in the electoral roll, the above law notwithstanding. That is to say, if the dislike for Indians became less marked and if the local Government was unwilling to injure the Indians, their names could be entered in the voters' lists without the slightest modification of the law. This is the advantage of a general law. Other instances of the same kind can be cited from among the laws in force in South Africa which have been referred to in previous chapters. The wise policy, therefore, is to enact as little class legislation as possible; and it would be wiser still to avoid it altogether. Once a law is enacted, many difficulties must be encountered before it can be reversed. It is only when public opinion is highly educated that the laws in force in a country can be repealed. A constitution under which laws are modified or repealed every now and then cannot be said to be stable or well organized.

We can now better appreciate the poison which was present in the anti-Asiatic laws in the Transvaal. They were all racial in character. The Asiatics as such could not vote; nor could they own land outside the locations set apart for them by the Government. The administrators could do nothing for the Indians so long as these laws were not removed from the statute-book. Lord Milner's committee could make a separate list of such laws only as were not general in character. Had they been general laws, all laws, enforced only against the Asiatics though not expressly directed against them, would have been repealed along with the rest. The officers in charge could never have argued their helplessness and said that they had no alternative but to enforce the laws so long as the new legislature did not abrogate them.

When these laws passed into the hands of the Asiatic Department it began to enforce them strictly. If the laws were at all worthy of being enforced, Government must arm itself with further powers in order to close the loopholes intentionally kept or left by inadvertence in favour of Asiatics. This looks quite simple and straight. Either the laws are bad in which case they should be repealed, or they are proper in which case their deficiencies should be remedied. The ministers had adopted the policy of enforcing the laws. The Indians had stood shoulder to shoulder with the British and risked their lives during the late war, but that was now a story three or four years old. The British Agent at Pretoria had put up a fight on behalf of the Indians, but that was during the old regime. The grievances of the Indians figured as one of the declared causes of the war, but that declaration was made by short-sighted statesmen who had no knowledge of local conditions. The local officials clearly observed that the anti-Asiatic laws enacted by the late Boer Government were neither adequately severe nor systematic. If the Indians could enter the Transvaal at will and carry on trade wherever they chose, British traders would suffer great loss. All these and similar arguments carried greater weight with the Europeans and their representatives in the ministry. They were all out to amass the maximum of wealth in a minimum of time; how could they stand the Indians becoming co-sharers with them? Hypocrisy pressed political theory into service in order to make out a plausible case. A bare-faced selfish or mercantile argument would not satisfy the intelligent Europeans of South Africa. The human intellect delights in inventing specious arguments in order to support injustice itself, and the South African Europeans were no exception to this general rule. These were the arguments advanced by General Smuts and others:

"South Africa is a representative of Western civilization while India is the centre of Oriental culture. Thinkers of the present generation hold that these two civilizations cannot go together. If nations representing these rival cultures meet even in small groups, the result will only be an explosion. The West is opposed to simplicity while Orientals consider that virtue to be of primary importance. How can these opposite views be reconciled? It is not the business of statesmen, practical men as they are, to adjudicate upon their relative merits. Western civilization may or may not be good, but Westerners wish to stick to it. They have made tireless endeavours to save that civilization. They have shed rivers of blood for its sake. They have suffered great hardships in its cause. It is therefore too late for them now to chalk out a new path for themselves. Thus considered, the Indian question cannot be resolved into one of trade jealousy or race hatred. The problem is simply one of preserving one's own civilization, that is of enjoying the supreme right of self-preservation and discharging the corresponding duty. Some public speakers may like to inflame the Europeans by finding fault with Indians, but political thinkers believe and say that the very qualities of Indians count for defects in South Africa. The Indians are disliked in South Africa for their simplicity, patience, perseverance, frugality and otherworldliness. Westerners are enterprising, impatient, engrossed in multiplying their material wants and in satisfying them, fond of good cheer, anxious to save physical labour and prodigal in habits. They are therefore afraid that if thousands of Orientals settled in South Africa, the Westerners must go to the wall. Westerners in South Africa are not prepared to commit suicide and their leaders will not permit them to be reduced to such straits."

I believe I have impartially recapitulated the arguments urged by men of the highest character among the Europeans. I have characterized their arguments as pseudo-philosophical, but I do not thereby wish to suggest that they are groundless. From a practical point of view, that is to say, from the standpoint of immediate self-interest they have much force. But from the philosophical point of view, they are hypocrisy pure and simple. In my humble opinion, no impartial person could accept such conclusions and no reformer would place his civilization in the position of helplessness in which those who urge these arguments have placed theirs. So far as I am aware, no Eastern thinker fears that if Western nations came in free contact with Orientals, Oriental culture would be swept away like sand by the onrushing tide of Western civilization. So far as I have a grasp of Eastern thought it seems to me that Oriental civilization not only does not fear but would positively welcome free contact with Western civilization. If contrary instances can be met with in the East, they do not affect the principle I have laid down, for a number of illustrations can be cited in its support. However that may be, Western thinkers claim that the foundation of Western civilization is the predominance of might over right. Therefore it is that the protagonists of that civilization devote most of their time to the conservation of brute force. These thinkers likewise assert that the nations which do not increase their material wants are doomed to destruction. It is in pursuance of these principles that Western nations have settled in South Africa and subdued the numerically overwhelmingly superior races of South Africa. It is absurd to imagine that they would fear the harmless population of India. The best proof of the statement that the Europeans have nothing to fear from the Asiatics is provided by the fact that had the Indians continued to work in South Africa for all time as mere labourers, no agitation would have been started against Indian immigration.

The only remaining factors are trade and colour. Thousands of Europeans have admitted in their writings that trade by Indians hits petty British traders hard, and that the dislike of the brown races has at present become part and parcel of the mentality of Europeans. Even in the United States of America, where the principle of statutory equality has been established, a man like Booker T. Washington who has received the best Western education, is a Christian of high character and has fully assimilated Western civilization, was not considered fit for admission to the court of President Roosevelt, and probably would not be so considered even today. The Negroes of the United States have accepted Western civilization. They have embraced Christianity. But the black pigment of their skin constitutes their crime, and if in the Northern

States they are socially despised, they are lynched in the Southern States on the slightest suspicion of wrongdoing.

The reader will thus see that there is not much substance in the 'philosophical' arguments discussed above. But he must not therefore conclude that all those who urge them do so in a hypocritical spirit. Many of them honestly hold these views to be sound. It is possible that if we were placed in their position, we too would advance similar arguments. We have a saying in India that as is a man's conduct, such is his understanding. Who is there but has observed that our arguments are but a reflection of our mentality, and that if they do not commend themselves to others, we become dissatisfied, impatient and even indignant?

I have deliberately discussed this question with much minuteness, as I wish the reader to understand different points of view and in order that the reader, who has so far not done so, may acquire the habit of appreciating and respecting varieties of standpoint. Such large-mindedness and such patience are essential to the understanding of Satyagraha and above all to its practice. Satyagraha is impossible in the absence of these qualities. I do not write this book merely for the writing of it. Nor is it my object to place one phase of the history of South Africa before the public. My object in writing the present volume is that the nation might know how Satyagraha, for which I live, for which I desire to live and for which I believe I am equally prepared to die, originated and how it was practised on a large scale; and knowing this, it may understand and carry it out to the extent that it is willing and able to do so.

To resume our narrative. We have seen that the British administrators decided to prevent fresh Indian immigrants from entering the Transvaal, and to render the position of the old Indian settlers so uncomfortable that they would feel compelled to leave the country in sheer disgust, and even if they did not leave it, they would be reduced to a state bordering on serfdom. Some men looked upon as great statesmen in South Africa had declared more than once that they could afford to keep the Indians only as hewers of wood and drawers of water. On the staff of the Asiatic Department was among others Mr Lionel Curtis who is now known to fame as the missionary for diarchy in India. This young man, as he then was, enjoyed the confidence of Lord Milner. He claimed to do everything according to scientific method, but he was capable of committing serious blunders. The Municipality of Johannesburg had suffered a loss of £14,000 in consequence of one such blunder committed by him. He suggested that if fresh Indian immigration was to be stopped, the first step to be taken to that end was the effective registration of the old Indian residents in South Africa. That done, no one could smuggle himself into the country by practising personation, and if any one did, he could be easily detected. The permits which were issued to Indians after the establishment of British rule in the Transvaal contained the signature of the holder or his thumb-impression if he was illiterate. Later on some one suggested the inclusion besides of a photograph of the holder, and this suggestion was carried out by administrative action, legislation being unnecessary. The Indian leaders therefore did not come to know of this innovation at once. When in course of time these novel features came to their notice, they sent memorials to the authorities, and waited upon them in deputations on behalf of the community. The official argument was that Government could not permit Indians to enter the country without regulation of some sort, and that therefore all Indians should provide themselves with uniform permits containing such details as might render it impossible for any one but the rightful holders to enter the country. It was my opinion that although we were not bound by law to take out such permits, the Government could insist on requiring them so long as the Peace Preservation Ordinance was in force. The Peace Preservation Ordinance in South Africa was something like the Defence of India Act in India. Just as the Defence of India Act was kept on the statute-book in India longer than necessary in order to harass the people, so was this Ordinance allowed to remain in force long after the necessity for it had passed in order to harass Indians in South Africa. As for the Europeans, it was a dead letter for all practical purposes. Now if permits must be taken out, they should contain some mark of identification. There was nothing wrong therefore that those who were illiterate should allow their thumb-impression to be taken. I did not at all like the inclusion of photographs in the permits. Musalmans again had religious objections to such a course.

The final upshot of the negotiations between the Indian community and the authorities was that the Indians consented to change their permits for new ones and agreed that fresh Indian immigrants should take out permits in the new form. Although the Indians were not bound in law, they voluntarily agreed to re-registration in the hope that new restrictions might not be imposed upon them, it might be clear to all concerned that the Indians did not wish to bring in fresh immigrants by unfair means, and the Peace Preservation Ordinance might no longer be used to harass new-comers. Almost all Indians thus changed their old permits for new ones. This was no small thing. The community completed like one man with the greatest promptitude this re-registration, which they were not legally bound to carry out. This was a proof of their veracity, tact, large-mindedness, commonsense and humility. It also showed that the community had no desire to violate in any way any law in force in the Transvaal. The Indians believed that if they behaved towards the Government with such courtesy, it would treat them well, show regard to them and confer fresh rights upon them. We shall see in the next chapter how the British Government in the Transvaal rewarded them for this great act of courtesy.

CHAPTER XI

THE REWARD OF GENTLENESS —
THE BLACK ACT

The year 1906 was well under way when this re-registration was completed. I had re-entered the Transvaal in 1903 and opened my office in Johannesburg about the middle of that year. Two years had thus passed in merely resisting the inroads of the Asiatic Department. We all expected now that re-registration would satisfy the Government and confidently looked forward to a period of comparative peace for the community. But that was not to be. The reader has been already introduced to Mr Lionel Curtis. This gentleman held, that the Europeans had not attained their objective simply because the Indians changed their old permits for new certificates of registration. It was not enough in his eyes, that great measures were achieved by mutual understanding. He was of opinion that these should have the force of law behind them, and that thus only could the principles underlying them be secured for all time. Mr Curtis wanted some such restrictions to be placed upon Indians as would produce a striking impression all over South Africa and ultimately serve as a model for the other Dominions of the Empire to imitate. He would not consider the Transvaal to be safe so long as even a single point in South Africa was open to Indians. Again, re-registration by mutual consent was calculated to increase the prestige of the Indian community while Mr Curtis was keen upon lowering it. He would not care to carry Indian opinion with him but would frighten us into submission to external restrictions backed up by rigorous legal sanctions. He therefore drafted an Asiatic Bill and advised the Government that so long as his Bill was not passed, there was no provision in the laws already in force to prevent the Indians from surreptitiously entering the Transvaal or to remove unauthorized residents from the country. Mr Curtis' arguments met with a ready response from the Government, and a draft Asiatic Law Amendment Ordinance to be introduced into the Legislative Council was published in the Transvaal Government Gazette.

Before dealing with this Ordinance in detail, it would be well to dispose of an important event in a few words. As I was the author of the Satyagraha movement, it is necessary to enable the reader fully to understand some events of my life. The Zulu 'rebellion' broke out in Natal just while attempts were thus being made to impose further disabilities upon Indians in the Transvaal. I doubted then and doubt even now if the outbreak could be described as a rebellion, but it has always been thus described in Natal. Now as in the Boer War, many European residents of Natal joined the army as volunteers. As I too was considered a resident of Natal, I thought I must do my bit in the war. With the community's permission, therefore, I made an offer to the Government to raise a Stretcher-bearer Corps for service with the troops. The offer was accepted. I therefore broke up my Johannesburg home and sent my family to Phoenix in Natal where my co-workers had settled and from where *Indian Opinion* was published. I did not close the office as I knew I would not be away for long.

I joined the army with a small corps of twenty or twenty-five men. Most of the provinces of India were represented even on this small body of men. The corps was on active service for a month. I have always been thankful to God for the work which then fell to our lot. We found that the wounded Zulus would have been left uncared for, unless we had attended to them. No European would help to dress their wounds. Dr Savage, who was in charge of the ambulance, was himself a very humane person. It was no part of our duty to nurse the wounded after we had taken them to the hospital. But we had joined the war with a desire to do all we could, no matter whether it did or did not fall within the scope of our work. The good Doctor told us that he could not induce Europeans to nurse the Zulus, that it was beyond his power to compel them and that he would feel obliged if we undertook this mission of mercy. We were only too glad to do this. We had to cleanse the wounds of several Zulus which had not been attended to for as many as five or six days and were therefore stinking horribly. We liked the work. The Zulus could not talk to us, but from their gestures and the expression of their eyes they seemed to feel as if God had sent us to their succour.

The work for which we had enlisted was fairly heavy, for sometimes during the month we had to perform a march of as many as forty miles a day.

The Corps was disbanded in a month. Its work was mentioned in despatches. Each member of the Corps was awarded the medal especially struck for the occasion. The Governor wrote a letter of thanks. The three sergeants of the Corps were Gujaratis, Shris Umiashankar Manchharam Shelat, Surendra Bapubhai Medh, and Harishankar Ishvar Joshi. All the three had a fine physique and worked very hard. I cannot just now recall the names of the other Indians, but I well remember that one of these was a Pathan, who used to express his astonishment on finding us carrying as large a load as, and marching abreast of, himself.

While I was working with the Corps, two ideas which had long been floating in my mind became firmly fixed. First, an aspirant after a life exclusively devoted to service must lead a life of celibacy. Secondly, he must accept poverty as a constant companion through life. He may not take up any occupation which would prevent him or make him shrink from undertaking the lowliest of duties or largest risks.

Letters and telegrams, asking me to proceed to the Transvaal at once, had poured in, even while I was serving with the Corps. On return from the war, therefore, I just met the friends at Phoenix and at once reached Johannesburg. There I read the draft Ordinance referred to above. I took the Transvaal Government Gazette Extraordinary of August 22, 1906 in which the Ordinance was published, home from the office. I went up a hill near the house in the company of a friend and began to translate the draft Ordinance into Gujarati for *Indian Opinion*. I shuddered as I read the sections of the Ordinance one after another. I saw nothing in it except hatred of Indians. It seemed to me that if the Ordinance was passed and the Indians meekly accepted it, that would spell absolute ruin for the Indians in South Africa. I clearly saw that this was a question of life and death for them. I further saw that even in the case of memorials and representations proving fruitless, the community must not sit with folded hands. Better die than submit to such a law. But how were we to die? What should we dare and do so that there would be nothing before us except a choice of victory or death? An impenetrable wall was before me, as it were, and I could not see my way through it. I must acquaint the reader with the details of the proposed measure, which shocked me so violently. Here is a brief summary of it.

Every Indian, man, woman or child of eight years or upwards, entitled to reside in the Transvaal, must register his or her name with the Registrar of Asiatics and take out a certificate of registration.

The applicants for registration must surrender their old permits to the Registrar, and state in their applications their name, residence, caste, age, etc. The Registrar was to note down important marks of identification upon the applicant's person, and take his finger and thumb impressions. Every Indian who failed thus to apply for registration before a certain date was to forfeit his right of residence in the Transvaal. Failure to appply would be held to be an offence in law for which the defaulter could be fined, sent to prison or even deported within the discretion of the court. Parents must apply on behalf of their minor children and bring them to the Registrar in order to give their finger impressions, etc. In case of parents failing to discharge this responsibility laid upon them, the minor on attaining the age of sixteen years must discharge it himself, and if he defaulted, he made himself liable to the same punishments as could be awarded to his parents. The certificate of registration issued to an applicant must be produced before any police officer whenever and wherever he may be required to do so. Failure thus to produce the certificate would be held to be an offence for which the defaulter could be fined or sent to prison. Even a person walking on public thoroughfares could be required to produce his certificate. Police officers could enter private houses in order to inspect certificates. Indians entering the Transvaal from some place outside it must produce their certificates before the inspector on duty. Certificates must be produced on demand in courts which the holder attended on business, and in revenue offices which issued to him a trading or bicycle licence. That is to say, if an Indian wanted any Government office to do for him something within its competence, the officer could ask to see his certificate before granting his request. Refusal to produce the certificate or to supply such particulars or means of identification as may be prescribed by regulation would be also held to be an offence for which the person refusing could be fined or sent to prison.

I have never known legislation of this nature being directed against free men in any part of the world. I know that indentured Indians in· Natal are subject to a drastic system of passes, but these poor fellows can hardly be classed as free men. However even the laws to which they are subject are mild in comparison to the Ordinance outlined above and the penalties they impose are a mere fleabite when compared with the penalties laid down in the Ordinance. A trader with assets running into *lakhs* could be deported and thus faced with utter ruin in virtue of the Ordinance. And the patient reader will see later on how persons were even deported for breaking some of its provisions. There are some drastic laws directed against criminal tribes in India, with which this Ordinance can be easily compared and will be found not to suffer by the comparison. The giving of finger prints, required by the Ordinance, was quite a novelty in South Africa. With a view to seeing some literature on the subject, I read a volume on finger impressions by Mr Henry, a police officer, from which I gathered that finger prints are required by law only from criminals. I was therefore shocked by this compulsory requirement regarding finger prints. Again, the registration of women and children under sixteen was proposed for the first time by this Ordinance.

The next day there was held a small meeting of the leading Indians to whom I explained the Ordinance word by word. It shocked them as it had shocked me. One of them said in a fit of passion: 'If any one came forward to demand a certificate from my wife, I would shoot him on that spot and take the consequences.' I quieted him, and addressing the meeting said, 'This is a very serious crisis. If the Ordinance were passed and if we acquiesced in it, it would be imitated all over South Africa. As it seems to me, it is designed to strike at the very root of our existence in South Africa. It is not the last step, but the first step with a view to hound us out of the country. We are therefore responsible for the safety, not only of the ten or fifteen thousand Indians in the Transvaal but of the entire Indian community in South Africa. Again, if we fully understand all the implications of this legislation, we shall find that India's honour is in our keeping. For the Ordinance seeks to humiliate not only ourselves but also the motherland. The humiliation consists in the degradation of innocent men. No one will take it upon himself to say that we have done anything to deserve such legislation. We are innocent, and insult offered to a single innocent member of a nation is tantamount to insulting the nation as a whole. It will not, therefore, do to be hasty, impatient or angry. That cannot save us from this onslaught. But God will come to our help, if we calmly think out and carry out in time measures of resistance, presenting a united front and bearing the hardship, which such resistance brings in its train.' All present realized the seriousness of the situation and resolved to hold a public meeting at which a number of resolutions must be proposed and passed. A Jewish theatre was hired for the purpose.

CHAPTER XII
THE ADVENT OF SATYAGRAHA

The meeting was duly held on September 11, 1906. It was attended by delegates from various places in the Transvaal. But I must confess that even I myself had not then understood all the implications of the resolutions I had helped to frame; nor had I gauged all the possible conclusions to which they might lead. The old Empire Theatre was packed from floor to ceiling. I could read in every face the expectation of something strange to be done or to happen. Mr Abdul Gani, Chairman of the Transvaal British Indian Association, presided. He was one of the oldest Indian residents of the Transvaal, and partner and manager of the Johannesburg branch of the well-known firm of Mamad Kasam Kamrudin. The most important among the resolutions passed by the meeting was the famous Fourth Resolution by which the Indians solemnly determined not to submit to the Ordinance in the event of its becoming law in the teeth of their opposition and to suffer all the penalties attaching to such non-submission.

I fully explained this resolution to the meeting and received a patient hearing. The business of the meeting was conducted in Hindi or Gujarati; it was impossible therefore that any one present should not follow the proceedings. For the Tamils and Telugus who did not know Hindi there were Tamil and Telugu speakers who fully explained everything in their respective languages. The resolution was duly proposed, seconded and supported by several speakers one of whom was Sheth Haji Habib. He too was a very old and experienced resident of South Africa and made an impassioned speech. He was deeply moved and went so far as to say that we must pass this resolution with God as witness and must never yield a cowardly submission to such degrading legislation. He then went on solemnly to declare in the name of God that he would never submit to that law, and advised all present to do likewise. Others also delivered powerful and angry speeches in supporting the resolution. When in the course of his speech Sheth Haji Habib came to the solemn declaration, I was at once startled and put on my guard. Only then did I fully realize my own responsibility and the responsibility of the community. The community had passed many a resolution before and amended such resolutions in the light of further reflection or fresh experience. There were cases in which resolutions passed had not been observed by all concerned. Amendments in resolutions and failure to observe resolutions on the part of persons agreeing thereto are ordinary experiences of public life all the world over. But no one ever imports the name of God into such resolutions. In the abstract there should not be any distinction between a resolution and an oath taken in the name of God. When an intelligent man makes a resolution deliberately he never swerves from it by a hair's breadth. With him his resolution carries as much weight as a declaration made with God as witness does. But the world takes no note of abstract principles and imagines an ordinary resolution and an oath in the name of God to be poles asunder. A man who makes an ordinary resolution is not ashamed of himself when he deviates from it, but a man who violates an oath administered to him is not only ashamed of himself, but is also looked upon by society as sinner. This imaginary distinction has struck such a deep root in the human mind that a person making a statement on oath before a judge is held to have committed an offence in law if the statement is proved to be false and receives drastic punishment.

Full of these thoughts as I was, possessing as I did much experience of solemn pledges, having profited by them, I was taken aback by Sheth Haji Habib's suggestion of an oath. I thought out the possible consequences of it in a moment. My perplexity gave place to enthusiasm. And although I had no intention of taking an oath or inviting others to do so when I went to the meeting, I warmly approved of the Sheth's suggestion. But at the same time it seemed to me that the people should be told

THE ADVENT OF SATYAGRAHA

of all the consequences and should have explained to them clearly the meaning of a pledge. And if even then they were prepared to pledge themselves, they should be encouraged to do so; otherwise I must understand that they were not still ready to stand the final test. I therefore asked the President for permission to explain to the meeting the implications of Sheth Haji Habib's suggestion. The President readily granted it and I rose to address the meeting. I give below a summary of my remarks just as I can recall them now:

"I wish to explain to this meeting that there is a vast difference between this resolution and every other resolution we have passed up to date and that there is a wide divergence also in the manner of making it. It is a very grave resolution we are making, as our existence in South Africa depends upon our fully observing it. The manner of making the resolution suggested by our friend is as much of a novelty as of a solemnity. I did not come to the meeting with a view to getting the resolution passed in that manner, which redounds to the credit of Sheth Haji Habib as well as it lays a burden of responsibility upon him. I tender my congratulations to him. I deeply appreciate his suggestion, but if you adopt it you too will share his responsibility. You must understand what is this reponsibility, and as an adviser and servant of the community, it is my duty fully to explain it to you.

"We all believe in one and the same God, the differrences of nomenclature in Hinduism and Islam notwithstanding. To pledge ourselves or to take an oath in the name of that God or with him as witness is not something to be trifled with. If having taken such an oath we violate our pledge we are guilty before God and man. Personally I hold that a man, who deliberately and intelligently takes a pledge and then breaks it, forfeits his manhood. And just as a copper coin treated with mercury not only becomes valueless when detected but also makes its owner liable to punishment, in the same way a man who lightly pledges his word and then breaks it becomes a man of straw and fits himself for punishment here as well as hereafter. Sheth Haji Habib is proposing to administer an oath of a very serious character. There is no one in this meeting who can be classed as an infant or as wanting in understanding. You are all well advanced in age and have seen the world; many of you are delegates and have discharged responsibilities in a greater or lesser measure. No one present, therefore, can ever hope to excuse himself by saying that he did not know what he was about when he took the oath.

"I know that pledges and vows are, and should be, taken on rare occasions. A man who takes a vow every now and then is sure to stumble. But if I can imagine a crisis in the history of the Indian community of South Africa when it would be in the fitness of things to take pledges that crisis is surely now. There is wisdom in taking serious steps with great caution and hesitation. But caution and hesitation have their limits, and we have now passed them. The Government has taken leave of all sense of decency. We would only be betraying our unworthiness and cowardice, if we cannot stake our all in the face of the conflagration which envelopes us and sit watching it with folded hands. There is no doubt, therefore, that the present is a proper occasion for taking pledges. But every one of us must think out for himself if he has the will and the ability to pledge himself. Resolutions of this nature cannot be passed by a majority vote. Only those who take a pledge can be bound by it. This pledge must not be taken with a view to produce an effect on outsiders. No one should trouble to consider what impression it might have upon the Local Government, the Imperial Government, or the Government of India. Every one must only search his own heart, and if the inner voice assures him that he has the requisite strength to carry him through, then only should he pledge himself and then only will his pledge bear fruit.

"A few words now as to the consequences. Hoping for the best, we may say that if a majority of the Indians pledge themselves to resistance and if all who take the pledge prove true to themselves, the Ordinance may not be passed and, if passed, may be soon repealed. It may

THE ADVENT OF SATYAGRAHA

be that we may not be called upon to suffer at all. But if on the one hand a man who takes a pledge must be a robust optimist, on the other hand he must be prepared for the worst. Therefore I want to give you an idea of the worst that might happen to us in the present struggle. Imagine that all of us present here numbering 3,000 at the most pledge ourselves. Imagine again that the remaining 10,000 Indians take no such pledge. We will only provoke ridicule in the beginning. Again, it is quite possible that in spite of the present warning some or many of those who pledge themselves may weaken at the very first trial. We may have to go to jail, where we may be insulted. We may have to go hungry and suffer extreme heat or cold. Hard labour may be imposed upon us. We may be flogged by rude warders. We may be fined heavily and our property may be attached and held up to auction if there are only a few resisters left. Opulent today we may be reduced to abject poverty tomorrow. We may be deported. Suffering from starvation and similar hardships in jail, some of us may fall ill and even die. In short, therefore, it is not at all impossible that we may have to endure every hardship that we can imagine, and wisdom lies in pledging ourselves on the understanding that we shall have to suffer all that and worse. If some one asks me when and how the struggle may end, I may say that if the entire community manfully stands the test, the end will be near. If many of us fall back under storm and stress, the struggle will be prolonged. But I can boldly declare, and with certainty, that so long as there is even a handful of men true to their pledge, there can only be one end to the struggle, and that is victory.

"A word about my personal responsibility. If I am warning you of the risks attendant upon the pledge, I am at the same time inviting you to pledge yourselves, and I am fully conscious of my responsibility in the matter. It is possible that a majority of those present here may take the pledge in a fit of enthusiasm or indignation but may weaken under the ordeal, and only a handful may be left to face the final test. Even then there is only one course open to some one like me, to die but not to submit to the law. It is quite unlikely but even if every one else flinched leaving me alone to face the music, I am confident that I would never violate my pledge. Please do not misunderstand me. I am not saying this out of vanity, but I wish to put you, especially the leaders upon the platform, on your guard. I wish respectfully to suggest it to you that if you have not the will or the ability to stand firm even when you are perfectly isolated, you must not only not take the pledge yourselves but you must declare your opposition before the resolution is put to the meeting and before its members begin to take pledges and you must not make yourselves parties to the resolution. Although we are going to take the pledge in a body, no one should imagine that default on the part of one or many can absolve the rest from their obligation. Every one should fully realize his responsibility, then only pledge himself independently of others and understand that he himself must be true to his pledge even unto death, no matter what others do."

I spoke to this effect and resumed my seat. The meeting heard me word by word in perfect quiet. Other leaders too spoke. All dwelt upon their own responsibility and the responsibility of the audience. The President rose. He too made the situation clear, and at last all present, standing with upraised hands, took an oath with God as witness not to submit to the Ordinance if it became law. I can never forget the scene, which is present before my mind's eye as I write. The community's enthusiasm knew no bounds. The very next day there was some accident in the theatre in consequence of which it was wholly destroyed by fire. On the third day friends brought me the news of the fire and congratulated the community upon this good omen, which signified to them that the Ordinance would meet the same fate as the theatre. I have never been influenced by such so-called signs and therefore did not attach any weight to the coincidence. I have taken note of it here only as a demonstration of the community's courage and faith. The reader will find in the subsequent chapters many more proofs of these two high qualities of the people.

THE ADVENT OF SATYAGRAHA

The workers did not let the grass grow under their feet after this great meeting. Meetings were held everywhere and pledges of resistance were taken in every place. The principal topic of discussion in *Indian Opinion* now was the Black Ordinance.

At the other end, steps were taken in order to meet the Local Government. A deputation waited upon Mr Duncan, the Colonial Secretary, and told him among other things about the pledges. Sheth Haji Habib, who was a member of the deputation, said, 'I cannot possibly restrain myself if any officer comes and proceeds to take my wife's finger prints. I will kill him there and then and die myself.' The Minister stared at the Sheth's face for a while and said, 'Government is reconsidering the advisability of making the Ordinance applicable to women, and I can assure you at once that the clauses relating to women will be deleted. Government have understood your feeling in the matter and desire to respect it. But as for the other provisions, I am sorry to inform you that Government is and will remain adamant. General Botha wants you to agree to this legislation after due deliberation. Government deem it to be essential to the existence of the Europeans. They will certainly consider any suggestions about details which you may make consistently with the objects of the Ordinance, and my advice to the deputation is that your interest lies in agreeing to the legislation and proposing changes only as regards the details.' I am leaving out here the particulars of the discussion with the Minister, as all those arguments have already been dealt with. The arguments were just the same, there was only a difference in phraseology as they were set forth before the Minister. The deputation withdrew, after informing him that his advice notwithstanding, acquiescence in the proposed legislation was out of the question, and after thanking Government for its intention of exempting women from its provisions. It is difficult to say whether the exemption of women was the first fruit of the community's agitation, or whether the Government as an afterthought made a concession to practical considerations which Mr Curtis had ruled out of his scientific methods. Government claimed that it had decided to exempt women independently of the Indian agitation. Be that as it might, the community established to their own satisfaction a cause and effect relation between the agitation and the exemption and their fighting spirit rose accordingly.

None of us knew what name to give to our movement. I then used the term 'passive resistance' in describing it. I did not quite understand the implications of 'passive resistance' as I called it. I only knew that some new principle had come into being. As the struggle advanced, the phrase 'passive resistance' gave rise to confusion and it appeared shameful to permit this great struggle to be known only by an English name. Again, that foreign phrase could hardly pass as current coin among the community. A small prize was therefore announced in *Indian Opinion* to be awarded to the reader who invented the best designation for our struggle. We thus received a number of suggestions. The meaning of the struggle had been then fully discussed in *Indian Opinion* and the competitors for the prize had fairly sufficient material to serve as a basis for their exploration. Shri Maganlal Gandhi was one of the competitors and he suggested the word 'Sadagraha,' meaning 'firmness in a good cause.' I liked the word, but it did not fully represent the whole idea I wished it to connote. I therefore corrected it to 'Satyagraha.' Truth (*Satya*) implies love, and firmness (*agraha*) engenders and therefore serves as a synonym for force. I thus began to call the Indian movement 'Satyagraha,' that is to say, the Force which is born of Truth and Love or non-violence, and gave up the use of the phrase 'passive resistance,' in connection with it, so much so that even in English writing we often avoided it and used instead the word 'Satyagraha' itself or some other equivalent English phrase. This then was the genesis of the movement which came to be known as Satyagraha, and of the word used as a designation for it. Before we proceed any further with our history we shall do well to grasp the differences between passive resistance and Satyagraha, which is the subject of our next chapter.

CHAPTER XIII
SATYAGRAHA V. PASSIVE RESISTANCE

As the movement advanced, Englishmen too began to watch it with interest. Although the English newspapers in the Transvaal generally wrote in support of the Europeans and of the Black Act, they willingly published contributions from well-known Indians. They also published Indian representations to Government in full or at least a summary of these, sometimes sent their reporters to important meetings of the Indians, and when such was not the case, made room for the brief reports we sent them.

These amenities were of course very useful to the community, but by and by some leading Europeans came to take interest in the movement as it progressed. One of these was Mr Hosken, one of the magnates of Johannesburg. He had always been free from colour prejudice but his interest in the Indian question deepened after the starting of Satyagraha. The Europeans of Germiston, which is something like a suburb of Johannesburg, expressed a desire to hear me. A meeting was held, and introducing me and the movement I stood for to the audience, Mr Hosken observed, "The Transvaal Indians have had recourse to passive resistance when all other means of securing redress proved to be of no avail. They do not enjoy the franchise. Numerically, they are only a few. They are weak and have no arms. Therefore they have taken to passive resistance which is a weapon of the weak." These observations took me by surprise, and the speech which I was going to make took an altogether different complexion in consequence. In contradicting Mr Hosken, I defined our passive resistance as 'soul force.' I saw at this meeting that a use of the phrase 'passive resistance' was apt to give rise to terrible misunderstanding. I will try to distinguish between passive resistance and soul force by amplifying the argument which I made before that meeting so as to make things clearer.

I have no idea when the phrase 'passive resistance' was first used in English and by whom. But among the English people, whenever a small minority did not approve of some obnoxious piece of legislation, instead of rising in rebellion they took the passive or milder step of not submitting to the law and inviting the penalties of such non-submission upon their heads. When the British Parliament passed the Education Act some years ago, the Non-conformists offered passive resistance under the leadership of Dr Clifford. The great movement of the English women for the vote was also known as passive resistance. It was in view of these two cases that Mr Hosken described passive resistance as a weapon of the weak or the voteless. Dr Clifford and his friends had the vote, but as they were in a minority in the Parliament, they could not prevent the passage of the Education Act. That is to say, they were weak in numbers. Not that they were averse to the use of arms for the attainment of their aims, but they had no hope of succeeding by force of arms. And in a well-regulated state, recourse to arms every now and then in order to secure popular rights would defeat its own purpose. Again some of the Non-conformists would generally object to taking up arms even if it was a practical proposition. The suffragists had no franchise rights. They were weak in numbers as well as in physical force. Thus their case lent colour to Mr Hosken's observations. The suffragist movement did not eschew the use of physical force. Some suffragists fired buildings and even assaulted men. I do not think they ever intended to kill any one. But they did intend to thrash people when an opportunity occurred, and even thus to make things hot for them.

But brute force had absolutely no place in the Indian movement in any circumstance, and the reader will see, as we proceed, that no matter how badly they suffered, the Satyagrahis never used physical force, and that too although there were occasions when they were in a position to use it effectively. Again, although the Indians had no franchise and were weak, these considerations had nothing to do with the organization of Satyagraha. This is not to say, that the Indians would have taken to Satyagraha even if they had possessed arms or the franchise. Probably there would not have been any scope for Satyagraha if they had the franchise. If they had arms, the opposite party would have thought twice before antagonizing them. One can therefore understand, that people who possess arms would have fewer occasions for offering Satyagraha. My point is that I can definitely assert that in planning the Indian movement there never was the slightest thought given to the possibility or otherwise of offering armed resistance. Satyagraha is soul force pure and simple, and whenever and to whatever extent there is room for the use of arms or physical force or brute force, there and to that extent is there so much less possibility for soul force. These are purely antagonistic forces in my view, and I had full realization of this antagonism even at the time of the advent of Satyagraha.

We will not stop here to consider whether these views are right or wrong. We are only concerned to note the distinction between passive resistance and Satyagraha, and we have seen that there is a great and fundamental difference between the two. If without understanding this, those who call themselves either passive resisters or Satyagrahis believe both to be one and the same thing, there would be injustice to both leading to untoward consequences. The result of our using the phrase 'passive resistance' in South Africa was, not that people admired us by ascribing to us the bravery and the self-sacrifice of the suffragists but we were mistaken to be a danger to person and property which the suffragists were, and even a generous friend like Mr Hosken imagined us to be weak. The power of suggestion is such, that a man at last becomes what he believes himself to be. If we continue to believe ourselves and let others believe, that we are weak and helpless and therefore offer passive resistance, our resistance would never make us strong, and at the earliest opportunity we would give up passive resistance as a weapon of the weak. On the other hand if we are Satyagrahis and offer Satyagraha believing ourselves to be strong, two clear consequences result from it. Fostering the idea of strength, we grow stronger and stronger every day. With the increase in our strength, our Satyagraha too becomes more effective and we would never be casting about for an opportunity to give it up. Again, while there is no scope for love in passive resistance, on the other hand not only has hatred no place in Satyagraha but is a positive breach of its ruling principle. While in passive resistance there is a scope for the use of arms when a suitable occasion arrives, in Satyagraha physical force is forbidden even in the most favourable circumstances. Passive resistance is often looked upon as a preparation for the use of force while Satyagraha can never be utilized as such. Passive resistance may be offered side by side with the use of arms. Satyagraha and brute force, being each a negation of the other, can never go together. Satyagraha may be offered to one's nearest and dearest; passive resistance can never be offered to them unless of course they have ceased to be dear and become an object of hatred to us. In passive resistance there is always present an idea of harassing the other party and there is a simultaneous readiness to undergo any hardships entailed upon us by such activity; while in Satyagraha there is not the remotest idea of injuring the opponent. Satyagraha postulates the conquest of the adversary by suffering in one's own person.

These are the distinctions between the two forces. But I do not wish to suggest that the merits, or if you like, the defects of passive resistance thus enumerated are to be seen in every movement which passes by that name. But it can be shown that these defects have been noticed in many cases of passive resistance. Jesus Christ indeed has been acclaimed as the prince of passive resisters but I submit in that case passive resistance must mean Satyagraha and Satyagraha alone. There are not many cases in history of passive resistance in that sense. One of these is that of the Doukhobors of Russia cited by Tolstoy. The phrase passive resistance was not employed to denote the patient suffering of oppression by thousands of devout Christians in the early days of Christianity. I would therefore class them as Satyagrahis. And if their conduct be described as passive resistance, passive resistance becomes synonymous with Satyagraha. It has been my object in the present chapter to show that Satyagraha is essentially different from what people generally mean in English by the phrase 'passive resistance.'

While enumerating the characteristics of passive resistance, I had to sound a note of warning in order to avoid injustice being done to those who had recourse to it. It is also necessary to point out that I do not claim for people calling themselves Satyagrahis all the merits which I have described as being characteristic of Satyagraha. I am not unaware of the fact that many a Satyagrahi so called is an utter stranger to them. Many suppose Satyagraha to be a weapon of the weak. Others have said that it is a preparation for armed resistance. But I must repeat once more that it has not been my object to describe Satyagrahis as they are but to set forth the implications of Satyagraha and the characteristics of Satyagrahis as they ought to be.

In a word, we had to invent a new term clearly to denote the movement of the Indians in the Transvaal and to prevent its being confused with passive resistance generally so called. I have tried to show in the present chapter the various principles which were then held to be a part and parcel of the connotation of that term.

CHAPTER XIV

DEPUTATION TO ENGLAND

In the Transvaal itself we took all necessary measures for resisting the Black Act such as approaching the Local Government with memorials, etc. The Legislative Council deleted the clause affecting women but the rest of the Ordinance was passed practically in the shape in which it was first drafted. The spirit of the community was then high and having closed its ranks it was unanimous in opposition to the Ordinance. No one therefore was despondent. We however still adhered to the resolution to exhaust all appropriate constitutional remedies in the first instance. The Transvaal was yet a Crown Colony, so that the Imperial Government was responsible for its legislation as well as its administration. Therefore the royal assent to measures passed by its legislature was not a mere formality, but very often it might so happen that the King, as advised by his ministers, might withhold his assent to such measures if they were found to be in conflict with the spirit of the British constitution. On the other hand, in the case of a Colony enjoying responsible government the royal assent to measures passed by its legislature is more often than not a matter of course.

I submitted to the community that if a deputation was to go to England, it was as well that they realized their responsibility in the matter still more fully, and with this end in view I placed three suggestions before our Association. First, although we had taken pledges at the meeting in the Empire Theatre, we should once again obtain individual pledges from leading Indians, so that if they had given way to doubt or weakness, they would be found out. One of the reasons advanced by me in support of this suggestion was, that if the deputation was backed up by Satyagraha, they would then have no fears and could boldly inform the Secretary of State for India and the Secretary of State for the Colonies about the resolution of the community. Secondly, arrangements for meeting the expenses of the deputation must be made in advance. And thirdly, the maximum number of members should be fixed. I made this last suggestion in order to correct the current misapprehension that a large number of members would be able to put in more work, and to bring this idea into relief that the members should join the deputation not because it was an honour to them but with a single-minded devotion to the cause. The three suggestions were accepted. Signatures were taken. Many signed the pledge, but still I saw even among those who had orally pledged themselves at the meeting, there were some who hesitated to sign it. When once a man has pledged himself he need not hesitate to pledge himself a hundred times. But yet it is no uncommon experience to find men weakening in regard to pledges deliberately taken and getting perplexed when asked to put down a verbal pledge in black and white. The necessary funds, too, were found. The greatest difficulty however was encountered in selecting the personnel of the deputation. I was to go, but who would go with me? The Committee took much time in arriving at a decision. Many a night passed, and we had a full experience of the bad habits which are generally prevalent in associations. Some proposed to cut the Gordian knot by asking me to go alone, but I flatly declined. There was for all practical purposes no Hindu-Muslim problem in South Africa. But it could not be claimed that there were no diffurences between the two sections and if these differences never assumed an acute form, that may have been to some extent due to the peculiar conditions in South Africa, but was largely and definitely due to the leaders having worked with devotion and frankness and thus given a fine lead to the community. My advice was that there must be a Musalman gentleman going with me, and that the personnel should be limited to two. But the Hindus at once said that as I represented the Indian community as a whole, there should be a representative of Hindu interests. Some even said that there should be one Konkani Musalman, one Meman, one Patidar, one Anavala and so on.

At last, all understood the real position, and only two of us, Mr H.O. Ali and myself were duly elected.

H. O. Ali could be considered a semi-Malay. His father was an Indian Musalman and his mother a Malay. His mother tongue, we might say, was Dutch. But he had been so well educated in English that he could speak Dutch and English equally well. He had also cultivated the art of writing to the newspapers. He was a member of the Transvaal British Indian Association and he had long been taking part in public affairs. He spoke Hindustani, too, freely.

We set to work as soon as we reached England. We got printed the memorial to be submitted to the Secretary of State which we had drafted in the steamer on our way to England. Lord Elgin was Secretary of State for the Colonies and Lord (then Mr) Morley Secretary of State for India. We met Dadabhai and through him the British Committee of the Indian National Congress. We placed our case before it and signified our intention to seek the co-operation of all the parties, as advised by Dadabhai. The Committee approved of our policy. Similarly we met Sir Muncherji Bhownuggree, who also was of much help. He as well as Dadabhai advised us to secure the Co-operation of some impartial and well-known Anglo-Indian who should introduce our deputation to Lord Elgin. Sir Muncherji suggested some names, too, one of which was that of Sir Lepel Griffin. Sir W. W. Hunter was now no longer alive; or else on account of his deep knowledge of the condition of Indians in South Africa he would have led the deputation himself or induced some influential member of the House of Lords to do so.

We met Sir Lepel Griffin. He was opposed to current political movements in India, but he was much interested in this question and agreed to lead the deputation not for the sake of courtesy but for the justice and righteousness of our cause. He read all the papers and became familiar with the problem. We likewise interviewed other Anglo-Indians, Members of Parliament, and as many others of any importance as were within our reach. The deputation waited upon Lord Elgin who heard everything with attention, expressed his sympathy, referred to his own difficulties and yet promised to do for us all he could. The same deputation met Mr Morley who also declared his sympathy and whose observations in replying to the deputation I have already summarized. Sir William Wedderburn was instrumental in calling a meeting of the Committee of the House of Commons for Indian Affairs in the drawing-room of the House and we placed our case before them too as best we could. We met Mr Redmond, the then leader of the Irish Party. In short, we met as many members of Parliament as we could, irrespective of the party to which they belonged. The British Committee of the Indian National Congress was of course very helpful. But according to English customs men belonging to a certain party and holding certain views only would join it, while there were many others who had nothing to do with the Committee but yet rendered us all possible assistance. We determined to organize a standing committee upon which all these could come together and thus be even more useful in watching over our interests and men of all parties liked our idea.

The burden of carrying on the work of an institution chiefly falls upon its secretary. The secretary should be such, that not only does he have full faith in the aims and the objects of the institution, but he should be able to devote nearly all his time to the achievement of these aims and has great capacity for work. Mr L. W. Ritch, who belonged to South Africa, was formerly articled to me and was now a student for the bar in London, satisfied all the requirements. He was there in England and was also desirous of taking up the work. We therefore ventured to form the South Africa British Indian Committee.

In England and other Western countries there is one, in my view, barbarous custom of inaugurating movements at dinners. The British Premier delivers in the Mansion House on the ninth of November an important speech in which he adumbrates his programme for the year and publishes his own forecast of the future, and which therefore attracts universal notice. Cabinet ministers among others are invited to dinner by the Lord Mayor of London, and when the dinner is over, bottles of wine are uncorked, all present drink to the health of the host and the guest, and speeches too are made while this merry business is in progress. The toast for the British Cabinet is proposed, and the Premier makes the important speech referred to in reply to it. And as in public, so in private, the person with whom some important conversations are to be held is, as a matter of custom, invited to dinner, and the topic of the day is broached either at or after dinner. We too had to observe this custom not once but quite a number of times, although of course we never touched meat or liquor. We thus invited our principal supporters to lunch. About a hundred covers were laid. The idea was to tender our thanks to our friends, to bid them good-bye and at the same time to constitute the Standing Committee. Here too, speeches were made, as usual, after dinner, and the Committee was also organized. We thus obtained greater publicity for our movement.

After a stay in England of about six weeks we returned to South Africa. When we reached Madeira, we received a cablegram from Mr Ritch to the effect that Lord Elgin had declared that he was unable without further consideration to advice His Majesty the King that the Transvaal Asiatic Ordinance should be brought into operation. Our joy knew no bounds. The steamer took about a fortnight to reach Cape Town from Madeira and we had quite a good time of it during these days and built many castles in the air about the coming redress of many more grievances. But the ways of Providence are inscrutable. We shall see in the next chapter how the castles we had laboriously built toppled down and passed into nothingness.

But I must place one or two sacred reminiscences on record before closing this chapter. We had utilized every single minute of our time in England. The sending of a large number of circulars etc., could not be done single-handed, and we were sorely in need of outside help. Money indeed does bring us this kind of help, but my experience ranging over forty years has taught me that assistance thus purchased can never compare with purely voluntary service. Fortunately for us we had many volunteer helpers.

Many an Indian youth who was in England for study surrounded us and some of them helped us day and night without any hope of reward or fame. I do not remember that any of them ever refused to do anything as being beneath his dignity, be it the writing of addresses or the fixing of stamps or the posting of letters. But there was an English friend named Symonds who cast all these into the shade. Whom the Gods love die young and so did this benevolent Englishman. I first met him in South Africa. He had been in India. When he was in Bombay in 1897, he moved fearlessly among the Indians affected by the plague and nursed them. It had become a second nature with him not to be daunted by death when ministering to sufferers from infectious diseases. He was perfectly free from any race or colour prejudice. He was independent in temperament. He believed that truth is always with the minority. It was this belief of his which first drew him to me in Johannesburg, and he often humorously assured me that he would withdraw his support of me if he ever found me in a majority, as he was of opinion that truth itself is corrupted in the hands of a majority. He had read very widely. He was private secretary to Sir George Farrar, one of the millionaires of Johannesburg. He was an expert stenographer. He happened to be in England when we were there. I did not know where he was, but the noble Englishman found us out as our public work had secured for us newspaper advertisement. He expressed his willingness to do for us anything he could. 'I will work as a servant if you like,' he said, 'and if you need a stenographer, you know you can scarcely come across the like of me.' We were in need of both these kinds of help, and I am not exaggerating when I say that this Englishman toiled for us day and night without any payment. He was always on the typewriter till twelve or one o'clock at night. Symonds would carry messages and post letters, always with a smile curling round his lips. His monthly income was about forty-five pounds, but he spent it all in helping his friends and others. He was about thirty years of age. He was unmarried and wanted to remain so all his life. I pressed him hard to accept some payment, but he flatly refused and said, 'I would be failing in my duty if I accepted any remuneration for this service.' I remember that on the last night he was awake till three o'clock while we were winding up our business and packing our things. He parted with us the next day after seeing us off on the steamer, and a sad parting it was. I have often experienced that benevolence is by no means peculiar to the brown skin.

For the benefit of young aspirants after public work, I note down the fact that we were so punctilious in keeping the accounts of the deputation that we preserved even such trifling vouchers as the receipts for the money spent in the steamers upon, say, soda water. Similarly we preserved the receipts for telegrams. I do not remember to have entered a single item under sundries when writing the detailed accounts. As a rule, sundries did not figure in our accounts at all, and if they did they were intended to cover a few pennies or shillings the manner of whose spending we could not recall at the time of writing the accounts at the end of the day.

I have clearly observed in this life the fact that we become trustees or responsible agents from the time that we reach years of discretion. So long as we are with our parents, we must account to them for moneys or business they entrust to us. They may be sure of our rectitude and may not ask us for accounts, but that does not affect our responsibility. When we become independent householders, there arises the responsibility to our family. We are not the sole proprietors of our acquisitions; our family is a co-sharer of them along with ourselves. We must account for every single pie for their sake. If such is our responsibility in private life, in public life it is all the greater. I have observed that voluntary workers are apt to behave as if they were not bound to render a detailed account of the business or moneys with which they are entrusted because like Caesar's wife they are above suspicion. This is sheer nonsense, as the keeping of accounts has nothing whatever to do with trustworthiness or the reverse. Keeping accounts is an independent duty, the performance of which is essential to clean work, and if the leading workers of the institution which we voluntarily serve do not ask us for accounts out of a sense of false courtesy or fear, they too are equally to blame. If a paid servant is bound to account for work done and money spent by him, the volunteer is doubly bound to do so, for his very work is as a reward to him. This is a very important matter, and as I know that this is generally not sufficiently attended to in many institutions, I have ventured to take up so much space here in adverting to the subject.

CHAPTER XV

CROOKED POLICY

As soon as we landed at Cape Town, and more so when we reached Johannesburg, we saw that we had over-rated the Madeira cablegram. Mr Ritch who sent it was not responsible for this. He cabled only what he had heard about the measure being disallowed. As we have already observed, the Transvaal was then, that is to say in 1906, a Crown Colony. Crown Colonies are represented in England by agents one of whose duties it is to instruct the Secretary of State for the Colonies in all matters affecting Colonial interests. The Transvaal was then represented by Sir Richard Solomon, the noted lawyer of South Africa. Lord Elgin had disallowed the Black Act in consultation with him. Responsible government was to be conferred on the Transvaal on January 1, 1907. Lord Elgin therefore assured Sir Richard that if an identical measure was passed by the Transvaal legislature constituted after the grant of responsible government, it would not be refused the royal assent. But so long as the Transvaal was a Crown Colony, the Imperial Government would be held directly responsible for such class legislation, and as racial discrimination was a departure from the fundamental principles of the British Empire, he could not but advise His Majesty to disallow the measure in question.

If the measure was to be thus disallowed only in name and if the Transvaal Europeans could at the same time have their own way, Sir Richard Solomon had no reason to object to such an excellent arrangement. I have characterized this as crooked policy, but I believe it could be given a still harsher name with perfect justice. The Imperial Government is directly responsible for the legislation of Crown Colonies, and there is no place in its constitution for discrimination on the ground of race or colour. So far so good. One can also understand that the Imperial Government could not all at once disallow measures passed by the legislatures of Colonies enjoying responsible government. But to hold private conferences with Colonial agents and in advance to promise the royal assent to legislation which is in open violation of the Imperial Constitution, — what is this if it is not a breach of faith and an injustice to those whose rights are thus pilfered? Really speaking Lord Elgin by his assurance encouraged the Transvaal Europeans in their anti-Indian activities. If he wanted to do this, he ought to have told the Indian deputation so in plain terms. As a matter of fact the Empire cannot escape responsibility even for the legislation of Colonies enjoying responsible government. Even such Colonies are bound to accept the fundamental principles of the British Constitution. As for example no such Colony can revive the institution of legalized slavery. If Lord Elgin disallowed the Black Act because it was an improper piece of legislation, and he could disallow it only on this ground, it was his clear duty privately to have warned Sir Richard Solomon that the Transvaal could not enact such an iniquitous law after the grant of responsible government, and if it had any intention of doing so, the Imperial Government would be constrained to reconsider the advisability of granting it any such superior status. Or he should have told Sir Richard that responsible government could be conferred only on the condition that the rights of the Indians were fully safeguarded. Instead of following such straightforward procedure, Lord Elgin made an outward show of friendliness to the Indians, while at the same time he really and secretly supported the Transvaal Government and encouraged it to pass once more the very law which he had vetoed himself. This is not the only or the first case of such tortuous policy followed by the British

Empire. Even an indifferent student of its history will easily recall similar incidents.

In Johannesburg, therefore, the sole topic of conversation was the trick played upon us by Lord Elgin and the Imperial Government. Our disappointment in South Africa was as deep as had been our joy in Madeira. Yet the immediate consequence of this deception was that the community became even more enthusiastic than before. Every one said that we must never fear as our struggle was independent of any help from the Imperial Government. We must look for assistance only to our own selves and to that God in Whose name we had pledged ourselves to resistance. And even crooked policy would in time turn straight if only we were true to ourselves.

Responsible government was established in the Transvaal. The first measure passed by the new Parliament was the budget; the second was the Asiatic Registration Act, which was, except for an alteration in the date specified in one of its clauses, which lapse of time made necessary, an exact replica of the original Ordinance, and was rushed through all its stages at a single sitting on March 21, 1907. The disallowance of the Ordinance, therefore, was forgotten as if it was a dream. The Indians submitted memorials, etc. as usual, but who would listen to them? The Act was proclaimed to take effect from July 1, 1907 and Indians were called upon to apply for registration under it before July 31. The delay in enforcing the Act was due not to any desire to oblige the Indians, but to the exigencies of the case. Some time must elapse before the formal sanction of the Crown to the measure was signified, and the preparation of the forms set forth in schedules and the opening of permit offices at various centres would also take time. The delay therefore was intended solely for the Transvaal Government's own convenience.

CHAPTER XVI
AHMAD MUHAMMAD KACHHALIA

When the deputation was on its way to England, I happened to talk about the anti-Asiatic legislation in the Transvaal with an Englishman who had settled in South Africa, and when I informed him of the object of our visit to England, he exclaimed, 'I see you are going to London in order to get rid of the dog's collar.' He thus compared the Transvaal permit to a dog's collar, but I did not quite understand then, and cannot exactly tell while recording that incident even now, whether he thus intended to express his contempt for the Indians and joy at their humiliation, or whether he only meant to show his strong feeling in the matter. According to the golden rule that a person's words must not be interpreted so as to do him an injustice, I take it that the gentleman used this graphic language only in order to evince his strong feeling. However that may be, the Transvaal Government on one side was preparing to throw the dog's collar on the Indians' necks, while on the other side the Indians were getting ready to put up a fight against the wicked policy of that Government and were concerting measures calculated to strengthen them in their resolution never to wear that collar. Of course, we were writing letters to friends in England as well as in India and trying thus to keep them in touch with the situation from day to day. But a Satyagraha struggle depends but little upon help from outside, and it is only internal remedies that are effective. The leaders' time therefore was chiefly taken up with the endeavours to keep all the elements of the community up to the mark.

One important question before us was what agency we should use for carrying on the struggle. The Transvaal British Indian Association had a large membership. Satyagraha had not yet seen the light of the day when it was established. The Association had resisted in the past, and must resist in the future, not one obnoxious law, but quite a host of them. Besides organizing resistance to obnoxious legislation, it had many other functions of a political and social nature to perform. Again all the members of the Association were not pledged to resist the Black Act through Satyagraha. At the same time we must take account of external risks to which the Association would be exposed in the event of its being identified with the Satyagraha struggle. What if the Transvaal Government declared the struggle to be seditious and all institutions carrying it on as illegal bodies? What would, in such a case, be the position of members who were not Satyagrahis? And what about the funds which were contributed at a time when Satyagraha was not so much as thought of? All these were weighty considerations. Lastly, the Satyagrahis were strongly of opinion that they not only must not entertain any ill-will against those who did not join the struggle whether for want of faith or weakness or any other reason whatever, but must maintain their present friendly relations with them unimpaired and even work side by side with them in all other movements except the Satyagraha struggle.

For all these reasons the community came to the conclusion that the Satyagraha struggle should not be carried on through any of the existing organizations. They might render all help in their power and resist the Black Act in every way open to them except that of Satyagraha, for which a new body named the 'Passive Resistance Association' was started by the Satyagrahis. The reader will see from this English name that the word Satyagraha had not yet been invented when this new Association came into being. Time fully justified the wisdom of constituting a fresh body for the work, and the Satyagraha movement might perhaps have suffered a setback if any of the existing organizations had been mixed up with it. Numerous members joined this new Association, and the community furnished it funds too with a lavish hand.

My experience has taught me that no movement ever stops or languishes for want of funds. This does not mean that any temporal movement can go on without money, but it does mean that wherever it has good men and true at its helm, it is bound to attract to itself the requisite funds. On the other hand, I have also observed that a movement takes its downward course from the time that it is afflicted with a plethora of funds. When therefore a public institution is managed from the interest of investments, I dare not call it a sin but I do say that it is a highly improper procedure. The public should be the bank for all public institutions, which should not last a day longer than the public wish. An institution run with the interest of accumulated capital ceases to be amenable to public opinion and becomes autocratic and self-righteous. This is not the place to dwell upon the corruption of many a social and religious institution managed with permanent funds. The phenomenon is so common that he who runs may read it.

But we must return to our narrative. Lawyers and English-educated persons do not by any means enjoy a monopoly of hair-splitting. I saw that even the uneducated Indians in South Africa were quite capable of drawing minute distinctions and making fine arguments. Some argued that the pledge taken in the Old Empire Theatre had been fulfilled as the old Ordinance was disallowed, and those who had weakened since then took shelter under this plea. The argument was not quite devoid of force, yet it could not impress those whose resistance was not to the law as a law but to the vicious principle underlying it. All the same it was found necessary to re-administer the oath of resistance for safety's sake just to reinforce the awakening of the community and to probe the extent of its weakness if any. Meetings therefore were held in every place, where the situation was explained, the oath was administered afresh and the spirit of the community was found to be as high as ever.

Meanwhile the fateful month of July was gradually drawing to an end, and on the last day of that month we had resolved to call a mass meeting of the Indians at Pretoria, the capital of the Transvaal. Delegates from other places besides were also invited to attend. The meeting was held in the open on the ground of Pretoria mosque. After the inauguration of Satyagraha our meetings were so largely attended that no building could accommodate them. The entire Indian population in the Transvaal did not exceed 13,000 souls, of whom over 10,000 lived in Johannesburg and Pretoria. An attendance at public meetings of two thousand from an aggregate population of ten thousand would be considered large and satisfactory in any part of the world. A movement of mass Satyagraha is impossible on any other condition. Where the struggle is wholly dependent upon internal strength, it cannot go on at all without mass discipline. The workers therefore did not consider such large attendance as anything surprising. From the very first they had decided to hold public meetings only in the open so that expense was nearly avoided and none had to go back from the place of meeting disappointed for want of accommodation. All these meetings, again, were mostly very quiet. The audiences heard everything attentively. If those who were far away from the platform could not hear a speaker, they would ask him to speak louder. The reader scarcely needs to be told that there were no chairs at these meetings. Every one sat on the ground. There was a very small platform designed to accommodate the chairman, the speaker and a couple of friends, and a small table and a few chairs or stools were placed upon it.

Mr Yusuf Ismail Mian, acting chairman of the British Indian Association, presided over this meeting. As the time for issuing permits under the Black Act was drawing nearer, the Indians were naturally anxious in spite of all their enthusiasm; but no less anxious than they were General Botha and General Smuts, all the might of the Transvaal Government at their back notwithstanding. No one would like to bend a whole community to his will by sheer force. General Botha therefore had sent Mr William Hosken to this meeting to admonish us. The reader has already made this gentleman's acquaintance in a previous chapter. The meeting received him warmly, and he said, "You know I am your friend. I need scarcely say that my feelings in this matter are with you. If at all I could, I would gladly make your opponents accede to your demands. But you hardly need to be told about the general hostility of the Transvaal Europeans to your community. I am here at General Botha's instance. He has asked me to be the bearer of his message to this meeting. He entertains a feeling of respect for you and understands your sentiments, but he says, 'he is helpless. All the Europeans in the Transvaal unanimously ask for such law, and he himself is convinced of the necessity for it. The Indians know fully well how powerful is the Transvaal Government. The law has again been endorsed by the Imperial Government. The Indians have done all they could and have acquitted themselves like men. But now that their opposition has failed, and the law has been passed, the community must prove their loyalty and love of peace by submitting to it. General Smuts will carefully look into any representations you make suggesting minior changes in the regulations framed in virtue of the Registration Act.' My own advice to you also is, that you should comply with the General's message. I know that the Transvaal Government is firm regarding this law. To resist it will be to dash your head against a wall. I wish that your community may not be ruined in fruitless opposition or invite needless suffering on their heads." I translated the speech to the meeting word by word, and further put them on their guard on my own behalf. Mr Hosken retired amidst cheers.

It was now time for the Indian speakers to address the meeting. One of these speakers was the late Ahmad Muhammad Kachhalia, the hero, not of this chapter alone, but of the present volume. I knew him only as a client and as an interpreter. He had never before now taken a leading part in public work. He had a working knowledge of English, which he had so far improved by practice that when he took his friends to English lawyers, he acted as interpreter himself. But interpretership was not a profession with him; he worked as interpreter only as a friend. He at first used to hawk piecegoods, and then to trade on a small scale in partnership with his brother. He was a Surti Meman and enjoyed great reputation in his class. His knowledge of Gujarati was also limited but in this too he had greatly advanced, being schooled by experience. He had such sharp intelligence that he very easily grasped anything that was put to him. He solved legal difficulties

with such facility as often astonished me. He would not
hesitate to argue law even with lawyers, and very often
his arguments were worthy of consideration for them.

I have never, whether in South Africa or in India,
come accross a man who could surpass Mr Kachhalia in
courage and steadfastness. He sacrificed his all for the
community's sake. He was always a man of his word. He
was a strict orthodox Musalman, being one of the trustees
of the Surti Meman mosque. But at the same time he looked upon Hindus and Musalmans with an equal eye. I do
not remember that he ever fanatically or improperly
sided with Musalmans as against Hindus. Perfectly fearless and impartial as he was, he never hesitated to point
out their faults to Hindus as well as Musalmans whenever
he found it necessary. His simplicity and humility were
worthy of imitation. My close contact with him for years
leads me to hold firmly to the opinion that a community
can rarely boast of having in their midst a man of the
stamp of Mr Kachhalia.

Mr Kachhalia was one of the speakers at the meeting.
He made a very short speech. He said, "Every Indian
knows what the Black Act is and what it implies. I have
heard Mr Hosken attentively, and so have you. His speech
has only confirmed me in my resolution. We know how
powerful the Transvaal Government is. But it cannot do
anything more than enact such a law. It will cast us into
prison, confiscate our property, deport us or hang us. All
this we will bear cheerfully, but we cannot simply put
up with this law." I observed that while saying this, Mr
Kachhalia was being deeply moved. His face reddened,
the veins on his neck and on the head were swollen with
the blood coursing rapidly through them, his body was
shaking, and moving the fingers of his right hand upon
his throat, he thundered forth: 'I swear in the name of
God that I will be hanged but I will not submit to this
law, and I hope that every one present will do likewise.'
So saying he took his seat. As he moved his fingers on his
throat, some of those seated on the platform smiled, and
I remember that I joined them in their smile. I was rather
doubtful whether Kachhalia Sheth would be able fully to

translate his brave words into action. I am ashamed of this doubt now, and every time I think of it. Kachhalia always remained to the fore among the many Indians who literally observed their pledge in that great struggle without a moment's flinching.

The meeting cheered him as he spoke. Others then knew him very much better than I did, as many of them were personally familiar with this obscure hero. They knew that Kachhalia only says what he means and means what he says. There were other spirited speeches too. But I have singled out Kachhalia Sheth's for mention, as it proved to be a prophecy of his subsequent career. Not everyone of the spirited speakers stood the final test. This great man died in 1918, four years after the struggle was over, serving the community till the last.

I will close this chapter with a reminiscence of Kachhalia Sheth which may not find a place elsewhere. The reader later on will hear of Tolstoy Farm where lived a number of Satyagrahi families. The Sheth sent his ten or twelve year old son Ali to be educated there as an example to others and in order that the boy might be brought up to a life of simplicity and service. It was due to the example he thus set that other Musalmans likewise sent their boys to the Farm. Ali was a modest, bright, truthful and straightforward boy. God took him unto Himself before his father. If it had been given to him to live, I doubt not he would have turned out to be the worthy son of an excellent father.

CHAPTER XVII
A RIFT IN THE LUTE

The first of July 1907 arrived, and saw the opening of permit offices. The community had decided openly to picket each office, that is to say, to post volunteers on the roads leading thereto, and these volunteers were to warn weak-kneed Indians against the trap laid for them there. Volunteers were provided with badges and expressly instructed not to be impolite to any Indian taking out a permit. They must ask him his name, but if he refused to give it they must not on any account be violent or rude to him. To every Indian going to the permit office, they were to hand a printed paper detailing the injuries which submission to the Black Act would involve, and explain what was written in it. They must behave to the police too with due respect. If the police abused or thrashed them, they must suffer peacefully; if the ill-treatment by the police was insufferable they should leave the place. If the police arrested them, they should gladly surrender themselves. If some such incident occurred in Johannesburg, it should be brought to my notice. At other places the local secretaries were to be informed, and asked for further instructions. Each party of pickets had a captain whose orders must be obeyed by the rest.

This was the community's first experience of that kind. All who were above the age of twelve were taken as pickets, so that there were many young men from 12 to 18 years of age enrolled as such. But not one was taken who was unknown to the local workers. Over and above all these precautions, people were informed by announcements at every public meeting and otherwise, that if any one desirous of taking out a permit was afraid of the pickets, he could ask the workers to detail a volunteer to escort him to the permit office and back. Some did avail themselves of this offer.

The volunteers in every place worked with boundless enthusiasm, and were ever alert and wide awake in the performance of their duties. Generally speaking there was not much molestation by the police. When sometimes there was such molestation, the volunteers quietly put up with it. They brought to bear upon their work quite an amount of humour, in which the police too sometimes joined. They devised various diversions in order to beguile their time. They were once arrested on a charge of obstructing the public traffic. As non-co-operation did not form a part of the Satyagraha struggle there, defence could be made in courts, though as a rule advocates for defence were not paid from public funds. The volunteers were declared innocent and acquitted by the court, which still further exalted their spirit.

Although the Indians who wanted to take out permits were thus saved from rudeness or violence from the volunteers in public, I must admit, that there arose a body of men in connection with the movement, who without becoming volunteers privately threatened those who would take out permits with violence or injury in other ways. This was a most painful development, and strong measures were adopted in order to stamp it out as soon as it was found out. The holding out of threats nearly ceased in consequence, though it was not quite rooted out. The threats left an impression behind them, and as I could see, thus far injured the cause. Those who were threatened instantly sought Government protection and got it. Poison was thus instilled into the community, and those who were weak already grew weaker still. The poison thus grew more virulent, as the weak are always apt to be revengeful.

These threats created but little impression; but the force of public opinion on the one hand, and on the other, the fear of one's name being known to the community through the presence of volunteers acted as powerful deterrents. I do not know a single Indian who held it proper to submit to the Black Act. Those who submitted did so out of an inability to suffer hardships or pecuniary losses, and were therefore ashamed of themselves. This sense of shame, as well as a fear of loss in trade following upon the displeasure of big Indian merchants, pressed heavily upon them, and some leading Indians found a way out of this twofold difficulty. They arranged with the permit office, that an officer should meet them in a private house after nine or ten o'clock at night and give them permits. They thought that in this case no one would know about their submission to the law for some time at least and that as they were leaders, others would follow suit, thus lightening their burden of shame. It did not matter if they were found out afterwards.

But the volunteers were so vigilant, that the community was kept informed of what happened every moment. There would be some even in the permit office who might give such information to the Satyagrahis. Others again, though weak themselves, would be unable to tolerate the idea of leaders thus disgracing themselves, and would inform the Satyagrahis from an idea that they too could face the music if others were firm. In this way the community once received information that certain men were going to take out permits in a certain shop on a certain night. The community therefore first tried to dissuade these men. The shop too was picketed. But human weakness cannot be long suppressed. Some leading men took permits in this way at ten or eleven o'clock at night, and there was a rift in the lute. The very next day their names were published by the community. But a sense of shame has its limits. Considerations of self-interest drive shame away and mislead men out of the strait and narrow path. By and by something like five hundred men took out permits. For some time permits were issued in private houses, but as the sense of shame wore out, some went publicly to the Asiatic office and obtained certificates of registration.

CHAPTER XVIII

THE FIRST SATYAGRAHI PRISONER

When the Asiatic Department found, that notwithstanding all their exertions, they could not get more than 500 Indians to register, they decided to arrest some one. In Germiston there lived many Indians, one of whom was Pandit Rama Sundara. This man had a brave look and was endowed with some gift of the gab. He knew a few Sanskrit verses by heart. Hailing from North India as he did, he naturally knew a few *dohas* and *chopais* from the Tulasi Ramayana, and owing to his designation Pandit, he also enjoyed some reputation among the people. He delivered a number of spirited speeches in various places. Some malevolent Indians in Germiston suggested to the Asiatic Department that many Indians there would take out permits if Rama Sundara was arrested, and the officers concerned could scarcely resist the temptation thus offered. So Rama Sundara was put under arrest, and this being the first case of its kind, the Government as well as the Indians were much agitated over it. Rama Sundara, who was till yesterday known only to the good people of Germiston, became in one moment famous all over South Africa. He became the cynosure of all eyes as if he were a great man put upon his trial. Government need not have taken, but it did take, special measures for the preservation of peace. In the Court too Rama Sundara was accorded due respect as no ordinary prisoner but a representative of his community. Eager Indian spectators filled the Court-room. Rama Sundara was sentenced to a month's simple imprisonment, and kept in a separate cell in the European ward in Johannesburg gaol. People were allowed to meet him freely. He was permitted to receive food from outside, and was entertained every day with delicacies prepared on behalf of the community. He was provided with everything he wanted. The day on which he was sentenced was celebrated with great eclat. There was no trace of depression, but on the other hand there was exultation and rejoicing. Hundreds were ready to go to jail. The officers of the Asiatic Department were disappointed in their hope of a bumper crop of registrants. They did not get a single registrant even from Germiston. The only gainer was the Indian community. The month was soon over. Rama Sundara was released and was taken in a procession to the place where a meeting had been arranged. Vigorous speeches were made. Rama Sundara was smothered with garlands of flowers. The volunteers held a feast in his honour, and hundreds of Indians envied Rama Sundara's luck and were sorry that they had not the chance of suffering imprisonment.

But Rama Sundara turned out to be a false coin. There was no escape from the month's imprisonment, as his arrest came as a surprise. In jail he had enjoyed luxuries to which he had been a stranger outside. Still accustomed as he was to licence, and addicted as he was to bad habits, the loneliness and the restraints of jail life were too much for him. In spite of all the attention showered upon him by the jail authorities as well as by the community, jail appeared irksome to him and he bid a final good-bye to the Transvaal and to the movement. There are cunning men in every community and in every movement and so there were in ours. These knew Rama Sundara through and through, but from an idea that even he might become an instrument of the community's providence, they never let me know his secret history until his bubble had finally burst. I subsequently found that he was an indentured labourer who had deserted before completing his term. There was nothing discreditable in his having been an indentured labourer. The reader will see towards the end how indentured labourers proved to be a most valuable acquisition to the movement, and what a large contribution they made towards winning the final victory. It was certainly wrong for him not to have finished his period of indenture.

I have thus detailed the whole history of Rama Sundara not in order to expose his faults, but to point a moral. The leaders of every clean movement are bound to see that they admit only clean fighters to it. But all their caution notwithstanding, undesirable elements cannot be kept out. And yet if the leaders are fearless and true, the entry of undesirable persons into the movement without their knowing them to be so does not ultimately harm the cause. When Rama Sundara was found out, he became a man of straw. The community forgot him, but the movement gathered fresh strength even through him. Imprisonment suffered by him for the cause stood to our credit, the enthusiasm created by his trial came to stay, and profiting by his example, weaklings slipped away out of the movement of their own accord. There were some more cases of such weakness besides this but I do not propose to deal with them in any detail, as it would not serve any useful purpose. In order that the reader may appreciate the strength and the weakness of the community at their real worth, it will be enough to say that there was not one Rama Sundara but several and yet I observed that the movement reaped pure advantage from all of them.

Let not the reader point the finger of scorn at Rama Sundara. All men are imperfect, and when imperfection is observed in some one in a larger measure than in others, people are apt to blame him. But that is not fair. Rama Sundara did not become weak intentionally. Man can change his temperament, can control it, but cannot eradicate it. God has not given him so much liberty. If the leopard can change his spots then only can man modify the peculiarities of his spiritual constitution. Although Rama Sundara fled away, who can tell how he might have repented of his weakness? Or rather was not his very flight a powerful proof of his repentance? There was no need for him to flee if he was shameless. He could have taken out a permit and steered clear of jail by submission to the Black Act. Further, if at all so minded, he could have become a tool of the Asiatic Department, misguided his friends and become *persona grata* with the Government. Why should we not judge him charitably and say that instead of doing anything of the kind, he being ashamed of his weakness hid his face from the community and even did it a service?

CHAPTER XIX
'INDIAN OPINION'

I propose to acquaint the reader with all the weapons, internal as well as external, employed in the Satyagraha struggle and now therefore proceed to introduce to him *Indian Opinion*, a weekly journal which is published in South Africa to this very day. The credit for starting the first Indian-owned printing press in South Africa is due to a Gujarati gentleman, Shri Madanjit Vyavaharik. After he had conducted the press for a few years in the midst of difficulties, he thought of bringing out a newspaper too. He consulted the late Shri Mansukhlal Nazar and myself. The paper was issued from Durban. Shri Mansukhlal Nazar volunteered to act as unpaid editor. From the very first the paper was conducted at a loss. At last we decided to purchase a farm, to settle all the workers, who must constitute themselves into a sort of commonwealth, upon it and publish the paper from the farm. The farm selected for the purpose is situated on a beautiful hill thirteen miles from Durban. The nearest railway station is at a distance of three miles from the farm and is called Phoenix. The paper was and is called *Indian Opinion*. It was formerly published in English, Gujarati, Hindi and Tamil. But the Hindi and Tamil sections were eventually discontinued, as the burden they imposed upon us seemed to be excessive, we could not find Tamil and Hindi writers willing to settle upon the farm and could not exercise a check upon them. The paper was thus being published in English and Gujarati when the Satyagraha struggle commenced. Among the settlers on the farm were Gujaratis, North Indians and Tamilians as well as Englishmen. After the premature death of Mansukhlal Nazar, his place as editor was taken by an English friend, Herbert Kitchin. Then the post of editor was long filled by Mr Henry S.L. Polak and during our incarceration the late Rev. Joseph Doke also acted as editor. Through the medium of this paper we could very well disseminate the news of the week among the community. The English section kept those Indians informed about the movement who did not know Gujarati, and for Englishmen in India, England and South Africa, *Indian Opinion* served the purpose of a weekly newsletter. I believe that a struggle which chiefly relies upon internal strength can be carried on without a newspaper, but it is also my experience that we could not perhaps have educated the local Indian community, nor kept Indians all over the world in touch with the course of events in South Africa in any other way, with the same ease and success as through *Indian Opinion*, which therefore was certainly a most useful and potent weapon in our struggle.

As the community was transformed in course of and as a result of the struggle, so was *Indian Opinion*. In the beginning we used to accept advertisements for it, and also execute job work in the printing press. I observed that some of our best men had to be spared for this kind of work. If we did receive advertisements for publication, there was constant difficulty in deciding which to accept and which to refuse. Again one would be inclined to refuse an objectionable advertisement, and yet be constrained to accept it, say because the advertiser was a leading member of the community and might take it ill if his advertisement was rejected. Some of the good workers had to be set apart for canvassing and realizing outstandings from advertisers, not to speak of the flattery which advertisers claimed as their due. Moreover, the view commended itself, that if the paper was conducted not because it yielded profit but purely with a view to service, the service should not be imposed upon the community by force but should be rendered only if the community wished. And the clearest proof of such wish would be forthcoming if they became subscribers in sufficiently large numbers to make the paper self-supporting. Finally it seemed that it was in every way better for all concerned that we should approach the generality of the community and explain to them the duty of keeping their newspaper going rather than set about to induce a few traders to place their advertisements with us in the name of service. On all these grounds we stopped advertisements in the paper with the gratifying result that those who were at first engrossed in the advertisement department could now devote their labours to improving the paper. The community realized at once their proprietorship of *Indian Opinion* and their consequent responsibility for maintaining it. The workers were relieved of all anxiety in that respect. Their only care now was to put their best work into the paper so long as the community wanted it, and they were not only not ashamed of requesting any Indian to subscribe to *Indian Opinion*, but thought it even their duty to do so. A change came over the internal strength and the character of the paper, and it became a force to reckon with. The number of subscribers which generally ranged between twelve and fifteen hundred increased day by day. The rates of subscription had to be raised and yet when the struggle was at its height, there were as many as 3,500 subscribers. The number of Indians who could read *Indian Opinion* in South Africa was at the outside 20,000, and therefore a circulation of over three thousand copies may be held to be quite satisfactory. The community had made the paper their own to such an extent, that if copies did not reach Johannesburg at the expected time, I would be flooded with complaints about it. The paper generally reached Johannesburg on Sunday morning. I know of many, whose first occupation after they received the paper would be to read the Gujarati section through from beginning to end. One of the company would read it, and the rest would surround him and listen. Not all who wanted to read the paper could afford to subscribe to it by themselves and some of them would therefore club together for the purpose.

Just as we stopped advertisements in the paper, we ceased to take job work in the press, and for nearly the same reasons. Compositors had now some time to spare, which was utilized in the publication of books. As here too there was no intention of reaping profits and as the books were printed only to help the struggle forward, they commanded good sales. Thus both the paper and the press made their contribution to the struggle, and as Satyagraha gradually took root in the community, there

CHAPTER XX

A SERIES OF ARRESTS

We have seen how the Government failed to reap any advantage from Rama Sundara's arrest. On the other hand they observed the spirit of the Indian community rising rapidly. The officers of the Asiatic Department were diligent readers of *Indian Opinion*. Secrecy had been deliberately ruled out of the movement. *Indian Opinion* was an open book to whoever wanted to gauge the strength and the weakness of the community, be he a friend, an enemy or a neutral. The workers had realized at the very outset that secrecy had no place in a movement, where one could do no wrong, where there was no scope for duplicity or cunning, and where strength constituted the single guarantee of victory. The very interest of the community demanded, that if the disease of weakness was to be eradicated, it must be first properly diagnosed and given due publicity. When the officers saw that this was the policy of *Indian Opinion*, the paper became for them a faithful mirror of the current history of the Indian community. They thus came to think the strength of the movement could not by any means be broken so long as certain leaders were at large. Some of the leading men were consequently served with a notice in Christmas week of 1907 to appear before the Magistrate. It must be admitted that this was an act of courtesy on the part of the officers concerned. They could have arrested the leaders by a warrant if they had chosen to do so. Instead of this they issued notices and this, besides being evidence of their courtesy, also betrayed their confidence that the leaders were willing and prepared to be arrested. Those who had thus been warned appeared before the Court on the date specified, Saturday December 28, 1907, to show cause why, having failed to apply for registration as required by law, they should not be ordered to leave the Transvaal within a given period.

One of these was one Mr Quinn, the leader of the Chinese residents of Johannesburg, who numbered three to four hundred, and were either traders or farmers. India is noted for its agriculture, but I believe that we in India are not as far advanced in agriculture as the Chinese are. The modern progress of agriculture in America and other countries defies description, but I consider it to be still in an experimental stage. China, on the other hand, is an old country like India and a comparison between India and China would be therefore fairly instructive. I observed the agricultural methods of the Chinese in Johannesburg and also talked with them on the subject, and this gave me the impression that the Chinese are more intelligent as well as diligent than we are. We often allow land to lie fallow thinking it is of no use, while the Chinese would grow good crops upon it, thanks to their minute knowledge of varying soils.

The Black Act applied to the Chinese as well as to the Indians whom they therefore joined in the Satyagraha struggle. Still from first to last the activities of the two communities were not allowed to be mixed up. Each worked through its own independent organization. This arrangement produced the beneficent result that so long as both the communities stood to their guns, each would be a source of strength to the other. But if one of the two gave way, that would leave the morale of the other unaffected or at least the other would steer clear of the danger of a total collapse. Many of the Chinese eventually fell away as their leader played them false. He did not indeed submit to the obnoxious law, but one morning some one came and told me that the Chinese leader had fled away without handing over charge of the books and moneys of the Chinese Association in his possession. It is always difficult for followers to sustain a conflict in the absence of their leader, and the shock is all the greater when the leader has disgraced himself. But when the arrests commenced, the Chinese were in high spirits.

Hardly any of them had taken out a permit, and therefore their leader Mr Quinn was warned to appear along with the Indians. For some time at any rate Mr Quinn put in very useful work.

I would like to introduce to the reader one out of the several leading Indians who constituted the first batch of prisoners, Shri Thambi Naidoo. Thambi Naidoo was a Tamilian born in Mauritius where his parents had migrated from Madras State. He was an ordinary trader. He had practically received no scholastic education whatever. But a wide experience had been his schoolmaster. He spoke and wrote English very well, although his grammar was not perhaps free from faults. In the same way he had acquired a knowledge of Tamil. He understood and spoke Hindustani fairly well and he had some knowledge of Telugu too, though he did not know the alphabets of these languages. Again, he had a very good knowledge of the Creole dialect current in Mauritius which is a sort of corrupt French, and he knew of course the language of the Negroes. A working knowledge of so many languages was not a rare accomplishment among the Indians of South Africa, hundreds of whom could claim a general acquaintance with all these languages. These men become such good linguists almost without effort. And that is because their brains are not fatigued by education received through the medium of a foreign tongue, their memory is sharp, and they acquire these different languages simply by talking with people who speak them and by observation. This does not involve any considerable strain on their brains but on the other hand the easy mental exercise leads to a natural development of their intellect. Such was the case with Thambi Naidoo. He had a very keen intelligence and could grasp new subjects very quickly. His ever-ready wit was astonishing. He had never seen India. Yet his love for the homeland knew no bounds. Patriotism ran through his very veins. His firmness was pictured on his face. He was very strongly built and he possessed tireless energy. He shone equally whether he had to take the chair at meetings and lead them, or whether he had to do porter's work. He would not be ashamed of carrying a load on the public roads.

Night and day were the same to him when he set to work. And none was more ready than he to sacrifice his all for the sake of the community. If Thambi Naidoo had not been rash and if he had been free from anger, this brave man could easily have assumed the leadership of the community in the Transvaal in the absence of Kachhalia. His irritability had not still worked for evil while the Transvaal struggle lasted, and his invaluable qualities had shone forth like jewels. But, later on, I heard that his anger and his rashness had proved to be his worst enemies, and eclipsed his good qualities. However that may be, the name of Thambi Naidoo must ever remain as one of the front rank in the history of Satyagraha in South Africa.

The Magistrate conducted each case separately, and ordered all the accused to leave the Transvaal within forty-eight hours in some cases and seven or fourteen days in others.

The time limit expired on January 10, 1908 and the same day we were called upon to attend court for sentence.

None of us had to offer any defence. All were to plead guilty to the charge of disobeying the order to leave the Transvaal within the stated period, issued by the Magistrate on failure to satisfy him that they were lawful holders of certificates of registration.

I asked leave to make a short statement, and on its being granted, I said I thought there should be a distinction made between my case and those that were to follow. I had just heard from Pretoria that my compatriots there had been sentenced to three months' imprisonment with hard labour, and had been fined a heavy amount, in lieu of payment of which they would receive a further period of three months' hard labour. If these men had committed an offence, I had committed a greater offence and I therefore asked the Magistrate to impose upon me the heaviest penalty. The Magistrate, however, did not agree to my request and sentenced me to two months' simple imprisonment. I had some slight feeling of awkwardness due to the fact that I was standing as an accused in the very Court where I had often appeared as counsel. But I well remember that I considered the former role as far more honourable than the latter, and did not feel the slightest hesitation in entering the prisoner's box.

In the court there were hundreds of Indians as well as brother members of the Bar in front of me. On the sentence being pronounced I was at once removed in custody and was then quite alone. The policeman asked me to sit on a bench kept there for prisoners, shut the door on me and went away. I was somewhat agitated and fell into deep thought. Home, the Courts where I practised, the public meeting,—all these passed away like a dream, and I was now a prisoner. What would happen in two months? Would I have to serve the full term? If the people courted imprisonment in large numbers, as they had promised, there would be no question of serving the full sentence. But if they failed to fill the prisons, two months would be as tedious as an age. These thoughts passed through my mind in less than one hundredth of the time that it has taken me to dictate them. And they filled me with shame. How vain I was! I, who had asked the people to consider the prisons as His Majesty's hotels, the suffering consequent upon disobeying the Black Act as perfect bliss, and the sacrifice of one's all and of life itself in resisting it as supreme enjoyment! Where had all this knowledge vanished today? This second train of thought acted upon me as a bracing tonic, and I began to laugh at my own folly. I began to think what kind of imprisonment would be awarded to the others and whether they would be kept with me in the prison. But I was disturbed by the police officer who opened the gate and asked me to follow him, which I did. He then made me go before him, following me himself, took me to the prisoners' closed van and asked me to take my seat in it. I was driven to Johannesburg jail.

In jail I was asked to put off my own private clothing. I knew that convicts were made naked in jail. We had all decided as Satyagrahis voluntarily to obey all jail regulations so long as they were not inconsistent with our self-respect or with our religious convictions. The clothes which were given to me to wear were very dirty. I did not like putting them on at all. It was not without pain that

A SERIES OF ARRESTS

I reconciled myself to them from an idea that I must put up with some dirt. After the officers had recorded my name and address, I was taken to a large cell, and in a short time was joined by my compatriots who came laughing and told me how they had received the same sentence as myself, and what took place after I had been removed. I understood from them that when my case was over, the Indians, some of whom were excited, took out a procession with black flags in their hands. The police disturbed the procession and flogged some of its members. We were all happy at the thought that we were kept in the same jail and in the same cell.

The cell door was locked at 6 o'clock. The door was not made of bars but was quite solid, there being high up in the wall a small aperture for ventilation, so that we felt as if we had been locked up in a safe.

No wonder the jail authorities did not accord us the good treatment which they had meted out to Rama Sundara. As Rama Sundara was the first Satyagrahi prisoner, the authorities had no idea how he should be treated. Our batch was fairly large and further arrests were in contemplation. We were therefore kept in the Negro ward. In Soth Africa only two classes of convicts are recognized, namely Whites and Blacks, i.e. the Negroes, and the Indians were classed with Negroes.

The next morning we found that prisoners without hard labour had the right to keep on their own private clothing, and if they would not exercise this right, they were given special jail clothing assigned to that class of prisoners. We decided that it was not right to put on our own clothing and that it was appropriate to take the jail uniform, and we informed the authorities accordingly. We were therefore given the clothes assigned to Negro convicts not punished with hard labour. But Negro prisoners sentenced to simple imprisonment are never numerous, and hence there was a shortage of simple imprisonment prisoners' clothing as soon as other Indians sentenced to simple imprisonment began to arrive. As the Indians did not wish to stand upon ceremony in this matter, they readily accepted clothing assigned to hard labour prisoners.

Some of those who came in later preferred to keep on their own clothing rather than put on the uniform of the hard labour convicts. I thought this improper, but did not care to insist upon their following the correct procedure in the matter.

From the second or third day Satyagrahi prisoners began to arrive in large numbers. They had all courted arrest and were most of them hawkers. In South Africa every hawker, Black or White, has to take out a licence, always to carry it with him and show it to the police when asked to do so. Nearly every day some policeman would ask to see the licences and arrest those who had none to show. The community had resolved to fill up the jail after our arrests. In this the hawkers took the lead. It was easy for them to be arrested. They only had to refuse to show their licences and that was enough to ensure their arrest. In this way the number of Satyagrahi prisoners swelled to more than a hundred in one week. And as a few were sure to arrive every day, we received the daily budget of news without a newspaper. When Satyagrahis began to be arrested in large numbers, they were sentenced to imprisonment with hard labour, either because the magistrates lost patience, or because, as we thought, they received some such instructions from the Government. Even today, I think we were right in our conjecture, as, if we leave out the first few cases in which simple imprisonment was awarded, never afterwards throughout the long drawn out struggle was there pronounced a sentence of simple imprisonment, even ladies having been punished with hard labour. If all the magistrates had not received the same orders or instructions, and if yet by mere coincidence they sentenced all men and women at all times to hard labour, that must be held to be almost a miracle.

In Johannesburg jail prisoners not condemned to hard labour got 'mealie pap' in the morning. There was no salt in it, but each prisoner was given some salt separately. At noon the prisoners were given four ounces of rice, four ounces of bread, one ounce of *ghi* and a little salt, and in the evening 'mealie pap' and some vegetable, chiefly potatoes of which two were given if they were small and only one if they were big in size. None of us were satisfied with this diet. The rice was cooked soft. We asked the prison medical officer for some condiments, and told him that condiments were allowed in the jails in India. 'This is not India', was the stern answer. 'There is no question of taste about prison diet and condiments therefore can not be allowed.' We asked for pulse on the ground that the regulation diet was lacking in muscle-building properties. 'Prisoners must not indulge in arguments on medical grounds,' replied the doctor. 'You do get muscle-building food, as twice a week you are served boiled beans instead of maize.' The doctor's argument was sound if the human stomach was capable of extracting the various elements out of various foods taken at various times in a week or fortnight. As a matter of fact he had no intention whatever of looking to our convenience. The Superintendent permitted us to cook our food ourselves. We elected Thambi Naidoo as our *chef*, and as such he had to fight many a battle on our behalf. If the vegetable ration issued was short in weight, he would insist on getting full weight. On vegetable days which were two in a week we cooked twice and on other days only once, as we were allowed to cook other things for ourselves only for the noon-day meal. We were somewhat better off after we began to cook our own food.

But whether or not we succeeded in obtaining these conveniences, every one of us was firm in his resolution of passing his term in jail in perfect happiness and peace. The number of Satyagrahi prisoners gradually rose to over 150. As we were all simple imprisonment convicts, we had no work to do except keeping the cells etc. clean. We asked the Superintendent for work, and he replied: 'I am sorry I cannot give you work, as, if I did, I should be held to have committed an offence. But you can devote as much time as you please to keeping the place clean.' We asked for some such exercise as drill, as we had observed even the Negro prisoners with hard labour being drilled in addition to their usual work. The Superintendent replied, 'If your warder has time and if he gives you drill, I will not object to it; nor will I require him to do it, as he is hard worked as it is, and your arrival in unexpectedly large numbers has made his work harder still.' The warder was a good man and this qualified permission was quite enough for him. He began to drill us every morning with great interest. This drill must be performed in the small yard before our cells and was therefore in the nature of a merry-go-round. When the warder finished the drill and went away, it was continued by a Pathan compatriot of ours named Nawabkhan, who made us all laugh with his quaint pronunciation of English words of command. He rendered 'Stand at ease' as 'sundlies.' We could not for the life of us understand what Hindustani word it was, but afterwards it dawned upon us that it was no Hindustani but only Nawabkhani English.

CHAPTER XXI

THE FIRST SETTLEMENT

We had thus been in jail for a fortnight, when fresh arrivals brought the news that there were going on some negotiations about a compromise with the Government. After two or three days Mr Albert Cartwright, editor of *The Transvaal Leader*, a Johannesburg daily, came to see me.

All the daily papers then conducted in Johannesburg were the property of one or the other of the European owners of the gold mines, but except in cases where the interests of these magnates were at stake, the editors were unfettered in the expression of their own views on all public questions. Only very able and well-known men were selected as editors. For instance the editor of *The Daily Star* had formerly been Private Secretary to Lord Milner, and later went to England to take Mr Buckle's place as editor of *The Times*. Mr Albert Cartwright of *The Transvaal Leader* was as broad-minded as he was able. He had almost always supported the Indian cause in his columns. He and I had become good friends. He saw General Smuts after I was sent to jail. General Smuts welcomed his mediation. Mr Cartwright thereupon met the Indian leaders, who said, 'We know nothing about legal technicalities, and cannot possibly talk about compromise so long as Gandhi is in prison. We desire settlement, but if Government wants it while our men are in jail, you should see Gandhi. We will ratify any arrangement which he accepts.'

Mr Cartwright thus came to see me and brought with him terms of settlement drafted or approved of by General Smuts. I did not like the vague language of the document, but was all the same prepared myself to put my signature to it with one alteration. However, I informed Mr Cartwright, that I could not sign it without consulting my fellow-prisoners, even if I took the consent of the Indians outside prison for granted.

The substance of the proposed settlement was that the Indians should register voluntarily, and not under any law; that the details to be entered in the new certificates of registration should be settled by Government in consultation with the Indian community, and, that if the majority of the Indians underwent voluntary registration, Government should repeal the Black Act, and take steps with a view to legalize the voluntary registration. The draft did not make quite clear the condition which required Government to repeal the Black Act. I therefore suggested a change calculated to place this beyond all doubt from my own standpoint.

Mr Cartwright did not like even this little addition and said, 'General Smuts considers this draft to be final. I have approved of it myself, and I can assure you that if you all undergo re-registration, the Black Act is bound to be repealed.'

I replied, 'Whether or not there is a settlement, we shall always be grateful to you for your kindness and help. I should not like to suggest a single unnecessary alteration in the draft. I do not object to such language as would uphold the prestige of Government. But where I myself am doubtful about the meaning, I must certainly suggest a change of language, and if there is to be a settlement after all, both the parties must have the right to alter the draft. General Smuts need not confront us with an ultimatum, saying that these terms are final. He has already aimed one pistol in the shape of the Black Act at the Indians. What can he hope to gain by aiming a second?'

Mr Cartwright had nothing to say against this argument, and he promised to place my suggestion for the change before General Smuts.

I consulted my fellow-prisoners. They too did not like the language, but agreed to the settlement if General Smuts would accept the draft with my amendment. New-comers to jail had brought a message from the leaders outside, that I should accept any suitable compromise without waiting for their consent. I got Messers Leuing Quinn and Thambi Naidoo to sign the draft along with myself and handed it to Mr Cartwright.

The second or third day, on January 30, 1908, Mr Vernon, the Superintendent of Police, Johannesburg, took me to Pretoria to meet General Smuts, with whom I had a good deal of talk. He told me what had passed between him and Mr Cartwright. He congratulated me on the Indian community having remained firm even after my imprisonment, and said, 'I could never entertain a dislike for your people. You know I too am a barrister. I had some Indian fellow students in my time. But I must do my duty. The Europeans want this law, and you will agree with me, that these are mostly not Boers, but Englishmen. I accept the alteration you have suggested in the draft. I have consulted General Botha also, and I assure you that I will repeal the Asiatic Act as soon as most of you have undergone voluntary registration. When the bill legalizing such registration is drafted, I will send you a copy for your criticism. I do not wish there should be any recurrence of the trouble, and I wish to respect the feelings of your people.'

So saying General Smuts rose. I asked him, 'Where am I to go? And what about the other prisoners?'

The General laughed and said, 'You are free this very moment. I am 'phoning to the prison officials to release the other prisoners tomorrow morning. But I must advise you not to go in for many meetings or demonstrations, as in that case Government will find itself in an awkward position.'

I replied, 'You may rest assured, that there will not be a single meeting simply for the sake of it. But I will certainly have to hold meetings in order to explain to the community how the settlement was effected, what is its nature and scope, and how it has added to our responsibilities.'

'Of such meetings,' said General Smuts, you may have as many as you please. It is sufficient that you have understood what I desire in the matter.'

It was then seven o'clock in the evening. I had not a single farthing in my pocket. The secretary of General Smuts gave me the railway fare to Johannesburg. There was no need to stop at Pretoria and announce the settlement to the Indians there. The leaders were all in Johannesburg, which was our headquarters. There was now only one more train for Johannesburg, and I was able to catch it.

CHAPTER XXII

OPPOSITION AND ASSAULT

I reached Johannesburg at about 9 p.m. and went direct to the Chairman, Sheth Yusuf Mian. He knew that I had been taken to Pretoria, and was hence rather expecting me. Still it was a pleasant surprise for him and others to find me unaccompanied by a warder. I suggested that a meeting should be called at once with such attendance as was possible at a very short notice. The Chairman and other friends agreed with me. As most of the Indians lived in the same quarter, it was not difficult to send round notice of the proposed meeting. The Chairman's house was near the mosque, and meetings were usually held on the grounds of the mosque. There was hence not much to be done by way of arrangement for the meeting. It was enough to have one light on the platform. The meeting was held that very night at about 11 or 12 p.m. The audience numbered nearly a thousand, in spite of the shortness of the notice and the late hour.

Before the meeting was held, I had explained the terms of the settlement to the leaders present. A few opposed the settlement. But all of them understood the situation after they had heard me. Every one of them, however, was troubled by one doubt, 'What if General Smuts broke faith with us? The Black Act might not be enforced but it would always hang over our heads like Damocles' sword. If in the meanwhile we registered voluntarily, we would have knowingly played in the adversary's hands, and surrendered the most powerful weapon in our possession for resisting the Act. The right order for the settlement was, that the Act should be repealed first and then we should be called upon to register voluntarily.'

I liked this argument. I felt proud of the keen commonsense and high courage of those who advanced it, and saw that such was the stuff of which Satyagrahis were made. In answer to that argument I observed: 'It is an excellent argument and deserves serious consideration. There would be nothing like it, if we registered voluntarily only after the Act was repealed. But then it would not be in the nature of a compromise. Compromise means that both the parties make large concessions on all points except where a principle is involved. Our principle is, that we would not submit to the Black Act, and therefore, would not, in virtue of it, do even such things as were otherwise unobjectionable; and to this principle we must adhere at all costs. The principle with the Government is, that in order to prevent the illegal entry of Indians into the Transvaal, it must get many Indians to take out non-transferable permits with marks of identification and thus set the suspicions of the Europeans at rest and allay all their fears; and the Government can never give it up on their part. We have admitted this principle of the Government by our conduct up to date, and therefore even if we feel like resisting it we may not do so until we find fresh grounds for such a departure. Our struggle aimed not at the abrogation of this principle but at removing the stigma which the Black Act sought to attach to the community. If, therefore, we now utilize the new and powerful force which has sprung up in the community for gaining a fresh point, it would ill become us, who claim to be Satyagrahis. Consequently, we cannot justly object to the present settlement. As for the argument that we must not surrender our weapons before the Act is repealed, it is easily answered. A Satyagrahi bids good-bye to fear. He is therefore never afraid of trusting the opponent. Even if the opponent plays him false twenty times, the Satyagrahi is ready to trust him for the twenty-first time, for an implicit trust in human nature is the very essence of his creed. Again to say that in trusting the Government we play into their hands is to betray an ignorance of the principles of Satyagraha. Suppose we register voluntarily, but the Government commits a breach of faith and fails to redeem its promise to repeal the Act. Could we not then resort to Satyagraha? If we refused to show at the proper time the certificates of registration we take out, our registration would count for nothing, and Government could not distinguish between ourselves and the Indians who might enter the Transvaal surreptitiously. Therefore, whether there is or there is not any law in force, the Government cannot exercise control over us without our co-operation. The existence of a law means, that if we refuse to accept the restriction sought to be imposed through it by the Government, we are liable to punishment, and generally it so happens, that the fear of punishment leads men to submit to the restriction. But a Satyagrahi differs from the generality of men in this, that if he submits to a restriction, he submits voluntarily, not because he is afraid of punishment, but because he thinks that such submission is essential to the common weal. And such is precisely our position regarding registration, which cannot be affected by any breach of faith, however flagrant, on the part of the Government. We are the creators of this position of ours, and we alone can change it. We are fearless and free, so long as we have the weapon of Satyagraha in our hands. And if any thinks that the community may not be as strong afterwards as it is today, I should say that he is not a Satyagrahi nor has he any understanding of Satyagraha. That would mean that the present strength of the community is not real strength but is in the nature of a momentary effervescence or intoxication, and if that is so, we do not deserve to win, and the fruits of victory will slip out of our hands even if we win. Suppose the Government first abrogates the Act and we then register voluntarily. Suppose further that the Government afterwards enacts the same obnoxious law and compels the Indians to register. What can then prevent the Government from pursuing such a course of action? And if we are doubtful about our strength today, then too shall we be in an equally bad case. From whatever standpoint, therefore, we examine the settlement, it may be said that the community not only will not lose but will on the other hand gain by the compromise. And I am also of opinion, that when our opponents recognize our humility and sense of justice, they would give up or at least mitigate their opposition.'

I was thus able fully to satisfy the one or two of the small company who struck a discordant note, but I did not then even dream of the storm which was to break out at the midnight meeting. I explained all the terms of the settlement to the meeting and said:

'The responsibility of the community is largely enhanced by this settlement. We must register voluntarily in order to show that we do not intend to bring a single Indian into the Transvaal surreptitiously or by fraud. If any one of us fails to register, he will not be punished at present; but that can only mean that the community does not accept the settlement. It is necessary, indeed, that you must here raise your hands as a mark of your agreeing to the settlement, but that is not enough. As soon as the arrangements for fresh registration are completed, every one of us who raises his hand should take out a certificate of registration at once, and just as many of you had volunteered before in order to explain to our compatriots why they should not register, even so should you now come forward to explain to the community why they must register. And it is only when we have thus worthily fulfilled our part that we shall reap the real fruit of our victory.'

As soon as I finished my speech a Pathan friend stood up and greeted me with a volley of questions:

'Shall we have to give ten finger-prints under the settlement?'

'Yes and no. My own view of the matter is, that all of us should give digit impressions without the least hesitation. But those, who have any conscientious objection to giving them or think it to be derogatory to their self-respect, will not be obliged to give those impressions.'

'What will you do yourself?'

'I have decided to give ten finger-prints. It may not be for me not to give them myself while advising others to do so.'

'You were writing a deal about the ten finger-prints. It was you who told us that they were required only from criminals. It was you who said that the struggle centred round the finger-prints. How does all that fit in with your attitude today?'

'Even now I fully adhere to everything that I have written before about finger-prints. Even now I say that in India finger-prints are required from criminal tribes. I have said before and say even now, that it would be a sin in virtue of the Black Act to give even our signatures not to talk of finger-prints. It is true that I have, —and I believe wisely,—laid great stress on this requisition of finger-prints. It was easier to rouse the community to a sense of the gravity of the situation by a reference to such a new and startling feature of the Act as the finger-prints than to minor items in which we had already yielded submission. And I saw from experience that the community grasped the situation at once. But circumstances have now changed. I say with all the force at my command, that what would have been a crime against the people yesterday is in the altered circumstances of today the hallmark of a gentleman. If you require me to salute you by force and if I submit to you, I will have demeaned myself in the eyes of the public and in your eyes as well as in my own. But if I of my own accord salute you as a brother or fellow-man, that evinces my humility and gentlemanliness, and it will be counted to me as righteousness before the Great White Throne. That is how I advise the community to give the finger-prints.'

'We have heard that you have betrayed the community and sold it to General Smuts for 15,000 pounds. We will never give the finger-prints nor allow others to do so. I swear with Allah as my witness, that I will kill the man who takes the lead in applying for registration.'

'I can understand the feelings of Pathan friends. I am sure that no one else believes me to be capable of selling the community. I have already said that finger-prints will not be demanded from those who have sworn not to give them. I will render all possible help to any Pathan or other who wishes to register without giving finger-prints, and I assure him that he will get the certificate all right without violence being done to his conscience. I must confess, however, that I do not like the threat of death which the friend has held out. I also believe that one may not swear to kill another in the name of the Most High. I therefore take it, that it is only in a momentary fit of passion that this friend has taken the oath. However that may be, whether or not he carries out his threat, as the principal party responsible for this settlement and as a servant of the community, it is my clear duty to take the lead in giving finger-prints, and I pray to God that He graciously permit me so to do. Death is the appointed end of all life. To die by the hand of a brother, rather than by disease or in such other way, cannot be for me a matter for sorrow. And if even in such a case I am free from the thoughts of anger or hatred against my assailant, I know that that will redound to my eternal welfare, and even the assailant will later on realize my perfect innocence.'

It is perhaps necessary to explain why these questions were asked. Although there were not entertained any feelings of hatred against those who had submitted to the Black Act, their action had been condemned in plain and strong terms on the public platform as well as in *Indian Opinion*. Life with them therefore was anything but pleasant. They never imagined that the bulk of the community would stand to their guns and make such a display of strength as to bring the Government to terms of compromise. But when over 150 Satyagrahis were already in prison and there was a talk about settlement, it was almost

OPPOSITION AND ASSAULT

too much for the 'blacklegs' to bear, and there were among them some who even wished that there should be no settlement and would try to wreck it if it was effected.

There were only a few Pathans living in the Transvaal, their total number hardly exceeding fifty. Some of them had come over as soldiers during the Boer War and they had settled in the country like many other Indian as well as European soldiers. Some of them were even my clients, and I was familiar with them otherwise too. The Pathans are an unsophisticated and credulous race. Brave they are as a matter of course. To kill and get killed is an ordinary thing in their eyes, and if they are angry with any one, they will thrash him and sometimes even kill him. And in this matter they are no respecters of persons. They will behave even to a blood-brother in an identical manner. Even though there were so few of them in the Transvaal, there would be a free fight whenever they quarrelled among themselves, and in such cases I had often to play the part of a peace-maker. A Pathan's anger becomes particularly uncontrollable when he has to deal with any one whom he takes to be a traitor. When he seeks justice he seeks it only through personal violence. These Pathans fully participated in the Satyagraha struggle; none of them had submitted to the Black Act. It was an easy thing to mislead them. It was quite possible to create a misunderstanding in their minds about the finger-prints and thus to inflame them. This single suggestion,—viz., why should I ask them to give finger-prints if I was not corrupt?—was enough to poison the Pathans' ears.

Again there was another party in the Transvaal which comprised such Indians as had entered the Transvaal surreptitiously without a permit or were interested in bringing others there secretly either without a permit at all or with a false permit. This party too knew that the settlement would be detrimental to their interest. None had to produce his permit so long as the struggle lasted, and therefore this group could carry on their trade without fear and easily avoid going to jail during the struggle. The longer the struggle was protracted, the better for them. Thus this clique also could have instigated the Pathans.

The reader will now see how the Pathans got thus excited all of a sudden.

The Pathan's questions, however, did not have any impression on the meeting. I had asked the meeting to vote on the settlement. The president and other leaders were firm. After this passage-at-arms with the Pathan, the president made a speech explaining the nature of the settlement and dwelling upon the necessity for endorsing it, and then proceeded to ascertain the sense of the meeting, which unanimously ratified the settlement with the exception of a couple of Pathans present.

I reached home at 2 or 3 a.m. Sleep was out of the question, as I had to rise early and go to the jail to get the others released. I reached the jail at 7 a.m. The Superintendent had received the necessary orders on the 'phone, and he was waiting for me. All the Satyagrahi prisoners were released in the course of one hour. The Chairman and other Indians were present to welcome them, and from jail all of us proceeded to the place of meeting where a second meeting was now held. That day and a couple of subsequent days were passed in feasting and educating the community on the settlement. With the lapse of time, if on the one hand the implications of the settlement became clearer misunderstandings on the other hand also began to thicken. We have already discussed the chief causes of misunderstanding. Then again the letter we had written to General Smuts was open to misrepresentation. The difficulty I experienced in meeting the various objections which were thus raised was infinitely greater than what I had felt while the struggle was actually in progress. In the days of struggle, the only difficulties felt crop up in our relations with the adversary, and these are always easily overcome, for then all internecine strife and internal discord are either suspended altogether or at least they lose their prominence in face of the common danger. But when the fight is over, internal jealousies are again fully in play, and if the differences with the adversary have been amicably settled, many take to the easy and grateful task of picking holes in the settlement. And in a democratic body it is only in the fitness of

OPPOSITION AND ASSAULT

things that one has to provide satisfactory answers for the questions of every one, big and small. Even in offering battle to the adversary one does not learn the valuable lessons which come home to oneself while thus dealing with misunderstandings and strivings between friends. There is a sort of intoxication and exultation in fighting the adversary. But misunderstandings and differences between friends are rare phenomena and are therefore all the more painful. Yet it is only on such occasions that one's mettle is put to a real test. Such has been my experience without any exception, and I believe that it is only when passing through such ordeals that I have made the largest gains in things of the spirit. Many, who had not understood the real nature of the struggle while it was still going on, understood it fully in course of and after the settlement. Serious opposition was confined to the Pathans and did not travel beyond them.

The registrar of Asiatics was soon ready to issue registration certificates under the new voluntary arrangement. The form of the certificates was altogether changed, and had been settled in consultation with the Satyagrahis.

On the morning of February 10, 1908 some of us got ready to go and take out certificates of registration. The supreme necessity of getting through the registration business with all possible expedition had been fully impressed on the community, and it had been agreed, that the leaders should be the first to take out certificates on the first day, with a view to break down shyness, to see if the officers concerned discharged their duties with courtesy and generally to have an eye over all the arrangements.

When I reached my office, which was also the office of the Satyagraha Association, I found Mir Alam and his companions standing outside the premises. Mir Alam was an old client of mine, and used to seek my advice in all his affairs. Many Pathans in the Transvaal employed labourers to manufacture straw or coir mattresses, which they sold at a good profit, and Mir Alam did the same. He was fully six feet in height and of a large and powerful build. Today for the first time I saw Mir Alam outside my office instead of inside it, and although his eyes met mine, he for the first time refrained from saluting me. I saluted him and he saluted me in return. As usual I asked him, 'How do you do?' and my impression is that he said he was all right. But he did not today wear his usual smile on the face. I noticed his angry eyes and took a mental note of the fact. I thought that something was going to happen. I entered the office. The Chairman Mr Yusuf Mian and other friends arrived, and we set out for the Asiatic Office. Mir Alam and his companions followed us.

The Registration Office was at Von Brandis Square, less than a mile away from my office. On our way to it we had to pass through high roads. As we were going along Von Brandis Street, outside the premises of Messrs Arnot and Gibson, not more than three minutes' walk from the Registration Office, Mir Alam accosted me and asked me, 'Where are you going?'

'I propose to take out a certificate of registration, giving the ten finger-prints,' I replied. 'If you will go with me, I will first get you a certificate, with an impression only of the two thumbs, and then I will take one for myself, giving the finger-prints.'

I had scarcely finished the last sentence when a heavy cudgel blow descended on my head from behind. I at once fainted with the words *He Rama* (O God!) on my lips, lay prostrate on the ground and had no notion of what followed. But Mir Alam and his companions gave me more blows and kicks, some of which were warded off by Yusuf Mian and Thambi Naidoo with the result that they too became a target for attack in their turn. The noise attracted some European passers-by to the scene. Mir Alam and his companions fled but were caught by the Europeans. The police arrived in the meanwhile and took them in custody. I was picked up and carried into Mr J. C. Gibson's private office. When I regained consciousness, I saw Mr Doke bending over me. 'How do you feel?' he asked me.

'I am all right,' I replied, 'but there is pain in the teeth and the ribs. Where is Mir Alam?'

'He has been arrested along with the rest.'

'They should be released.'

'That is all very well. But here you are in a stranger's office with your lip and cheek badly lacerated. The police are ready to take you to the hospital, but if you will go to my place, Mrs Doke and I will minister to your comforts as best we can.'

'Yes, please take me to your place. Thank the police for their offer but tell them that I prefer to go with you.'

Mr Chamney the Registrar of Asiatics too now arrived on the scene. I was taken in a carriage to this good clergyman's residence in Smit Street and a doctor was called in. Meanwhile I said to Mr Chamney: 'I wished to come to your office, give ten finger-prints and take out the first certificate of registration, but God willed it otherwise. However I have now to request you to bring the papers and allow me to register at once. I hope that you will not let any one else register before me.'

'Where is the hurry about it?' asked Mr Chamney. 'The doctor will be here soon. You please rest yourself and all will be well. I will issue certificates to others but keep your name at the head of the list.'

'Not so,' I replied. 'I am pledged to take out the first certificate if I am alive and if it is acceptable to God. It is therefore that I insist upon the papers being brought here and now.'

Upon this Mr Chamney went away to bring the papers.

The second thing for me to do was to wire to the Attorney-General that I did not hold Mir Alam and others guilty for the assault committed upon me, that in any case I did not wish them to be prosecuted and that I hoped they would be discharged for my sake. But the Europeans of Johannesburg addressed a strong letter to the Attorney-General saying that whatever views Gandhi might hold as regards the punishment of criminals, they could not be given effect to in South Africa. Gandhi himself might not take any steps, but the assault was committed not in a private place but on the high roads and was therefore a public offence. Several Englishmen too were in a position to tender evidence and the offenders must be prosecuted. Upon this the Attorney-General re-arrested

Mir Alam and one of his companions who were sentenced to three months' hard labour. Only I was not summoned as a witness.

But let us return to the sick room. Dr Thwaites came in while Mr Chamney was still away. He examined me and stitched up the wounds in the cheek and on the upper lip. He prescribed some medicine to be applied to the ribs and enjoined silence upon me so long as the stitches were not removed. He restricted my diet to liquids only. He said that none of the injuries was serious, that I should be able to leave my bed and take up my ordinary activities in a week, but that I should be careful not to undertake much physical strain for two months more. So saying he left.

Thus speech was forbidden me, but I was still master of my hands. I addressed a short note as follows to the community through the Chairman and sent it for publication:

'I am well in the brotherly and sisterly hands of Mr and Mrs Doke. I hope to take up my duty shortly.

'Those who have committed the act did not know what they were doing. They thought that I was doing what was wrong. They have had their redress in the only manner they know. I therefore request that no steps be taken against them.

'Seeing that the assault was committed by a Musalman or Musalmans, the Hindus might probably feel hurt. If so, they would put themselves in the wrong before the world and their Maker. Rather let the blood spilt today cement the two communities indissolubly—such is my heartfelt prayer. May God grant it.

'Assault or no assault, my advice remains the same. The large majority of Asiatics ought to give finger-prints. Those who have real conscientious scruples will be exempted by the Government. To ask for more would be to show ourselves as children.

'The spirit of Satyagraha rightly understood should make the people fear none and nothing but God. No cowardly fear therefore should deter the vast majority of sober-minded Indians from doing their duty. The promise of repeal of the Act against voluntary registration having been given, it is the sacred duty of every good Indian to help the Government and the Colony to the uttermost.'

Mr Chamney returned with the papers and I gave my finger-prints but not without pain. I then saw that tears stood in Mr Chamney's eyes. I had often to write bitterly against him, but this showed me how man's heart may be softened by events.

The reader will easily imagine that all this did not take more than a few minutes. Mr Doke and his good wife were anxious that I should be perfectly at rest and peaceful, and were therefore pained to witness my mental activity after the assault. They were afraid that it might react in a manner prejudicial to my health. They, therefore, by making signs and similar devices, removed all persons from near my bed, and asked me not to write or do anything. I made a request in writing, that before and in order that I might lie down quietly, their daughter Olive, who was then only a little girl, should sing for me my favourite English hymn, 'Lead, kindly light.' Mr Doke liked this very much and acceded to my request with a sweet smile. He called Olive by signs and asked her to stand at the door and sing the hymn in a low tone. The whole scene passes before my eyes as I dictate this, and the melodious voice of little Olive reverberates in my ears.

I have included in this chapter much that, I think and the reader too will think, is irrelevant to my subject. Yet I cannot close this chapter without adding one reminiscence, too sacred to be omitted. How shall I describe the service rendered to me by the Doke family?

Mr Joseph Doke was a Baptist minister then 46 years old and had been in New Zealand before he came to South Africa. Some six months before this assault, he came to my office and sent in his card. On seeing the word 'Reverend' before his name, I wrongly imagined that he had come, as some other clergymen did, to convert me to Christianity or to advise me to give up the struggle or perhaps to express patronizing sympathy with the movement. Mr Doke entered, and we had not talked many miniutes before I saw how sadly I had misjudged him and mentally apologized to him. I found him familiar with all the facts of the struggle which were published in newspapers. He said, 'Please consider me as your friend in this struggle. I consider it my religious duty to render you such help as I can. If I have learnt any lesson from the life of Jesus, it is this that one should share and lighten the load of those who are heavily laden.' We thus got acquainted with each other, and every day marked an advance in our mutual affection and intimacy. The name of Mr Doke will often recur in course of the present volume, but it was necessary to say a few words by way of introducing him to the reader before I describe the delicate attention I received at the hands of the Dokes.

Day and night one or other member of the family would be waiting upon me. The house became a sort of caravanserai so long as I stayed there. All classes of Indians flocked to the place to inquire after my health, and when later permitted by the doctor, to see me, from the humble hawker basket in hand with dirty clothes and dusty boots right up to the Chairman of the Transvaal British Indian Association. Mr Doke would receive all of them in his drawing room with uniform courtesy and consideration, and so long as I lived with the Dokes, all their time was occupied either with nursing me or with receiving the hundreds of people who looked in to see me. Even at night Mr Doke would quietly peep twice or thrice into my room. While living under his hospitable roof, I never so much as felt that it was not my home, or that my nearest and dearest could have looked after me better than the Dokes.

And it must not be supposed that Mr Doke had not to suffer for according public support to the Indians in their struggle and for harbouring me under his roof. Mr Doke was in charge of a Baptist church, and depended for his livelihood upon a congregation of Europeans, not all of whom entertained liberal views and among whom dislike of the Indians was perhaps as general as among other Europeans. But Mr Doke was unmoved by it. I had discussed this delicate subject with him in the very beginning of our acquaintance. And he said, 'My dear friend, what do you think of the religion of Jesus? I claim to be a humble follower of Him, who cheerfully mounted the cross for the faith that was in Him, and whose love was as wide as the world. I must take a public part in your struggle if I am at all desirous of representing Christ to the Europeans who, you are afraid, will give me up as punishment for it. And I must not complain if they do thus give me up. My livelihood is indeed derived from them, but you certainly do not think that I am associated with them for living's sake, or that they are my cherishers. My cherisher is God; they are but the instruments of His Almighty will. It is one of the unwritten conditions of my connection with them, that none of them may interfere with my religious liberty. Please therefore stop worrying on my account. I am taking my place beside you in this struggle not to oblige the Indians but as a matter of duty. The fact, however, is that I have fully discussed this question with my dean. I gently informed him, that if he did not approve of my relations with the Indians, he might permit me to retire and engage another minister instead. But he not only asked me not to trouble myself about it but even spoke some words of encouragement. Again you must not imagine, that all Europeans alike entertain hatred against your people. You can have no idea of the silent sympathy of many with your tribulations, and you will agree with me that I must know about it situated as I am.'

After this clear explanation, I never referred to the subject again. And later on when Mr Doke died in the pursuit of his holy calling in Rhodesia, at a time when the Satyagraha struggle was still in progress, the Baptists called a meeting in their church, to which they invited the late Mr Kachhalia and other Indians as well as myself, and which they asked me to address.

About ten days afterwards I had recovered enough strength to move about fairly well, and I then took my leave of this godly family. The parting was a great wrench to me no less than to the Dokes.

CHAPTER XXIII

EUROPEAN SUPPORT

As the number of Europeans of position, who actively sided with the Indians in their struggle, was fairly large, it will not perhaps, be out of place to introduce them here to the reader all at once, so that when their names occur later on in this narrative, they will not be strange to him, and I shall not have to stop in the midst of the narrative in order to introduce them. The order in which the names have been arranged is not the order of the merit of service rendered, nor that of the public estimation in which the bearers of the names were held. I mention the friends in order of the time when I got acquainted with them and in connection with the various branches of the struggle where they helped the Indians.

The first name is that of Mr Albert West, whose association with the community dated from before the struggle and whose association with me commenced earlier still. When I opened my office in Johannesburg my wife was not with me. The reader will remember that in 1903 I received a cable from South Africa and suddenly left India, expecting to return home within a year. Mr West used to frequent the vegetarian restaurant in Johannesburg where I regularly had my meals both morning and evening, and we thus became acquainted with each other. He was then conducting a printing press in partnership with another European. In 1904 a virulent plague broke out among the Indians in Johannesburg. I was fully engaged in nursing the patients, and my visits to the restaurant became irregular. Even when I went, I went there before the other guests in order to avoid any possible danger from their coming in contact with me. Mr West became anxious when he did not find me there for two days in succession as he had read in the papers that I was attending to the plague patients. The third day, at 6 o'clock in the morning I was scarcely ready to go out when Mr

EUROPEAN SUPPORT

West knocked at my door. When I opened it, I saw Mr West with his beaming face.

'I am so glad to see you,' he exclaimed. 'I had been worrying about you, not finding you at the restaurant. Do tell me if I can do anything for you.'

'Will you nurse the patients?' I asked jocularly.

'Why not? I am quite ready.'

Meanwhile I had thought out my plans, and said, 'No other answer could be expected of you, but there are already many helping with the nursing, and besides, I propose to put you to still harder work. Madanjit is here on plague duty, and there is no one to look after the *Indian Opinion* press. If you go to Durban and take charge of the press, it will be really a great help. I cannot of course offer you any tempting terms. Ten pounds a month and half the profits if any is all that I can afford.'

'That is rather a tough job. I must have my partner's permission, and then there are some dues to be collected. But never mind. Will you wait till evening for my final answer?'

'Yes, we meet in the park at 6 o'clock.'

So we met. Mr West had obtained his partner's permission. He entrusted me with the recovery of his dues, and left for Durban by the evening train the next day. In a month I had his report that not only was the press not profitable at all but it was actually a losing concern. There were large arrears to be collected but the books had been badly kept. Even the list of the names and addresses of subscribers was incomplete. There was also mismanagement in other respects. Mr West did not write all this as a matter of complaint. As he did not care for profit, he assured me that he would not give up what he had undertaken, but gave me clearly to understand that the paper would not be paying its way for a long time to come.

Shri Madanjit had come to Johannesburg to canvass subscribers for the paper as well as to confer with me as regards the management of the press. Every month I had to meet a small or large deficit, and I was therefore desirous of having a more definite idea of my possible liabilities.

Madanjit had no experience of printing press business and I had been thinking since the beginning, that it would be well to associate a trained hand with him. The plague broke out in the meantime, and as Madanjit was just the man for such a crisis, I put him on to nursing. And I closed with West's unexpected offer and told him that he was to go not temporarily while the epidemic lasted, but for good. Hence his report on the prospects of the paper just referred to.

The reader knows how at last both the paper and the press were removed to Phoenix, where West drew a monthly allowance of £3 instead of £10 as previously arranged. West was himself fully agreeable to all these changes. I never observed in him the least anxiety as to how he would be able to maintain himself. I recognized in him a deeply religious spirit, although he was not a student of religion. He was a man of perfectly independent temperament. He would say what he thought of all things, and would not hesitate to call a spade a spade. He was quite simple in habits. He was unmarried when we first met, and I know that he lived a life of spotless purity. Some years later he went to England to see his parents and returned a married man. By my advice he brought with him his wife, mother-in-law and unmarried sister, who all lived in extreme simplicity and in every way fraternized with the Indians in Phoenix. Miss Ada West (or Devi Behn as we used to call her) is now 35 years old, is still unmarried and leads a most pious life. She too rendered to the pioneers at Phoenix services of no mean order. At one time or another she looked after the little children, taught them English, cooked in the common kitchen, swept the houses, kept accounts and did composing and other work in the press. Whatever task came to her, she never hesitated in doing it. She is not now in Phoenix, but that is because since my return to India the press has been unable to meet even her small personal expenditure. West's mother-in-law is now over eighty years old. She is a fine hand at sewing, and used to help the settlement with her skill as a tailor. Every one in Phoenix called her Granny and felt that she was really related so to him. I need scarcely say anything about Mrs

West. When many members of the Phoenix settlement were in jail, the Wests along with Maganlal Gandhi took over the whole management of the institution. West would see to the press and the paper, and in the absence of others and myself, dispatch to Gokhale the cables which were to be sent from Durban. When even West was arrested (though he was soon released), Gokhale got nervous and sent over Andrews and Pearson.

Then there was Mr Ritch. I have already written about him. He had joined my office before the struggle and proceeded to England for the bar with a view to filling my place when I was not available. He was the moving spirit of the South African British Indian Committee in London.

The third was Mr Polak, whose acquaintance like that of West I casually made in the restaurant. He likewise left at once the sub-editorship of *The Transvaal Critic* to join the staff of *Indian Opinion*. Every one knows how he went to India and to England in connection with the struggle. When Ritch went to England, I called Polak from Phoenix to Johannesburg, where he became my articled clerk and then a full-fledged attorney. Later on he married. People in India are familiar with Mrs Polak, who not only never came in her husband's way but was a perfect helpmate to him during the struggle. The Polaks did not see eye to eye with us in the Non-co-operation movement, but they are still serving India to the best of their ability.

The next was Mr Hermann Kallenbach, whom too I came to know before the struggle. He is a German, and had it not been for the Great War, he would be in India today. He is a man of strong feelings, wide sympathies and childlike simplicity. He is an architect by profession, but there is no work, however lowly, which he would consider to be beneath his dignity. When I broke up my Johannesburg establishment, I lived with him, but he would be hurt if I offered to pay him my share of the household expenses, and would plead that I was responsible for considerable savings in his domestic economy. This was indeed true. But this is not the place to describe my personal relations with European friends. When we thought of accommodating the families of Satyagrahi prisoners in Johannesburg in one place, Kallenbach lent the use of his big farm without any rent. But more of that later. When Gokhale came to Johannesburg, the community put him up at Kallenbach's cottage which the illustrious guest liked very much. Kallenbach went with me as far as Zanzibar to see Gokhale off. He was arrested along with Polak and suffered imprisonment. Finally, when I left South Africa to see Gokhale in England, Kallenbach was with me. But when I returned to India, he was not permitted to go with me to India on account of the war. He was like all other Germans interned in England. When the war was over Kallenbach returned to Johannesburg and recommenced the practice of his profession.

Let me now introduce the reader to a noble girl, I mean Miss Sonja Schlesin. I cannot resist the temptation of placing here on record Gokhale's estimate of her character. He had a wonderful power of judging men. I went with him from Delagoa Bay to Zanzibar, and the voyage gave us a fine opportunity of quiet talks. Gokhale had come in contact with the Indian and European leaders in South Africa. And while minutely analysing for me the characters of the principal persons of the drama, I perfectly remember that he gave the pride of place among them all, Europeans as well as Indians, to Miss Schlesin: 'I have rarely come across such purity, single-minded devotion to work and great determination as I have seen in Miss Schlesin. I was simply astonished how she had sacrificed her all for the Indian cause without expecting any reward whatever. And when you add to all this her great ability and energy, these qualities combine to make her a priceless asset to your movement. I need hardly say it and yet I say that you must cherish her.' I had a Scottish girl, Miss Dick, working with me as stenotypist, who was the very picture of loyalty and purity. Many a bitter experience has been my portion in life, but I have also had the good fortune to claim a large number of Europeans and Indians of high character as my associates. Miss Dick left me when she married, and then Mr Kallenbach introduced Miss Schlesin to me and said, 'This girl has been entrusted to me by her mother. She is clever and honest, but she is very mischievous and impetuous. Perhaps she is even insolent. You keep her if you can manage her. I do not place her with you for the mere pay.' I was ready to allow £20 a month to a good stenotypist, but I had no idea of Miss Schlesin's ability. Mr Kallenbach proposed that I should pay her £6 a month to begin with, and I readily agreed. Miss Schlesin soon made me familiar with the mischievous part of herself. But in a month's time she had achieved the conquest of my heart. She was ready to work at all times whether by day or at night. There was nothing difficult or impossible for her. She was then only sixteen years of age, but she captivated my clients as well as the fellow Satyagrahis by her frankness and readiness to serve. This young girl soon constituted herself the watchman and warder of the morality not only of my office but of the whole movement. Whenever she was in doubt as to the ethical propriety of any proposed step, she would freely discuss it with me and not rest till she was convinced of it. When all the leaders except Sheth Kachhalia were in jail, Miss Schlesin had control of large funds and was in charge of the accounts. She handled workers of various temperaments. Even Sheth Kachhalia would have recourse to her and seek her advice. Mr Doke was then in charge of *Indian Opinion*. But even he, hoary-headed veteran as he was, would get the articles he wrote for *Indian Opinion* passed by her. And he once told me, 'If Miss Schlesin had not been there, I do not know how I could have satisfied even my own self with my work. I cannot sufficiently appreciate the value of her assistance, and very often I have accepted the corrections or additions she suggested knowing them to be appropriate.' Pathans, Patels, ex-indentured men, Indians of all classes and ages surrounded her, sought her advice and followed it. Europeans in South Africa would generally never travel in the same railway compartment as Indians, and in the Transvaal they are even prohibited from doing so. Yet Miss Schlesin would deliberately sit in the third class compartment for Indians like other Satyagrahis and even resist the guards who interfered with her. I feared and Miss Schlesin hoped that she might be arrested some day. But although the Transvaal Government were aware of her ability, her mastery over the 'strategy' of the movement, and the hold she had acquired over the Satyagrahis, they adhered to the policy and the chivalry of not arresting her. Miss Schlesin never asked for or desired an increase in her monthly allowance of £6. I began giving her £10 when I came to know of some of her wants. This too she accepted with reluctance, and flatly declined to have anything more. 'I do not need more, and if I take anything in excess of my necessities, I will have betrayed the principle which has attracted me to you,' she would say, and silence me. The reader will perhaps ask what was Miss Schlesin's education. She had passed the Intermediate examination of the Cape University, and obtained first class diploma in shorthand etc. She graduated after the struggle was over, and is now head mistress in a Government Girls' School in the Transvaal.

Herbert Kitchin was an English electrician with a heart pure as crystal. He worked with us during the Boer War and was for some time editor of *Indian Opinion*. He was a lifelong *brahmachari*.

The persons I have thus far mentioned were such as came in close contact with me. They could not be classed among the leading Europeans of the Transvaal. However, this latter class too was very largely helpful, and the most influential of such helpers was Mr Hosken, ex-President of the Association of Chambers of Commerce of South Africa and a member of the Legislative Assembly of the Transvaal, whose acquaintance the reader has already made and who was Chairman of the Committee of European sympathizers with the Satyagraha movement. When the movement was in full swing, direct communications between Satyagrahis and the local Government were obviously out of the question, not because of any objection on principle on the part of the Satyagrahis to deal directly with Government but because the latter would naturally not confer with the breakers of its laws. And this committee acted as mediator between the Indians and the Government.

I have already introduced Mr Albert Cartwright to the reader. Then there was Rev. Charles Phillips who joined and assisted us even as Mr Doke did. Mr Phillips had long been Congregational minister in the Transvaal. His good wife too did us much service. A third clergyman who had given up orders to take up the editorship of the Bloemfontein daily *The Friend* and who supported the Indian cause in his paper in the teeth of European opposition was Rev. Dewdney Drew, one of the best speakers in South Africa. A similarly spontaneous helper was Mr Vere Stent, editor of *The Pretoria News*. A mass meeting of Europeans was once held in the Town Hall of Pretoria under the presidency of the Mayor to condemn the Indian movement and to support the Black Act. Mr Vere Stent alone stood up in opposition to the overwhelming majority of anti-Indians and refused to sit down in spite of the president's orders. The Europeans threatened to lay hands on him, yet he stood unmoved and defiant like a lion, and the meeting disperesed at last without passing its resolution.

There were other Europeans whose names I could mention and who never missed an opportunity of doing us a good turn, although they did not formally join any association. But I propose to close this chapter with a few words about three ladies. One of these was Miss Hobhouse, the daughter of Lord Hobhouse, who at the time of the Boer War reached the Transvaal against the wishes of Lord Milner, and who single-handed moved among the Boer women, encouraged them and bade them to stand firm when Lord Kitchener had set up his famous or rather infamous 'concentration camps' in the Transvaal and the Free State. She believed the English policy in respect of the Boer War to be totally unrighteous, and therefore like the late Mr Stead she wished and prayed to God for England's defeat in the war. Having thus served the Boers, she was shocked to learn that the same Boers, who had only recently resisted injustice with all their might, were now led into doing injustice to the Indians through ignorant prejudice. The Boers looked up to her with great respect and affection. She was very intimate

with General Botha, and did her best to commend to the
Boers the policy of repealing the Black Act.

The second lady was Miss Olive Schreiner, to whom
I have already referred in a previous chapter. The name
Schreiner is one to conjure with in South Africa, so much
so that when Miss Schreiner married, her husband adopted her name so that (I was told) her relation with the
Schreiners might not be forgotten among the Europeans
of South Africa. This was not due to any false pride, as
Miss Schreiner was as simple in habits and humble in
spirit as she was learned. I had the privilege of being familiar with her. She knew no difference between her Negro
servants and herself. Authoress of *Dreams* and many other
works as she was, she never hesitated to cook, wash the
pots or handle the broom. She held that far from affecting
it adversely, such useful physical labour stimulated her
literary ability and made for a sense of proportion and
discrimination in thought and language. This gifted lady
lent to the Indian cause the whole weight of her influence
over the Europeans of South Africa.

The third lady was Miss Molteno, an aged member
of that ancient family of South Africa, who also did her
best for the Indians.

The reader may ask what fruit all this sympathy of
the Europeans bore. Well, this chapter has not been written
to describe the practical consequences of their sympathy.
The work detailed above of some of these friends bears
witness to a portion of the result. The very nature of Satyagraha is such that the fruit of the movement is contained
in the movement itself. Satyagraha is based on self-help,
self-sacrifice and faith in God. One of my objects in enumerating the names of European helpers is to mark the Satyagrahis' gratefulness to them. This history would be justly
considered incomplete without such mention. I have not
tried to make the list exhaustive, but have tendered the
Indians' thanks to all in selecting a few for especial mention.
Secondly, as a Satyagrahi I hold to the faith, that all activity
pursued with a pure heart is bound to bear fruit, whether
or not such fruit is visible to us. And last but not the least, I

have tried to show that all truthful movements spontaneously attract to themselves all manner of pure and disinterested help. If it is not clear already, I should like to make it clear that no other effort whatever was made during the struggle to enlist European sympathy beyond the effort, if effort it can be called, involved in adherence to Truth and Truth alone. The European friends were attracted by the inherent power of the movement itself.

CHAPTER XXIV
FURTHER INTERNAL DIFFICULTIES

We have had some idea of our internal difficulties in Chapter XXII. When I was assaulted in Johannesburg, my family lived in Phoenix and were naturally anxious about me. But it was not possible for them to expend money on the journey from Phoenix to Johannesburg. It was therefore necessary for me to see them after my recovery.

I was often on the move between the Transvaal and Natal in connection with my work. From the letters of Natal friends I was aware that in Natal too the settlement had been grossly misunderstood. And I had received a sheaf of correspondence addressed to *Indian Opinion* in which adverse criticism was passed on the settlement. Although the Satyagraha struggle was still confined to the Transvaal Indians, we must seek the support and enlist the sympathies of the Natal Indians also. The Transvaal struggle was not a mere local affair and the Indians in the Transvaal were really fighting the battle on behalf of all the Indians in South Africa. And therefore also I must go to Durban and remove the misunderstandings prevalent there. So I took the first opportunity to run up to Durban.

A public meeting of the Indians was called in Durban. Some friends had warned me beforehand that I would be attacked at this meeting and that I should therefore not attend it at all or at least take steps for defending myself. But neither of the two courses was open to me. If a servant when called by his master fails to respond through fear, he forfeits his title to the name of servant. Nor does he deserve the name if he is afraid of the master's punishment. Service of the public for service's sake is like walking on the sword's edge. If a servant is ready enough for praise he may not flee in the face of blame. I therefore presented myself at the meeting at the appointed time. I explained to the meeting how the settlement had been effected, and also answered the questions put by the audience. The meeting was held at 8 o'clock in the evening. The proceedings were nearly over when a Pathan rushed to the platform with a big stick. The lights were put out at the same time. I grasped the situation at once. Sheth Daud Muhammad the chairman stood up on the chairman's table and tried to quell the disturbance. Some of those on the platform surrounded me to defend my person. The friends who feared an assault had come to the place prepared for eventualities. One of them had a revolver in his pocket and he fired a blank shot. Meanwhile Parsi Rustomji who had noticed the gathering clouds went with all possible speed to the police station and informed Superintendent Alexander, who sent a police party. The police made a way for me through the crowd and took me to Parsi Rustomji's place.

The next day Parsi Rustomji brought all the Pathans of Durban together in the morning, and asked them to place before me all their complaints against me. I met them and tried to conciliate them, but with little success. They had a preconceived notion that I had betrayed the community, and until this poison was removed, it was useless reasoning with them. The canker of suspicion cannot be cured by arguments or explanations.

I left Durban for Phoenix the same day. The friends who had guarded me the previous night would not let me alone, and informed me that they intended to accompany me to Phoenix. I said, 'I cannot prevent you if you will come in spite of me. But Phoenix is a jungle. And what will you do if we the only dwellers in it do not give you even food?' One of the friends replied, 'That won't frighten us. We are well able to look after ourselves. And so long as we are a-soldiering, who is there to prevent us

FURTHER INTERNAL DIFFICULTIES

from robbing your pantry?' We thus made a merry party for Phoenix.

The leader of this self-appointed guard was Jack Moodaley, a Natal-born Tamilian well known among the Indians as a trained boxer. He and his companions believed that no man in South Africa, whether white or coloured, was a match for him in that branch of sport.

In South Africa I had for many years been in the habit of sleeping in the open at all times except when there was rain. I was not prepared now to change the habit, and the self-constituted guard decided to keep watch all night. Though I had tried to laugh these men out of their purpose, I must confess that I was weak enough to feel safer for their presence. I wonder if I could have slept with the same ease if the guard had not been there. I suppose I should have been startled by some noise or other. I believe that I have an unflinching faith in God. For many years I have accorded intellectual assent to the proposition that death is only a big change in life and nothing more, and should be welcome whenever it arrives. I have deliberately made a supreme attempt to cast out from my heart all fear whatsoever including the fear of death. Still I remember occasions in my life when I have not rejoiced at the thought of approaching death as one might rejoice at the prospect of meeting a long lost friend. Thus man often remains weak notwithstanding all his efforts to be strong, and knowledge which stops at the head and does not penetrate into the heart is of but little use in the critical times of living experience. Then again the strength of the spirit within mostly evaporates when a person gets and accepts support from outside. A Satyagrahi must be always on his guard against such temptations.

While in Phoenix I did just one thing. I wrote a great deal with a view to removing misunderstandings about the compromise, including an imaginary dialogue for *Indian Opinion* in which I disposed of in ample detail the objections advanced and criticisms passed against the settlement. I believe that this dialogue produced a good effect. It was found that the Transvaal Indians, whose misunderstanding of the settlement, if persistent, would have led to really disastrous results, did not long misunderstand it. It was only for the Transvaal Indians to accept or to reject the settlement. They were on their trial as well as myself as their leader and servant. In the end there were hardly any Indians who had not registered themselves voluntarily. There was such a rush of the applicants for registration that the officers concerned were hard pressed with work, and in a very short time the Indians had fulfilled their part of the settlement. Even the Government had to admit this, and I could see that the misunderstanding, though of an acute nature, was quite limited in its extent. There was no doubt a great deal of stir when some Pathans violently took the law into their own hands. But such violent stir, when analysed, often turns out to have no bottom at all and is equally often only temporary. And yet it is a power in the world today as we are apt to be unnerved in the face of violence. If however we calmly think about it, we shall find that there is no reason for nervousness. Just suppose that Mir Alam and his friends, instead of only wounding, had actually destroyed my body. And suppose also that the community had deliberately remained calm and unperturbed, and forgiven the offenders perceiving that according to their lights they could not behave otherwise than they did. Far from injuring the community, such a noble attitude would have greatly benefited them. All misunderstanding would have disappeared, and Mir Alam and party would have had their eyes opened to the error of their ways. As for me, nothing better can happen to a Satyagrahi than meeting death all unsought in the very act of Satyagraha, i.e., pursuing Truth. All these propositions are true only of a struggle like the Satyagraha movement, where there is no room for hatred, where self-reliance is the order of the day, where no one has to look expectantly at another, where there are no leaders and hence no followers, or where all are leaders and all are followers, so that the death of a fighter, however eminent, makes not for slackness but on the other hand intensifies the struggle.

Such is the pure and essential nature of Satyagraha, not realized in practice, because not every one of us has shed hatred. In actual practice the secret of Satyagraha is not understood by all, and the many are apt unintelligently to follow the few. Again as Tolstoy observed, the Transvaal struggle was the first attempt at applying the principle of Satyagraha to masses or bodies of men. I do not know any historical example of pure mass Satyagraha. I cannot however formulate any definite opinion on the point, as my knowledge of history is limited. But as a matter of fact we have nothing to do with historical precedents. Granted the fundamental principles of Satyagraha, it will be seen that the consequences I have described are bound to follow as night the day. It will not do to dismiss such a valuable force with the remark that it is difficult or impossible of application. Brute force has been the ruling factor in the world for thousands of years, and mankind has been reaping its bitter harvest all along, as he who runs may read. There is little hope of anything good coming out of it in the future. If light can come out of darkness, then alone can love emerge from hatred.

CHAPTER XXV
GENERAL SMUTS' BREACH OF FAITH(?)

The reader has seen something of the internal difficulties, in describing which I had to draw largely upon my own life story, but that could not be avoided, as my own difficulties regarding Satyagraha became equally the difficulties of the Satyagrahis. We now return to the external situation.

I am ashamed of writing the caption of this chapter as well as the chapter itself, for it deals with the obliquity of human nature. Already in 1908 General Smuts ranked as the ablest leader in South Africa, and today he takes a high place among the politicians of the British Empire, and even of the world. I have no doubt about his great abilities. General Smuts is as able a general and administrator as he is a lawyer. Many other politicians have come and gone in South Africa, but from 1907 up to date the reins of Government have practically been held throughout by this gentleman, and even today he holds a unique position in the country. It is now nine years since I left South Africa. I do not know what epithet the people of South Africa now bestow upon General Smuts. His Christian name is Jan, and South Africa used to call him 'slim Janny.' Many English friends had asked me to beware of General Smuts, as he was a very clever man and a trimmer, whose words were intelligible only to himself and often of a kind that either party could interpret them in a sense favourable to himself. Indeed on a suitable occasion he would lay aside the interpretations of both the parties, put a fresh interpretation upon them, carry it out and support it by such clever arguments that the parties for the time would be led to imagine that they were wrong themselves and General Smuts was right in construing the words as he did. As regards the events I am now going to describe, we believed and said, when they happened, that General Smuts had played us false. Even today, I look upon the incident as a breach of faith from the Indian community's standpoint. However I have placed a mark of interrogation after the phrase, as in point of fact the General's action did not perhaps amount to an intentional breach of faith. It could not be described as breach of faith if the intention was absent. My experience of General Smuts in 1913-14 did not then seem bitter and does not seem so to me today, when I can think of the past events with a greater sense of detachment. It is quite possible that in behaving to the Indians as he did in 1908 General Smuts was not guilty of a deliberate breach of faith.

These prefatory words were necessary in justice to General Smuts, as well as in defence of the use of the phrase 'breach of faith' in connection with his name and of what I am going to say in the present chapter.

We have seen in the last chapter how the Indians registered voluntarily to the satisfaction of the Transvaal Government. The Government must now repeal the Black Act, and if they did, the Satyagraha struggle would come

GENERAL SMUTS' BREACH OF FAITH (?)

to an end. This did not mean the end of the entire mass of anti-Indian legislation in the country or the redress of all the Indian grievances, for which the Indians must still continue their constitutional agitation. Satyagraha was directed solely to the scattering of the new and ominous cloud on the horizon in the shape of the Black Act, which, if accepted by the Indians, would have humiliated them and prepared the way for their final extinction first in the Transvaal and then throughout South Africa. But instead of repealing the Black Act, General Smuts took a fresh step forward. He maintained the Black Act on the statute book and introduced into the legislature a measure, validating the voluntary registrations effected and the certificates issued subsequent to the date fixed by the Government in terms of that Act, taking the holders of the voluntary registration certificates out of its operation, and making further provision for the registration of Asiatics. Thus there came into force two concurrent pieces of legislation with one and the same object, and freshly arriving Indians as well as even later applicants for registration were still subject to the Black Act.

I was astounded when I read the Bill. I did not know how I would face the community. Here was excellent food for the Pathan friend who had severely criticized me at the midnight meeting. But I must say that far from shaking it, this blow made my faith in Satyagraha stronger than ever. I called a meeting of our Committee and explained the new situation to them. Some of the members tauntingly said, 'There you are. We have often been telling you that you are very credulous, and believe in everything that any one says. It would not matter much if you were so simple in your private affairs, but the community has to suffer for your credulity in public matters. It is very difficult now to rouse the same spirit as actuated our people before. You know what stuff we Indians are made of, men whose momentary enthusiasm must be taken at the flood. If you neglect the temporary tide, you are done for.'

There was no bitterness in these taunting words. Such things had been addressed to me on other occasions. I replied with a smile: 'Well, what you call my credulity is part and parcel of myself. It is not credulity but trust, and it is the duty of every one of us, yours as well as mine, to trust our fellowmen. And even granting that it is really a defect with me, you must take me as you find me with my defects no less than with my qualities. But I cannot concede that the enthusiasm of the community is a mere temporary effervescence. You must remember that you, as well as I, are members of the community. I should consider it an insult if you thus characterized my enthusiasm. I take it that you too regard yourselves as exceptions to the general rule you seek to formulate. But if you don't you do the community the injustice of imagining that others are as weak-kneed as yourselves. In great struggles like ours there is always a tide and an ebb. However clear may be your understanding with the adversary, what is there to prevent him from breaking faith? There are many among us who pass promissory notes to others. What can be clearer and more free from doubt than a man's putting his signature to a document? Yet suits must be filed against them; they will oppose the suits and offer all kinds of defence. At last there are decrees and writs of attachment which take a long time and cost great trouble to execute. Who can guarantee against the repetition of such flagrant behaviour? I would therefore advise you patiently to deal with the problem before us. We have to consider what we can do in case the struggle has to be resumed, that is to say, what each Satyagrahi can do absolutely regardless of the conduct of others. Personally I am inclined to think, that if only we are true to ourselves, others will not be found wanting, and even if they are inclined to weakness, they will be strengthened by our example.'

I believe this was enough to conciliate the well-intentioned sceptics who were doubtful about the resumption of the struggle. About this time Mr Kachhalia began to show his mettle and come to the front. On every point he would announce his considered opinion in the fewest words possible and then stick to it through thick and thin. I do not remember a single occasion on which he betrayed weakness or doubt about the final result. A time came when Yusuf Mian was not ready to continue at the helm in troubled waters. We all with one voice acclaimed Kachhalia as our captain and from that time forward to the end he held unflinchingly to his responsible post. He fearlessly put up with hardships which would have daunted almost any other man in his place. As the struggle advanced, there came a stage when going to jail was a perfectly easy task for some and a means of getting well-earned rest, whereas it was infinitely more difficult to remain outside, minutely to look into all things, to make various arrangements and to deal with all sorts and conditions of men.

Later on the European creditors of Kachhalia caught him as in a noose. Many Indian traders are entirely dependent in their trade on European firms, which sell them *lakhs* of rupees worth of goods on credit on mere personal security. That Europeans should repose such trust in Indian traders is an excellent proof of the general honesty of Indian trade. Kachhalia likewise owed large sums to many European firms, which asked him at once to meet their dues, being instigated thereto directly or indirectly by the Government. The firms gave Kachhalia to understand that they would not press for immediate payment if he left the Satyagraha movement. But if he did not, they were afraid of losing their money as he might be arrested any time by the Government, and therefore demanded immediate satisfaction in cash. Kachhalia bravely replied, that his participation in the Indian struggle was his personal affair, which had nothing to do with his trade. He considered that his religion, the honour of his community and his own self-respect were bound up with the struggle. He thanked his creditors for the support they had extended to him, but refused to attach any undue importance to that support or indeed to his trade. Their money was perfectly safe with him, and as long as he was alive he would repay them in full at any cost. But if anything happened to him, his stock as well as the book debts owing to him were at their disposal. He therefore wished that his creditors would continue to trust him as before. This was a perfectly fair argument, and Kachhalia's firmness was an additional reason for his creditors to trust him, but on this occasion it failed to impress them. We can rouse from his slumbers a man who is really asleep, but not him who only makes a pretence of sleep all the while that he is awake, and so it was with these European traders, whose sole object was to bring undue pressure to bear upon Kachhalia. Otherwise their money was perfectly safe.

A meeting of the creditors was held in my office on January 22, 1909. I told them clearly that the pressure to which they were subjecting Kachhalia was purely political and unworthy of merchants, and they were incensed at my remark. I showed them Kachhalia Sheth's balance sheet and proved that they could have their 20 s. in the pound. Again if the creditors wanted to sell the business to some one else, Kachhalia was ready to hand over the goods and the book debts to the purchaser. If this did not suit them, the creditors could take over the stock in Kachhalia's shop at cost price, and if any part of their dues still remained unsatisfied, they were free to take over book debts due to him sufficient to cover the deficit. The reader can see that in agreeing to this arrangement the European merchants had nothing to lose. I had on many previous occasions effected such arrangements with the creditors of some of my clients who were hard pressed. But the merchants at this juncture did not seek justice. They were out to bend Kachhalia. Kachhalia would not bend, bankruptcy proceedings were instituted against him, and he was declared an insolvent, though his estate showed a large excess of assets over liabilities.

Far from being a blot upon his escutcheon this insolvency was perfectly honourable to him. It enhanced his prestige among the community and all congratulated him upon his firmness and courage. But such heroism is rarely found. The man in the street cannot understand how insolvency can cease to be insolvency, cease to be a disgrace and become an honour and an ornament, but Kachhalia realized it at once. Many traders had submitted to the Black Act merely from a fear of insolvency. Kachhalia could have warded off the insolvency if he had wished, not by leaving the struggle,— that was out of the question, —but by borrowing from his many Indian friends who would have gladly helped him over the crisis. But it would not have been becoming in him to have saved his trade by such means. The danger of being any day clapped into gaol he shared in common with all Satyagrahis. It would therefore be hardly proper for him to borrow from a fellow Satyagrahi to pay his European creditors. But among his friends there were 'blacklegs' also whose help was available. Indeed one or two of them actually offered assistance. But to accept their offer would have been tantamount to an admission that there was wisdom in submitting to the obnoxious Act. We therefore decided to decline their proffered aid.

Again we thought that if Kachhalia allowed himself to be declared an insolvent, his insolvency would serve as a shield for others, for if not in all, at least in an overwhelmingly large majority of cases of insolvency, the creditor stands to lose something. He is quite pleased if he realizes 10 s. in the pound, and considers 15 s. quite as good as 20 s. in the pound. For big traders in South Africa generally reap a profit not of 6¼ but of 25 per cent. They therefore consider 15 s. as good as full payment. But as 20 s. in the pound is hardly ever realized from a bankrupt's estate, creditors are not anxious to reduce their debtor to a state of insolvency. As soon, therefore, as Kachhalia was declared an insolvent, there was every likelihood that the European traders would cease to threaten other Satyagrahi traders who were their debtors. And that was exactly what happened. The Europeans wanted to compel Kachhalia either to give up the struggle or else to pay them in full in cash. They failed to achieve any of these two objects, and the actual result was the very reverse of what they had expected. They were dumbfounded by this first case of a respectable Indian trader welcoming insolvency and were quiet ever afterwards. In a year's time the creditors realized 20 s. in the pound from Kachhalia Sheth's stock-in-trade, and this was the first case in South Africa to my knowledge in which creditors were paid in full from the insolvent debtor's estate. Thus even while the struggle was in progress, Kachhalia commanded great respect among the European merchants, who showed their readiness to advance to him any amount of goods in spite of his leading the movement. But Kachhalia was every day gaining in strength and in an intelligent appreciation of the struggle. No one could now tell how long the struggle would last. We had therefore resolved after the insolvency proceedings that the Sheth should not make any large commitments in trade during the continuance of the movement, but confine his operations within such moderate limits as would suffice to provide him with his daily bread. He therefore did not avail himself of the European merchants' offer.

I need scarcely say that all these incidents in the life of Kachhalia Sheth did not happen soon after the Committee meeting referred to above, but I have found place for them here in the shape of a connected narrative. Chronologically, Kachhalia became Chairman some time after the resumption of the struggle (September 10, 1908) and his insolvency came about five months later.

But to return to the Committee meeting. When the meeting was over, I wrote a letter to General Smuts, saying that his new bill constituted a breach of the compromise, and drawing his attention to the following passage in his Richmond speech delivered within a week of the settlement: 'The Indians' second contention was that they would never register until the law had been repealed. . . . He had told them that the law would not be repealed so long as there was an Asiatic in the country who had not registered. . . . Until every Indian in the country had registered the law would not be repealed.' Politicians do not reply at all to questions which land them in difficulty, or if they do, they resort to circumlocution. General Smuts was a past master of this art. You may write to him as often as you please, you may make any number of speeches you like, but if he is unwilling to reply, nothing that you do can draw him out. The law of courtesy, which requires a gentleman to reply to letters received, could not bind

GENERAL SMUTS' BREACH OF FAITH (?)

General Smuts, and I did not receive any satisfactory reply to my letters.

I met Albert Cartwright who had been our mediator. He was deeply shocked and exclaimed, 'Really I cannot understand this man at all. I perfectly remember that he promised to repeal the Asiatic Act. I will do my best, but you know that nothing can move General Smuts when he has once taken up a stand. Newspaper articles are as nothing to him. So I am afraid I may not be of much help to you.' I also met Mr Hosken who wrote to General Smuts but who received only a very unsatisfactory reply. I wrote articles in *Indian Opinion* under the caption of 'Foul Play', but what was that to the redoubtable General? One may apply any bitter epithets one likes to a philosopher or a heartless man but in vain. They will follow the even tenor of their way. I do not know which of these two appelations would fit General Smuts. I must admit that there is a sort of philosophy about his attitude. When I was corresponding with him and writing in the paper against him, I remember I had taken General Smuts to be a heartless man. But this was only the beginning of the struggle, only its second year, while it was to last as long as eight years, in course of which I had many occasions of meeting him. From our subsequent talks I often felt that the general belief in South Africa about General Smuts' cunning did him perhaps less than justice. I am however sure of two things. First, he has some principles in politics, which are not quite immoral. Secondly, there is room in his politics for cunning and on occasions for perversion of truth.

CHAPTER XXVI

RESUMPTION OF THE STRUGGLE

If on the one hand we were trying to induce General Smuts to fulfil his part of the settlement, we were on the other hand enthusiastically engaged in 'educating' the community. We found the people everywhere ready to resume the struggle and go to jail. Meetings were held in every place, where we explained the correspondence which was being carried on with the Government. The weekly diary in *Indian Opinion* kept the Indians fully abreast of current events, and they were warned of the impending failure of the voluntary registration, and asked to hold themselves in readiness to burn the certificates if the Black Act was not repealed after all, and thus let the Government note that the community was fearless and firm and ready to go to prison. Certificates were collected from every place with a view to making a bonfire of them.

The Government bill we have referred to in the previous chapter was about to pass through the Legislature, to which a petition was presented on behalf of the Indians but in vain. At last an 'ultimatum' was sent to the Government by the Satyagrahis. The word was not the Satyagrahis' but of General Smuts who thus chose to style the letter they had addressed to him signifying the determination of the community. The General said, 'The people who have offered such a threat to the Government have no idea of its power. I am only sorry that some agitators are trying to inflame poor Indians who will be ruined if they succumb to their blandishments.' As the newspaper reporter wrote on this occasion, many members of the Transvaal Assembly reddened with rage at this 'ultimatum' and unanimously and enthusiastically passed the bill introduced by General Smuts.

The so-called ultimatum may be thus summarized: 'The point of the agreement between the Indians and General Smuts clearly was that if the Indians registered voluntarily, he on his part should bring forward in the

Legislature a bill to validate such registration and to repeal the Asiatic Act. It is well known that the Indians have registered voluntarily to the satisfaction of the Government, and therefore the Asiatic Act must be repealed. The community has sent many communications to General Smuts and taken all possible legal steps to obtain redress but thus far to no purpose. At a time when the bill is passing through the Legislature, it is up to the leaders to apprise the Government of the discontent and strong feeling prevalent in the community. We regret to state, that if the Asiatic Act is not repealed in terms of the settlement, and if Government's decision to that effect is not communicated to the Indians before a specific date, the certificates collected by the Indians would be burnt, and they would humbly but firmly take the consequences.'

One reason why this letter was held to be an ultimatum was that it prescribed a time limit for reply. Another reason was that the Europeans looked upon the Indians as savages. If the Europeans had considered the Indians to be their equals, they would have found this letter perfectly courteous and would have given it most serious consideration. But the fact that the Europeans thought Indians to be barbarians was a sufficient reason for the Indians to write such letter. The Indians must either confess to their being barbarians and consent to be suppressed as such, or else they must take active steps in repudiation of the charge of barbarism. This letter was the first of such steps. If there had not been behind the letter an iron determination to act up to it, it would have been held an impertinence, and the Indians would have proved themselves to be a thoughtless and foolish race.

The reader will perhaps point out that the charge of barbarism was repudiated in 1906 when the Satyagraha pledge was taken. And if so, there was nothing new about this letter which might warrant my giving it so much importance and dating the denial of the charge from it. This is true so far as it goes; but on thinking a little more deeply, it will appear that the repudiation really began with this letter. It should be remembered that the Satyagraha pledge came in almost by accident, and the subsequent imprisonments followed as an inevitable corollary. The community then gained largely in stature but unconsciously. But when this letter was written, there was a deliberate intention of claiming full knowledge and high prestige. Now as well as before the object aimed at was the repeal of the Black Act. But there was change in the style of language used, in the methods of work selected and in other things besides. When a slave salutes a master and a friend salutes a friend, the form is the same in either case, but there is a world of difference between the two, which enables the detached observer to recognize the slave and the friend at once.

There was much discussion among ourselves when the ultimatum was forwarded. Would not the demand for reply within a stated period be considered impudent? Might it not be that it would stiffen the Government and lead them to reject our terms which otherwise they might have accepted? Would it not be sufficient indirectly to announce the community's decision to the Government? After giving due weight to all these considerations we unanimously came to the conclusion that we must do what we thought to be right and proper for us to do. We must run the risk of being charged with discourtesy, as well as the risk of Government refusing in a huff what otherwise they might have granted. If we do not admit our inferiority as human beings in any sense whatever and if we believe that we possess the capacity for unlimited suffering for any length of time, we must adopt a straightforward course without hesitation.

The reader will perhaps see that there was some novelty and distinction about the step now taken, which had its reverberations in the Legislature and in European circles outside. Some congratulated the Indians on their courage while others got very angry, and asked for condign punishment to be awarded to the Indians for their insolence. Either section acknowledged the novelty of the Indians' fresh move by its conduct. This letter created greater stir than even the commencement of the Satyagraha movement, which too was a novelty when it was started. The reason is obvious. When Satyagraha was started, no one knew what the Indians were capable of, and therefore neither such a letter nor the language in which it was couched would have been fitting for that initial stage. But now the community had had its baptism of fire. Every one had seen that the Indians had the capacity of suffering the hardships incidental to an attempt to get their wrongs righted, and therefore the language of the 'ultimatum' appeared in the light of a natural growth and not at all inappropriate in the circumstances.

CHAPTER XXVII

A BONFIRE OF CERTIFICATES

The ultimatum was to expire on the same day that the new Asiatic Bill was to be carried through the Legislature. A meeting had been called some two hours after the expiry of the time limit to perform the public ceremony of burning the certificates. The Satyagraha Committee thought that the meeting would not be fruitless even if quite unexpectedly perhaps a favourable reply was received from the Government, as in that case the meeting could be utilized for announcing the Government's favourable decision to the community.

The Committee however believed that the Government would not reply to the ultimatum at all. We had all reached the place of meeting early, and arranged for the Government's reply by wire, if any, to be brought promptly to the meeting, which was held at four o'clock on the grounds of the Hamidia Mosque at Johannesburg (August 16, 1908). Every inch of space available was taken up by Indians of all classes. The Negroes of South Africa take their meals in iron cauldrons resting on four legs. One such cauldron of the largest size available in the market had been requisitioned from an Indian trader's shop and set up on a platform in a corner of the grounds in order to burn the certificates.

As the business of the meeting was about to commence, a volunteer arrived on a cycle with a telegram from the Government in which they regretted the determination of the Indian community and announced their inability to change their line of action. The telegram was read to the audience which received it with cheers, as if they were glad that the auspicious opportunity of burning the certificates did not after all slip out of their hands as it would have if the Government had complied with the demands formulated in the ultimatum. It is difficult to pronounce any categorical opinion on the propriety or the reverse of such a feeling of gladness without a knowledge of the motives which prompted each of the audience who greeted the Government reply with applause. This much however can be said, that these cheers were a happy sign of the enthusiasm of the meeting. The Indians had now some consciousness of their strength.

The meeting began. The chairman put the meeting on their guard and explained the whole situation to them. Appropriate resolutions were adopted. I clearly detailed the various stages of the protracted negotiations and said, 'If there is any Indian who has handed his certificate to be burnt but wants it to be returned to him, let him step forward and have it. Merely burning the certificates is no crime, and will not enable those who court imprisonment to win it. By burning the certificates we only declare our solemn resolution never to submit to the Black Act and divest ourselves of the power of even showing the certificates. But it is open to any one to take a copy tomorrow of the certificate that may be burned to ashes today, and if there are any persons here who contemplate such a cowardly act or doubt their own ability to stand the ordeal, there is still time for them to have their certificates back, and these can be given back to them. No one need be ashamed of getting his certificate back just now, as in doing so he will be exhibiting a certain kind of courage. But it would be not only shameful but also detrimental to the best interests of the community to get a copy of the certificate afterwards. Again let us take note that this is going to be a protracted struggle. We know that some of us have fallen out of the marching army, and the burden of those who remain has been made heavier to that extent. I would advise you to ponder over all these considerations and only then to take the plunge proposed today.'

Even during my speech there were voices saying, 'We do not want the certificates back, burn them.' Finally I suggested that if any one wanted to oppose the resolution, he should come forward, but no one stood up. Mir Alam too was present at this meeting. He announced that he had done wrong to assault me as he did, and to the great joy of the audience, handed his original certificate to be burnt, as he had not taken a voluntary certificate. I took hold of his hand, pressed it with joy, and assured him once more that I had never harboured in my mind any resentment against him.

The Committee had already received upwards of 2,000 certificates to be burnt. These were all thrown into the cauldron, saturated with paraffin and set ablaze by Mr Yusuf Mian. The whole assembly rose to their feet and made the place resound with the echoes of their continuous cheers during the burning process. Some of those who had still withheld their certificates brought them in numbers to the platform, and these too were consigned to the flames. When asked why he handed his certificate only at the last moment, one of these friends said that he did so as it was more appropriate and would create a greater impression on the onlookers. Another frankly admitted his want of courage and a feeling that the certificates might not be burnt after all. But he could not possibly withhold the cerificate after he had seen the bonfire and gave it up, from an idea that the fate of all might well be his own fate too. Such frankness was a matter of frequent experience during the struggle.

The reporters of English newspapers present at the meeting were profoundly impressed with the whole scene and gave graphic descriptions of the meeting in their papers. A description of the meeting was sent to *The Daily Mail* (London) by its Johannesburg correspondent, in course of which he compared the act of the Indians in burning their certificates with that of the Boston Tea Party. I do not think this comparison did more than justice to the Indians, seeing that if the whole might of the British

Empire was ranged against the hundreds of thousands of able Europeans in America, here in South Africa a helpless body of 13,000 Indians had challenged the powerful Government of the Transvaal. The Indians' only weapon was a faith in the righteousness of their own cause and in God. There is no doubt that this weapon is all-sufficient and all-powerful for the devout, but so long as that is not the view of the man in the street, 13,000 unarmed Indians might appear insignificant before the well-armed Europeans of America. As God is the strength of the weak, it is as well that the world despises them.

CHAPTER XXVIII
CHARGE OF FORCING FRESH ISSUE

During the same year in which the Black Act was passed General Smuts carried through the Legislature another bill called the Transvaal Immigrants Restriction Bill (Act 15 of 1907), which was ostensibly of general application but was chiefly aimed at the Indians. This Act generally followed the lines of similar legislation in Natal, but it treated as prohibited immigrants those who could pass education tests but were ineligible for registration under the Asiatic Act, and was thus indirectly made an instrument for preventing the entry of a single Indian newcomer.

It was absolutely essential for the Indians to resist this fresh inroad on their rights, but the question was whether it should be made a plank in the Satyagraha struggle. The community was not bound as to when and regarding what subjects they should offer Satyagraha, in deciding which question they must only not transgress the limits prescribed by wisdom and appreciation of their own capacity. Satyagraha offered on every occasion seasonable or otherwise would be corrupted into Duragraha. And if any one takes to Satyagraha without having measured his own strength and afterwards sustains a defeat, he not only disgraces himself but he also brings the matchless weapon of Satyagraha into disrepute by his folly.

CHARGE OF FORCING FRESH ISSUE 189

The Satyagraha Committee saw that the Indians' Satyagraha was being offered only against the Black Act, and that if the Black Act was once repealed, the Immigration Restriction Act would lose the sting to which I have referred. Still if the Indians did not take any steps regarding the Immigration Act from an idea that a separate movement against it was unnecessary, their silence might be misconstrued as implying their consent to the total prohibition of Indian immigration in the future. The Immigration Act too must therefore be opposed, and the only question was: Should this also be included in the Satyagraha struggle? The community's view was that it was their duty to include in the Satyagraha any fresh attacks on their rights made while the struggle was in progress. If they did not feel strong enough to do so that was altogether a different matter. The leaders came to the conclusion that their lack or deficiency of strength should not be made a pretext for letting the Immigration Act alone, and that therefore this Act too must be covered by the Satyagraha struggle.

Correspondence was therefore carried on with the Government on this subject. We could not thereby induce General Smuts to agree to a change in the law, but it provided him with a fresh handle for vilifying the community and really speaking myself. General Smuts knew that many more Europeans, besides those who were publicly helping us, were privately sympathetic to our movement, and he naturally wished that their sympathy should be alienated if possible. He therefore charged me with raising a fresh point, and he told as well as wrote to our supporters that they did not know me as he did. If he yielded an inch, I would ask for an ell and therefore it was that he was not repealing the Asiatic Act. When Satyagraha was started, there was no question whatever about fresh immigrants. Now when he was legislating to prevent the fresh entry of any more Indians in the interest of the Transvaal, there too I had threatened Satyagraha. He could not any more put up with this 'cunning.' I might do my worst, and every Indian might be ruined, but he would not repeal the Asiatic Act, nor would the Transvaal

Government give up the policy they had adopted regarding the Indians, and in this just attitude they were entitled to the support of all Europeans.

A little reflection will show how totally unjust and immoral this argument was. When there was nothing like the Immigrants Restriction Act at all in existence, how were the Indians or myself to oppose it? General Smuts talked glibly about his experience of what he called my 'cunning' and yet he could not cite a single case in point in support of his statement. And I do not remember to have ever resorted to cunning during all those years that I lived in South Africa. I may now go even farther and say without the least hesitation that I have never had recourse to cunning in all my life. I believe that cunning is not only morally wrong but also politically inexpedient, and have therefore always discountenanced its use even from the practical standpoint. It is hardly necessary for me to defend myself. I would even be ashamed of defending myself before the class of readers for whom this is written. If even now they have not seen that I am free from cunning, nothing that I could write in self-defence could convince them of that fact. I have penned these few sentences only with a view to give the reader an idea of the difficulties which were encountered during the Satyagraha struggle and of the imminent danger to the movement if the Indians even by a hair's breadth swerved from the strait and narrow path. The rope-dancer, balancing himself upon a rope suspended at a height of twenty feet, must concentrate his attention upon the rope, and the least little error in so doing means death for him, no matter on which side he falls. My eight years' experience of Satyagraha in South Africa has taught me that a Satyagrahi has to be if possible even more single-minded than the rope-dancer. The friends before whom General Smuts levelled this charge at me knew me well, and therefore the charge had an effect over them just the opposite of what General Smuts had desired. They not only did not give me up or the movement but grew even more zealous in supporting us, and the Indians saw later on that they would have come in for no end of trouble if

CHARGE OF FORCING FRESH ISSUE

their Satyagraha had not been extended to the Immigration Act also.

My experience has taught me that a law of progression applies to every righteous struggle. But in the case of Satyagraha the law amounts to an axiom. As the Ganga advances, other streams flow into it, and hence at the mouth it grows so wide that neither bank is to be seen and a person sailing upon the river cannot make out where the river ends and the sea begins. So also as a Satyagraha struggle progresses onward, many another element helps to swell its current, and there is a constant growth in the results to which it leads. This is really inevitable, and is bound up with the first principles of Satyagraha. For in Satyagraha the minimum is also the maximum, and as it is the irreducible minimum, there is no question of retreat, and the only movement possible is an advance. In other struggles, even when they are righteous, the demand is first pitched a little higher so as to admit of future reduction, and hence the law of progression does not apply to all of them without exception. But I must explain how the law of progression comes into play when the minimum is also the maximum as in Satyagraha. The Ganga does not leave its course in search of tributaries. Even so does the Satyagrahi not leave his path which is sharp as the sword's edge. But as the tributaries spontaneously join the Ganga as it advances, so it is with the river that is Satyagraha. Seeing that the Immigration Act was included in the Satyagraha, some Indians ignorant of the principles of Satyagraha insisted upon the whole mass of the anti-Indian legislation in the Transvaal being similarly treated. Others again suggested a mobilization of Indians all over South Africa and the offering of Satyagraha against all anti-Indian legislation in Natal, the Cape Colony, the Orange Free State etc., while the Transvaal struggle was on. Both the suggestions involved a breach of principle. I distinctly said, that it would be dishonest now, having seen the opportunity, to take up a position which was not in view when Satyagraha was started. No matter how strong we were, the present struggle must close when the demands for which it was commenced were accepted.

I am confident, that if we had not adhered to this principle, instead of winning, we would not only have lost all along the line, but also forfeited the sympathy which had been enlisted in our favour. On the other hand if the adversary himself creates new difficulties for us while the struggle is in progress, they become automatically included in it. A Satyagrahi, without being false to his faith, cannot disregard new difficulties which confront him while he is pursuing his own course. The adversary is not a Satyagrahi,— Satyagraha against Satyagraha is impossible,—and is not bound by any limit of maximum or minimum. He can therefore try if he wishes to frighten the Satyagrahi by raising novel issues. But the Satyagrahi has renounced all fear, tackles by Satyagraha the later difficulties as well as the former and trusts that it will help him to hold his own against all odds. Therefore as a Satyagraha struggle is prolonged, that is to say by the adversary, it is the adversary who stands to lose from his own standpoint, and it is the Satyagrahi who stands to gain. We shall come across other illustrations of the working of this law in the later stages of this struggle.

CHAPTER XXIX

SORABJI SHAPURJI ADAJANIA

Now as Satyagraha was made to embrace the Immigration Act as well, Satyagrahis had to test the right of educated Indians to enter the Transvaal. The Committee decided that the test should not be made through any ordinary Indian. The idea was that some Indian, who did not come within the four corners of the definition of a prohibited immigrant in the new Act in so far as the definition was acceptable to the community, should enter the Transvaal and go to jail. We had thus to show that Satyagraha is a force containing within itself seeds of progressive self-restraint. There was a section in the Act to the effect that any person who was not conversant with a European language should be treated as a prohibited immigrant. The Committee therefore proposed that some Indian who knew English but who had not been to the

Transvaal before should enter the country. Several young Indians volunteered for the purpose, out of whom Sorabji Shapurji Adajania was selected.

Sorabji was a Parsi. There were not perhaps more than a hundred Parsis in the whole of South Africa. I held in South Africa the same views about the Parsis as I have expressed in India. There are not more than a hundred thousand Parsis in the world, and this alone speaks volumes for their high character that such a small community has long preserved its prestige, clung to its religion and proved itself second to none in the world in point of charity. But Sorabji turned out to be pure gold. I was but slightly acquainted with him when he joined the struggle. His letters as regards participation in Satyagraha left a good impression on me. As I am a lover of the great qualities of the Parsis, I was not and I am not unaware of some of their defects as a community. I was therefore doubtful whether Sorabji would be able to stand to his guns in critical times. But it was a rule with me not to attach any weight to my own doubts where the party concerned himself asserted the contrary. I therefore recommended to the Committee that they should take Sorabji at his word, and eventually Sorabji proved himself to be a first class Satyagrahi. He not only was one of the Satyagrahis who suffered the longest terms of imprisonment, but also made such deep study of the struggle that his views commanded respectful hearing from all. His advice always betrayed firmness, wisdom, charity and deliberation. He was slow to form an opinion as well as to change an opinion once formed. He was as much of an Indian as of a Parsi, and was quite free from the ban of narrow communalism. After the struggle was over Doctor Mehta offered a scholarship in order to enable some good Satyagrahi to proceed to England for bar. I was charged with the selection. There were two or three deserving candidates, but all the friends felt that there was none who could approach Sorabji in maturity of judgment and ripeness of wisdom, and he was selected accordingly. The idea was, that on his return to South Africa he should take my place and serve the community. Sorabji went to England with

the blessings of the community, and was duly called to
the bar. He had already come in contact with Gokhale
in South Africa, and his relations with him became closer
in England. Sorabji captivated Gokhale who asked him
to join the Servants of India Society when he returned
to India. Sorabji became extremely popular among the
students. He would share the sorrows of all, and his soul
was not tarnished by the luxury and the artificiality in
England. When he went to England, he was above thirty,
and he had only a working knowledge of English. But
difficulties vanish at the touch of man's perseverance.
Sorabji lived the pure life of a student and passed his
examinations. The bar examinations in my time were
easy. Barristers now-a-days have to study comparatively
very much harder. But Sorabji knew not what it was to
be defeated. When the ambulance corps was established
in England, he was one of the pioneers as also one of those
who remained in it till the last. This corps too had to offer
Satyagraha in which many members fell back but Sorabji
was at the head of those who would not give in. Let me
state in passing that this Satyagraha of the ambulance
corps was also crowned with victory.

After being called to the bar in England Sorabji
returned to Johannesburg where he began to practice law
as well as to serve the community. Every letter I received
from South Africa was full of praise for Sorabji: 'He is
as simple in habits as ever, and free from the slightest
trace of vanity. He mixes with all, rich as well as poor.'
But God seems to be as cruel as he is merciful. Sorabji
caught galloping phthisis and died in a few months, leaving the Indians whose love he had freshly acquired to
mourn his loss. Thus within a very short period God bereft
the community of two outstanding personalities, Kachhalia and Sorabji. If I were asked to choose between the two,
I would be at a loss to decide. In fact, each was supreme
in his own field. And Sorabji was as good an Indian as
he was a good Parsi, even as Kachhalia was as good
an Indian as he was a good Musalman.

Thus Sorabji entered the Transvaal, having previously informed the Government of his intention to test

his right to remain in the country under the Immigrants Restriction Act. The Government were not at all prepared for this and could not at once decide what to do with Sorabji, who publicly crossed the border and entered the country. The Immigration Restriction Officer knew him. Sorabji told him that he was deliberately entering the Transvaal for a test case, and asked him to examine him in English or to arrest him just as he pleased. The Officer replied that there was no question of examining him as he was aware of his knowledge of English. He had no orders to arrest him. Sorabji might enter the country and the Government, if they wished, would arrest him where he went.

Thus contrary to our expectation Sorabji reached Johannesburg and we welcomed him in our midst. No one had hoped that the Government would permit him to proceed even an inch beyond the frontier station of Volksrust. Very often it so happens that when we take our steps deliberately and fearlessly, the government is not ready to oppose us. The reason for this lies in the very nature of government. A government officer does not ordinarily make his department so much his own as to arrange his ideas on every subject beforehand and make preparations accordingly. Again, the officer has not one but many things to attend to, and his mind is divided between them. Thirdly, the official suffers from the intoxication of power, is thus apt to be careless and believes that it is child's play for the authorities to deal with any movement whatever. On the other hand, the public worker knows his ideal as well as the means to achieve his end, and if he has definite plans, he is perfectly ready to carry them out, and his work is the only subject of his thoughts day and night. If therefore he takes the right steps with decision, he is always in advance of the government. Many movements fail, not because governments are endowed with extraordinary power but because the leaders are lacking in the qualities just referred to.

In short, whether through the negligence or the set design of the Government Sorabji reached as far as Johannesburg, and the local officer had neither any idea of his duty in a case like this nor any instructions from his superiors on the point. Sorabji's arrival increased our enthusiasm, and some young men thought that the Government were defeated and would soon come to terms. They saw their mistake very soon, however. They even realized that a settlement could perhaps be purchased only by the self-devotion of many a young man.

Sorabji informed the Police Superintendent, Johannesburg, about his arrival and let him know that he believed himself entitled to remain in the Transvaal in terms of the new Immigration Act, as he had ordinary knowledge of English, in respect of which he was ready to submit to an examination by the officer if he so desired. No reply to this letter was received, or rather the reply came after some days in the form of a summons.

Sorabji's case came before the Court on July 8, 1908. The court house was packed full of Indian spectators. Before the case began, we held a meeting of the Indians present on the grounds of the Court and Sorabji made a fighting speech, in which he announced his readiness to go to jail as often as necessary for victory and to brave all dangers and risks. In the meanwhile, I had got fairly familiar with Sorabji and assured myself that he would do credit to the community. The Magistrate took up the case in due course. I defended Sorabji, and at once asked for his discharge on the ground of the summons being defective. The public Prosecutor also made an argument, but on the 9th the Court upheld my contention and discharged Sorabji who, however, immediately received warning to appear before the Court the next day, Friday, July 10, 1908.

On the 10th, the Magistrate ordered Sorabji to leave the Transvaal within seven days. After the Court's order was served upon him, Sorabji informed Superintendent J. A. G. Vernon that it was not his desire to leave. He was accordingly brought to the Court once more, on the 20th, charged with failing to obey the Magistrate's order, and sentenced to a month's imprisonment with hard labour. The Government, however, did not arrest the local Indians as they saw that the more arrests there were the higher did the Indians' spirit rise. Again Indians were sometimes discharged thanks to legal technicalities in the cases instituted against them and this also served to redouble the ardour of the community. Government had carried through the Legislature all the laws they wanted. Many Indians had indeed burnt the certificates but they had proved their right to remain in the country by their registration. Government therefore saw no sense in prosecuting them simply to send them to jail, and thought that the workers would cool down finding no outlet for their energies in view of the masterly inactivity of the Government. But they were reckoning without their host. The Indians took fresh steps to test the Government's patience, which was soon exhausted.

CHAPTER XXX

SHETH DAUD MAHOMED ETC. ENTER THE STRUGGLE

When the Indians saw through the Government's game of tiring them out by fabian tactics they felt bound to take further steps. A Satyagrahi is never tired so long as he has the capacity to suffer. The Indians were therefore in a position to upset the calculations of the Government.

There were several Indians in Natal who possessed ancient rights of domicile in the Transvaal. They had no need to enter the Transvaal for trade, but the community held that they had the right of entry. They also had some knowledge of English. Again there was no breach of the principles of Satyagraha in educated Indians like Sorabji entering the Transvaal. We therefore decided that two classes of Indians should enter the Transvaal; first, those who had previously been domiciled in the country, and secondly, those who had received English education.

Of these Sheth Daud Mahomed and Parsi Rustomji were big traders, and Surendra Medh, Pragji Khandubhai Desai, Ratansi Mulji Sodha, Harilal Gandhi and others were 'educated' men. Daud Sheth came in spite of his wife being dangerously ill.

Let me introduce Sheth Daud Mahomed to the reader. He was president of the Natal Indian Congress, and one of the oldest Indian traders that came to South Africa. He was a Sunni Vora from Surat. I have seen but few Indians in South Africa who equalled him in tact. He had excellent powers of understanding. He had not had much literary education but he spoke English and Dutch well. He was skilful in his business intercourse with European traders. His liberality was widely known. About fifty guests would dine with him every day. He was one of the chief contributors to Indian collections. He had the priceless jewel of a son who far surpassed him in character. The boy's heart was pure as crystal. Daud Sheth never came in the way of his son's aspirations. Indeed it would be no exaggeration to say, that the father almost worshipped the son. He wished that none of his own defects should reappear in the boy and had sent him to England for education. But Daud Sheth lost this treasure of a son in his prime. Phthisis claimed Husen for its victim. This was a sore wound that never healed. With Husen died the high hopes which the Indians had cherished about him. He was a most truthful lad, and Hindu and Musalman were to him as the left and the right eye. Even Daud Sheth is now no more with us. Who is there upon whom Death does not lay his hands?

I have already introduced Parsi Rustomji to the reader. The names of several other friends who joined this 'Asiatic invasion' have been left out as I am writing this without consulting any papers, and I hope they will excuse me for it. I am not writing these chapters to immortalize names but to explain the secret of Satyagraha, and to show how it succeeded, what obstacles beset its path and how they were removed. Even where I have mentioned names I have done so in order to point out to the reader how men who might be considered illiterate distinguished themselves in South Africa, how Hindus, Musalmans, Parsis and Christians there worked harmoniously together and how traders, 'educated' men and others fulfilled their duty. Where a man of high merit has been mentioned, praise has been bestowed not upon him but only upon his merit.

When Daud Sheth thus arrived on the frontiers of the Transvaal with his Satyagrahi 'army,' the Government was ready to meet him. The Government would become an object of ridicule if it allowed such a large troop to enter the Transvaal, and was therefore bound to arrest them. So they were arrested, and on August 18, 1908 brought before the Magistrate who ordered them to leave the Transvaal within seven days. They disobeyed the order of course, were rearrested at Pretoria on the 28th and deported without trial. They re-entered the Transvaal on the 31st and finally on September 8 were sentenced at Volksrust to a fine of fifty pounds or three months' imprisonment with hard labour. Needless to say, they cheerfully elected to go to gaol.

The Transvaal Indians were now in high spirits. If they could not compel the release of their Natal compatriots, they must certainly share their imprisonment. They therefore cast about for means which would land them in jail. There were several ways in which they could have their heart's desire. If a domiciled Indian did not show his registration certificate, he would not be given a trading licence and it would be an offence on his part if he traded without licence. Again one must show the certificate if one wanted to enter the Transvaal from Natal, and would be arrested if one had none to show. The certificates had already been burnt and the line was therefore clear. The Indians employed both these methods. Some began to hawk without a licence while others were arrested for not showing certificates upon entering the Transvaal.

The movement was now in full swing. Every one was on his trial. Other Natal Indians followed Sheth Daud Mahomed's example. There were many arrests in Johannesburg also. Things came to such a pass that any one who wished could get himself arrested. Jails began to be filled, 'invaders' from Natal getting three months and the Transvaal hawkers anything from four days to three months.

Among those who thus courted arrest was our 'Imam Saheb,' Imam Abdul Kadar Bavazir, who was arrested for hawking without a licence and sentenced on July 21, 1908 to imprisonment for four days with hard labour. Imam Saheb's health was so delicate that people laughed when they heard of his courting arrest. Some people came to me and asked me not to take Imam Saheb for fear he might bring discredit upon the community. I disregarded this warning. It was none of my business to gauge the strength or weakness of Imam Saheb. Imam Saheb never walked barefooted, was fond of the good things of the earth, had a Malay wife, kept a well-furnished house and went about in a horse carriage. Very true, but who could read the depths of his mind? After he was released, Imam Saheb went to jail again, lived there as an ideal prisoner and took his meals after a spell of hard labour. At home he would have new dishes and delicacies every day; in jail he took mealie pap and thanked God for it. Not only was he not defeated, but he became simple in habits. As a prisoner he broke stones, worked as a sweeper and stood in a line with other prisoners. At Phoenix he fetched water and even set types in the press. Every one at the Phoenix Ashram was bound to acquire the art of type-setting. Imam Saheb learnt type-setting to the best of his ability. Now-a-days he is doing his bit in India.

But there were many such who experienced self-purification in jail.

Joseph Royeppen, barrister-at-law, a graduate of Cambridge University had been born in Natal of parents who were indentured labourers, but had fully adopted the European style of living. He would not go barefooted even in his house, unlike Imam Saheb who must wash his feet before prayers and must also pray barefooted. Royeppen left his law books, took up a basket of vegetables and was arrested as an unlicensed hawker. He too suffered imprisonment. 'But should I travel third class?' asked Royeppen. 'If you travel first or second how can I ask any of the rest to travel third? Who in jail is going to recognize the barrister in you?' I replied, and that was enough to satisfy Royeppen.

Many lads sixteen years old went to jail. One Mohanlal Manji Ghelani was only fourteen.

The jail authorities left no stone unturned to harass the Indians, who were given scavenger's work, but they did it with a smile on their face. They were asked to break stones, and they broke stones with the name of Allah or Rama on their lips. They were made to dig tanks and put upon pick-axe work in stony ground. Their hands became hardened with the work. Some of them even fainted under unbearable hardships, but they did not know what it was to be beaten.

One must not suppose, that there were no internal jealousies or quarrels in jail. Food constitutes the eternal apple of discord, but we successfully avoided bickerings even over food.

I too was arrested again. At one time there were as many as seventy-five Indian prisoners in Volksrust jail. We cooked our own food. I became the cook as only I could adjudicate on the conflicting claims to the ration supplied. Thanks to their love for me my companions took without a murmur the half-cooked porridge I prepared without sugar.

Government thought that if they separated me from the other prisoners it might perhaps chasten me as well as the others. They therefore took me to Pretoria jail where I was confined in a solitary cell reserved for dangerous prisoners. I was taken out only twice a day for exercise. In Pretoria jail no *ghi* was provided to the Indians, unlike as in Volksrust. But I do not propose here to deal with our hardships in jail, for which the curious may turn to the account of my experiences of jail life in South Africa.

But yet the Indians would not take a defeat. Government was in a quandary. How many Indians could be sent to jail after all? And then it meant additional expenditure. The Government began to cast about for other means of dealing with the situation.

CHAPTER XXXI

DEPORTATIONS

The obnoxious Acts provided for three kinds of punishment, *viz.*, fine, imprisonment and deportation. The Courts were empowered simultaneously to award all the punishments, and all magistrates were given jurisdiction to impose the maximum penalties. At first deportation meant taking the 'culprit' into the limits of Natal, the Orange Free State or Portuguese East Africa beyond the Transvaal frontier and leaving him there. As for instance the Indians who crossed over from Natal were taken beyond the limits of Volksrust station and there left to their own devices. Deportation of this kind was a farce pure and simple, as it involved only a little inconvenience, and instead of disheartening them it only encouraged the Indians still further.

The local Government therefore had to find out fresh means of harassing the Indians. The jails were already overcrowded. The Government thought that the Indians would be thoroughly demoralized and would surrender at discretion if they could be deported to India. There was some ground for this belief of the Government who accordingly sent a large batch of Indians to India. These deportees suffered great hardships. They had nothing to eat except what Government chose to provide for them on the steamers, and all of them were sent as deck passengers. Again some of them had their landed as well as other property and their business in South Africa, many had their families there, while others were also in debt. Not many men would be ready to lose their all and turn into perfect bankrupts.

All this notwithstanding, many Indians remained perfectly firm. Many more however weakened and ceased to court arrest, although they did not weaken to the extent of getting duplicates of the burnt certificates. Some few were even terrorized into registering afresh.

Still there was a considerable number of stalwarts who were so brave that some of them, I believe, would have mounted the gallows with a smile on their face. And if they cared little for life, they cared still less for property.

But many of those who were deported to India were poor and simple folk who had joined the movement from mere faith. That these should be oppressed so heavily was almost too much to bear. However it was difficult to see our way to assist them. Our funds were meagre, and then there was the danger of losing the fight altogether if we proceeded to give monetary help. Not a single person was permitted to join the movement from pecuniary inducement; for otherwise the movement would have been choked up by men coming in on the strength of such selfish hopes. We felt it was incumbent upon us, however, to help the deportees with our sympathies.

I have seen from experience that money cannot go as far as fellow-feeling, kind words and kind looks can. If a man, who is eager to get riches gets the riches from another but without sympathy, he will give him up in the long run. On the other hand, one who has been conquered by love is ready to encounter no end of difficulties with him who has given him his love.

We therefore resolved to do for the deportees all that kindness could do. We comforted them with the promise, that proper arrangements would be made for them in India. The reader must remember that many of them were ex-indentured labourers, and had no relations in India. Some were even born in South Africa, and to all India was something like a strange land. It would be sheer cruelty if these helpless people upon being landed in India were left to shift for themselves. We therefore assured them that all suitable arrangements would be made for them in India.

But this was not enough. The deportees could not be comforted so long as some one was not sent with them to be their companion and guide. This was the first batch of deportees, and their steamer was to start in a few hours. There was not much time for making a selection. I thought of P. K. Naidoo, one of my co-workers, and asked him:

'Will you escort these poor brothers to India?'

'Why not?'

'But the steamer is starting just now.'

'Let it.'

'What about your clothes? And food?'

'As for clothes, the suit I have on will suffice, and I will get the food from the steamer all right.'

This was a most agreeable surprise for me. The conversation took place at Parsi Rustomji's. There and then I procured some clothes and blankets for Naidoo and sent him on.

'Take care and look after these brothers on the way. See first to their comforts and then to your own. I am cabling to Shri Natesan at Madras, and you must follow his instructions.'

'I will try to prove myself a true soldier.' So saying P. K. Naidoo left for the pier. Victory must be certain with such valiant fighters, I said to myself. Naidoo was born in South Africa and had never been to India before. I gave him a letter of recommendation to Shri Natesan and also sent a cablegram.

In those days Shri Natesan perhaps stood alone in India as a student of the grievances of Indians abroad, their valued helper, and a systematic and well-informed exponent of their case. I had regular correspondence with him. When the deportees reached Madras, Shri Natesan rendered them full assistance. He found his task easier for the presence of an able man like Naidoo among the deportees. He made local collections and did not allow the deportees to feel for a moment that they had been deported.

These deportations by the Transvaal Government were as illegal as they were cruel. People are generally unaware that governments often deliberately violate their own laws. In face of emergency there is no time for undertaking fresh legislation. Governments therefore break the laws and do what they please. Afterwards they either enact new laws or else make the people forget their breach of the law.

DEPORTATIONS

The Indians started a powerful agitation against this lawlessness of the local Government, which was adversely commented upon in India too so that the Government every day found it more and more difficult to deport poor Indians. The Indians took all possible legal steps and successfully appealed against the deportations, with the result that Government had to stop the practice of deporting to India.

But the policy of deportations was not without its effect upon the Satyagrahi 'army.' Not all could overcome the fear of being deported to India. Many more fell away, and only the real fighters remained.

This was not the only step taken by the Government to break the spirit of the community. As I have stated in the last chapter, Government had done their utmost to harass the Satyagrahi prisoners, who were put to all manner of tasks including breaking stones. But that was not all. At first all prisoners were kept together. Now the Government adopted the policy of separating them, and accorded harsh treatment to them in every jail. Winter in the Transvaal is very severe; the cold is so bitter, that one's hands are almost frozen while working in the morning. Winter therefore was a hard time for the prisoners, some of whom were kept in a road camp where no one could even go and see them. One of these prisoners was a young Satyagrahi eighteen years old of the name of Swami Nagappan, who observed the jail rules and did the task entrusted to him. Early in the morning he was taken to work on the roads where he contracted double pneumonia of which he died after he was released (July 7, 1909). Nagappan's companions say that he thought of the struggle and struggle alone till he breathed his last. He never repented of going to jail and embraced death for his country's sake as he would embrace a friend. Nagappan was 'illiterate' according to our standards. He spoke English and Zulu from experience. Perhaps he also wrote broken English, but he was by no means an educated man. Still if we consider his fortitude, his patience, his patriotism, his firmness unto death, there is nothing left which we might desire him to possess. The Satyagraha movement went on successfully though it was not joined by any highly educated men, but where would it have been without soldiers like Nagappan?

As Nagappan died of ill-treatment in jail, the hardships of deportation proved to be the death of Narayanaswami (October 16, 1910). Still the community stood unmoved; only weaklings slipped away. But even the weaklings had done their best. Let us not despise them. Those who march forward are generally apt to look down upon those who fall back and to consider themselves very brave fellows, whereas often the facts are just the reverse. If a man who can afford to contribute fifty rupees subscribes only twenty-five and if he who can afford to pay only five rupees contributes that amount in full, he who gives five must be held to be a more generous donor than the other who gives five times as much. Yet very often he who contributes twenty-five is needlessly elated at the false notion of his superiority over the contributor of five rupees. In the same way, if a man who falls back through weakness has done his utmost, he is really superior to another who leaves him behind but has not put his whole soul into the march. Therefore even those, who slipped away when they found things too hot for them, did render service to the community. A time now came when greater calls were made on our patience and courage. But the Transvaal Indians were not found wanting even so. The stalwarts who held to their posts were equal to the service required of them.

Thus day by day the trial grew more and more severe for the Indians. Government became more and more violent in proportion to the strength put forth by the community. There are always special prisons where dangerous prisoners or prisoners whom Government wants to bend are kept, and so there were in the Transvaal. One of these was the Diepkloof Convict Prison, where there was a harsh jailer, and where the labour exacted from prisoners was also hard. And yet there were Indians who successfully performed their allotted task. But though they were prepared to work, they would not put up with the insult offered to them by the jailer and therefore went on hunger strike. They solemnly declared that they would take no food until either the jailer was removed from the prison, or else they themselves were transferred to another prison. This was a perfectly legitimate strike. The strikers were quite honest and not likely to take food secretly. The reader must remember that there was not much room in the Transvaal for such public agitation as a case of this nature would evoke in India. Again jail regulations in the Transvaal were particularly drastic. Outsiders did not seek interviews with prisoners even on occasions of this nature. A Satyagrahi, when once he found himself in jail, had generally to shift for himself. The struggle was on behalf of the poor and was conducted as a poor men's movement. And therefore the vow which these strikers took was fraught with great risk. However, they were firm and succeeded in getting themselves transferred to another prison after a seven days' fast. As hunger strikes were a rarity in those days, these Satyagrahis are entitled to special credit as pioneers (November, 1910).

CHAPTER XXXII

A SECOND DEPUTATION

Thus the Satyagrahis were being imprisoned or deported. There was sometimes a lull and then a storm, but both the parties had somewhat weakened. The Government saw that they could not hope to subdue the Satyagrahi stalwarts by sending them to jail, and the policy of deportations had only put themselves in a false position. The Government also lost some cases which were taken to the courts. The Indians on their part were not in a position to put up a strong fight. There was not a sufficient number of Satyagrahis for the purpose. Some Indians were war-weary, while others had become entirely defeatist and therefore looked upon the staunch Satyagrahis as so many fools. The 'fools' however knew themselves to be wise and had full faith in God, in their cause and in the righteousness of the means they had selected to promote it. They were confident that great is Truth and it shall prevail in the end.

Meanwhile, there was continuous movement in South African politics. The Boers and the British were anxious to secure a higher status by effecting a union of the various Colonies in the sub-continent. General Hertzog stood for a total breach of the British connection while others preferred to keep up a nominal association with the British Empire. Englishmen would never agree to a total secession, and any higher status in view could only be attained through the British Parliament. The Boers and the British in South Africa therefore decided that a deputation should visit England on their behalf and present their case before the British Cabinet.

The Indians observed that in case of a union of the Colonies their last state would be worse than their first. All the Colonies were ever desirous of suppressing the Indians, and it was clear in view of their anti-Indian tendency that it would go very hard with the community when they came closer together. In order that not a single avenue might remain unexplored, the Indians resolved to send once again a deputation to England, although there was every likelihood of their small voice being drowned in the loud roar of British and Boer lions. On this occasion Sheth Haji Habib, a Memon gentleman from Porbandar, was appointed as my colleague on the deputation. The Sheth carried on a long established trade in the Transvaal and was a man of wide experience. He had not received English education, yet he easily understood English, Dutch, Zulu and other languages. His sympathies were with the Satyagrahis but he could not be described as a full Satyagrahi himself. Mr Merriman the famous veteran statesman of South Africa was our fellow passenger on board S.S. *Kenilworth Castle*, which took us to England, leaving Cape Town on June 23, 1909. He was going with a view to the unification of the Colonies. General Smuts and others were already in England. A separate deputation of the Indians in Natal also visited England about this time in connection with their special grievances.

At this time Lord Crewe was Secretary of State for the Colonies and Lord Morley Secretary of State for India. There were many discussions, and we interviewed a large number of people. There was hardly a journalist or member of either House whom it was possible to meet but whom we did not meet. Lord Ampthill rendered us invaluable help. He used to meet Mr Merriman, General Botha and others and at last he brought a message from the General. Said he: 'General Botha appreciates your feelings in the matter, and is willing to grant you minor demands. But he is not ready to repeal the Asiatic Act or to amend the Immigrants Restriction Act. He also refuses to remove the colour bar which has been set up in the law of the land. To maintain the racial bar is a matter of principle with the General and even if he felt like doing away with it the South African Europeans would never listen to him. General Smuts is of the same mind as General Botha, and this is their final decision and final offer. If you ask for more you will only be inviting trouble for yourself as well as for your people. Therefore whatever you do, do it after giving due consideration to this attitude of the Boer leaders. General Botha has asked me to tell you this and give you an idea of your responsibility.'

And after delivering the message Lord Ampthill said, 'You see that General Botha concedes all your practical demands, and in this work-a-day world we must always give and take. We cannot have everything that we desire. I would therefore strongly advice you to close with this offer. If you wish to fight for principle's sake, you may do so later on. You and the Sheth think over this, and let me have your reply at your convenience.'

Upon hearing this I looked to Sheth Haji Habib, who said, 'Tell him from me that I accept General Botha's offer on behalf of the conciliation party. If he makes these concessions, we will be satisfied for the present and later on struggle for principle. I do not like the community to suffer any more. The party I represent constitutes the majority of the community, and it also holds the major portion of the community's wealth.'

I translated the Sheth's sentences word by word, and then on behalf of the Satyagrahis I said: 'We are both highly obliged to you for the trouble you have taken. My colleague is right when he says that he represents a numerically and financially stronger section. The Indians for whom I speak are comparatively poor and inferior in numbers, but they are resolute unto death. They are fighting not only for practical relief but for principle as well. If they must give up either of the two, they will jettison the former and fight for the latter. We have an idea of General Botha's might, but we attach still greater weight to our pledge, and therefore we are ready to face the worst in the act of abiding by it. We will be patient in the confidence that if we stick to our solemn resolution, God in Whose name we have made it will see to its fulfilment.

'I can grasp your position fully. You have done much for us. We will not take it ill if you now withhold your support from a handful of Satyagrahis. Nor will we forget the debt of gratitude under which you have laid us. But we trust that you will excuse us for our inability to accept your advice. You may certainly tell General Botha how the Sheth and myself have received his offer and inform him that the Satyagrahis though in a minority will observe their pledge and hope in the end to soften his heart by their self-suffering and to induce him to repeal the Asiatic Act.'

Lord Ampthill replied:

'You must not suppose that I will give you up. I too must play the gentleman's part. Englishmen are not willing at once to relinquish any task they have undertaken. Yours is a righteous struggle, and you are fighting with clean weapons. How possibly can I give you up? But you can realize my delicate position. The suffering, if any, must be borne by you alone, and therefore it is my duty to advise you to accept any settlement possible in the circumstances. But if you, who have to suffer, are prepared to undergo any amount of suffering for principle's sake, I must not only not come in your way but even congratulate you. I will therefore continue as President of your Committee and help you to the best of my ability. But you must remeber that I am but a junior member of the House of Lords, and do not command much influence. However, you may rest assured that what little influence I possess will be continually exerted on your behalf.'

We were both pleased to hear these words of encouragement.

One delightful feature of this interview has perhaps not escaped the reader. As I have already observed Sheth Haji Habib and myself held divergent views, and yet there was such friendship and mutual confidence between us, that the Sheth did not hesitate to communicate his difference of opinion through me. He relied upon me to present his case to Lord Ampthill all right.

I will close this chapter with a not quite relevant paragraph. During my stay in England I had occasion to talk with many Indian anarchists. My booklet *Indian Home Rule* written during my return voyage to South Africa on board S.S. *Kildonan Castle* (November 1909) and published soon afterwards in *Indian Opinion* had its birth from the necessity of having to meet their arguments as well as to solve the difficulties of Indians in South Africa who held similar views. I had also discussed the main points of the book with Lord Ampthill in order that he might not feel for one moment that I had misused his name and his help for my work in South Africa by suppressing my views. This discussion with Lord Ampthill has always remained imprinted on my memory. He found time to meet me in spite of illness in his family, and although he did not agree with my views as expressed in *Hind Swaraj*, he accorded his support to our struggle till the last, and my relations with him were always cordial.

CHAPTER XXXIII
TOLSTOY FARM—I

The deputation which now returned from England did not bring good news. But I did not mind what conclusions the community would draw from our conversations with Lord Ampthill. I knew who would stand by us till the end. My ideas about Satyagraha had now matured and I had realized its universality as well as its excellence. I was therefore perfectly at ease. *Hind Swaraj* was written in order to demonstrate the sublimity of Satyagraha and that book is a true measure of my faith in its efficacy. I was perfectly indifferent to the numerical strength of the fighters on our side.

But I was not free from anxiety on the score of finance. It was indeed hard to prosecute a long protracted struggle without funds. I did not realize then as clearly as I do now that a struggle can be carried on without funds, that money very often spoils a righteous fight and that God never gives a Satyagrahi or *mumukshu** anything beyond his strict needs. But I had faith in God who did not even then desert me but raised me from the slough of despondency. If on the one hand I had to tell the Indians on our landing in South Africa that our mission had failed, on the other hand God relieved me from the financial difficulty. As I set my foot in Cape Town I received a cable from England that Mr (afterwards Sir) Ratanji Jamshedji Tata had given Rs. 25,000 to the Satyagraha funds. This sum amply sufficed for our immediate needs and we forged ahead.

But this or even the largest possible gift of money could not by itself help forward a Satyagraha struggle, a fight on behalf of Truth consisting chiefly in self-purification and self-reliance. A Satyagraha struggle is impossible without capital in the shape of character. As a splendid palace deserted by its inmates looks like a ruin, so does a man without character, all his material belongings notwithstanding. The Satyagrahis now saw that no one could

---
*Pilgrim bound for the eternal city. V. G. D.

tell how long the struggle would last. On the one hand there were the Boer Generals determined not to yield even an inch of ground and on the other there was a handful of Satyagrahis pledged to fight unto death or victory. It was like a war between ants and the elephant who could crush thousands of them under each of his feet. The Satyagrahis could not impose a time limit upon their Satyagraha. Whether it lasted one year or many, it was all the same to them. For them the struggle itself was victory. Fighting meant imprisonment or deportation for them. But what about their families in the meanwhile? No one would engage as an employee a man who was constantly going to jail and when he was released, how was he to maintain himself as well as those dependent on him? Where was he to lodge and where was his house rent to come from? Even a Satyagrahi may be excused if he feels troubled at heart from want of his daily bread. There cannot be many in the world who would fight the good fight in spite of being compelled to condemn their nearest and dearest to the same starvation which they suffered in their own person.

Till now the families of jail-going Satyagrahis were maintained by a system of monthly allowances in cash according to their need. It would not have done to grant an equal sum to all. A Satyagrahi who had a family of five persons dependent upon him could not be placed on a par with another who was a *brahmachari* without any family responsibilities. Nor was it possible to recruit only *brahmacharis* for our 'army.' The principle generally observed was, that each family was asked to name the minimum amount adequate to their needs and was paid accordingly on trust. There was considerable room here for fraud, of which some rogues might not fail to take advantage. Others who were honest but who were accustomed to live in a particular style naturally expected such help as would enable them to keep it up. I saw that at this rate the movement could not be conducted for any length of time. There was always the risk of injustice being done to the deserving, and undue advantage being taken by the unscrupulous. There was only one solution for this difficulty, namely, that all the families should be kept at one place and should become members of a sort of co-operative commonwealth. Thus there would be no scope for fraud, nor would there be injustice to any. Public funds would be largely saved and the families of Satyagrahis would be trained to live a new and simple life in harmony with one another. Indians belonging to various provinces and professing divers faiths would have an opportunity of living together.

But where was the place suitable for a settlement of this nature? To live in a city would have been like straining at a gnat and swallowing a camel. The house rent alone would perhaps amount to the same sum as the food bill, and it would not be easy to live a simple life amidst the varied distractions of a city. Again in a city it would be impossible to find a place where many families could prosecute some useful industry in their own homes. It was therefore clear that the place selected should be neither too far from nor too near a city. There was of course Phoenix, where *Indian Opinion* was being printed and where there was also some cultivation being carried on. Phoenix was also convenient in many other ways, but it was three hundred miles away from Johannesburg and to be reached by a journey of thirty hours. It was therefore difficult and expensive to take the families such a distance and bring them back again. Besides, the families would not be ready to leave their homes for such a far off place, and even if they were ready it seemed impossible to send them as well as the Satyagrahi prisoners on their release.

The place required then must be in the Transvaal and near Johannesburg. Mr Kallenbach, whose acquaintance the reader has already made, bought a farm of about 1,100 acres and gave the use of it to Satyagrahis free of any rent or charge (May 30, 1910). Upon the farm there were nearly one thousand fruit-bearing trees and a small house at the foot of a hill with accommodation for half-a-dozen persons. Water was supplied from two wells as well as from a spring. The nearest railway station, Lawley, was about a mile from the farm and Johannesburg was twenty-one miles distant. We decided to build houses upon this Farm and to invite the families of Satyagrahis to settle there.

CHAPTER XXXIV

TOLSTOY FARM—II

Upon the Farm oranges, apricots and plums grew in such abundance that during the season the Satyagrahis could have their fill of the fruit and yet have a surplus.

The spring was about 500 yards away from our quarters, and the water had to be fetched on carrying poles.

Here we insisted that we should not have any servants either for the household work or as far as might be even for the farming and building operations. Everything therefore from cooking to scavenging was done with our own hands. As regards accommodation for families, we resolved from the first that the men and women should be housed separately. The houses therefore were to be built in two separate blocks, each at some distance from the other. For the time it was considered sufficient to provide accommodation for ten women and sixty men. Then again we had to erect a house for Mr Kallenbach and by its side a school house, as well as a workshop for carpentry, shoemaking etc.

The settlers hailed from Gujarat, Tamilnad, Andhradesh and North India, and there were Hinus, Musalmans, Parsis and Christians among them. About forty of them were young men, two or three old men, five women and twenty to thirty children of whom four or five were girls.

The Christian and other women were meat-eaters. Mr Kallenbach and I thought it desirable to exclude meat from the Farm. But how could we ask people, who had no scruples in the matter, who had been habituated to taking meat since childhood and who were coming over here in their days of adversity, to give up meat even temporarily? But if they were given meat, would not that swell our cost of living? Again should those who were accustomed to take beef be given that too? How many separate kitchens must be run in that case? What was my duty on this point? Having been instrumental in giving monetary help to these families, I had already given my support to meat-eating as well as beef-eating. If I made a rule that meat-eaters should not be helped, I would have to prosecute the Satyagraha struggle through vegetarians only, which was absurd as the movement had been organized on behalf of all classes of Indians. I did not take long clearly to visualize my duty in these circumstances. If the Christians and Musalmans asked even for beef, that too must be provided for them. To refuse them admission to the Farm was absolutely out of the question.

But where love is, there God is also. The Musalman friends had already granted me permission to have a purely vegetarian kitchen. I had now to approach Christian sisters whose husbands or sons were in jail. I had often come in such intimate contact with the Christian friends who were now in jail and who had on similar occasions consented to having a vegtarian dietary. But this was the first time that I had to deal at close quarters with their families in their absence. I represented to the sisters the difficulty of housing accommodation as well as of finance and my own deep-rooted sentiment in the matter. At the same time I assured them that even beef would be provided for them if they wanted it. The sisters kindly consented not to have meat, and the cooking department was placed in their charge. I with or without another man was detailed to assist them. My presence acted as a check upon petty bickerings. The food was to be the simplest possible. The time as well as the number of meals was fixed. There was to be one single kitchen, and all were to dine in a single row. Every one was to see to the cleaning of his own dish and other things. The common pots were to be cleaned by different parties in turn. I must state that Satyagrahis lived on Tolstoy Farm for a long time, but neither the women nor the men ever asked for meat. Drink, smoking etc. were of course totally prohibited.

As I have already stated, we wanted to be self-reliant as far as possible even in erecting buildings. Our architect was Mr Kallenbach of course, and he got hold of a European mason. A Gujarati carpenter, Narayandas Damania, volunteered his services free of charge and brought other carpenters to work at reduced rates. As regards unskilled labour, the settlers worked with their own hands. Some of us who had supple limbs literally worked wonders. A fine Satyagrahi of the name of Vihari did half of the carpenter's work. The lion-like Thambi Naidoo was in charge of sanitation and marketing for which he had to go to Johannesburg.

One of the settlers was Pragji Khandubhai Desai who had never been accustomed to discomfort all his life, but who had here to put up with bitter cold, a hot sun and sharp rains. In the beginning we lived in tents for about two months while the buildings were under construction. The structures were all of corrugated iron and therefore did not take long to raise. The timber too could be had ready made in all sizes required. All we had to do was to cut it to measure. There were not many doors or windows to be prepared. Hence it was that quite a number of buildings could be erected within such a short space of time. But all this labour was a heavy tax on Pragji's physical constitution. The work on the Farm was certainly harder than in jail. One day Pragji actually fainted thanks to fatigue and heat. But he was not the man to give in. He fully trained up his body here, and in the end he stood abreast as a good worker with the best of us.

Then there was Joseph Royeppen, a barrister free from barrister's pride. He could not undertake very hard work. It was difficult for him to take down loads from the railway train and to haul them on the cart, but he did it as best he could.

The weak became strong on Tolstoy Farm and labour proved to be a tonic for all.

Every one had to go to Johannesburg on some errand or other. Children liked to go there just for the fun of it. I also had to go there on business. We therefore made a rule that we could go there by rail only on the public business of our little commonwealth, and then too travel third class. Any one who wanted to go on a pleasure trip must go on foot, and carry home-made provisions with him. No one might spend anything on his food in the city. Had it not been for these drastic rules, the money saved by living in a rural locality would have been wasted in railway fares and city picnics. The provisions carried were of the simplest: home-baked bread made from coarse wheat flour ground at home, from which the bran was not removed, groundnut butter also prepared at home, and home-made marmalade. We had purchased an iron handmill for grinding wheat. Groundnut butter was made by roasting and then grinding groundnuts, and was four times cheaper than ordinary butter. As for the oranges, we had plenty of them on the Farm. We scarcely used cow's milk on the Farm and generally managed with condensed milk.

But to return to the trips. Any one who wished to go to Johannesburg went there on foot once or twice a week and returned the same day. As I have already stated, it was a journey of 21 miles and back. We saved hundreds of rupees by this one rule of going on foot, and those who thus went walking were much benefited. Some newly acquired the habit of walking. The general practice was that the sojourner should rise at two o'clock and start at half past two. He would reach Johannesburg in six to seven hours. The record for the minimum time taken on the journey was 4 hours 18 minutes.

The reader must not imagine that this discipline operated upon the settlers at all as a hardship. On the other hand it was accepted cheerfully. It would have been impossible to have a single settler if force had been employed. The youngsters thoroughly enjoyed the work on the Farm and the errands to the city. It was difficult to prevent them from playing their pranks while engaged in work. No more work was given to them than what they willingly and cheerfully rendered, and I never found that the work thus done was unsatisfactory either in quantity or in quality.

A paragraph may be devoted to our sanitary arrangements. In spite of the large number of settlers, one could not find refuse or dirt anywhere on the Farm. All rubbish was buried in trenches sunk for the purpose. No water was permitted to be thrown on the roads. All waste water was collected in buckets and used to water the trees. Leavings of food and vegetable refuse were utilized as manure. A square pit one foot and a half deep was sunk near the house to receive the nightsoil, which was fully covered with the excavated earth and which therefore did not give out any smell. There were no flies, and no one would imagine that nightsoil had been buried there. We were thus not only spared a nuisance, but the source of possible nuisance was converted into invaluable manure for the Farm. If nightsoil was properly utilized, we would get manure worth *lakhs* of rupees and also secure immunity from a number of diseases. By our bad habits we spoil our sacred river banks and furnish excellent breeding grounds for flies with the result that the very flies which through our criminal negligence settle upon uncovered nightsoil defile our bodies after we have bathed. A small spade is the means of salvation from a great nuisance. Leaving nightsoil, cleaning the nose or spitting on the road is a sin against God as well as humanity, and betrays a sad want of consideration for others. The man who does not cover his waste deserves a heavy penalty even if he lives in a forest.

The work before us was to make the Farm a busy hive of industry, thus to save money and in the end to make the families self-supporting. If we achieved this goal, we could battle with the Transvaal Government for an indefinite period. We had to spend some money on shoes. The use of shoes in a hot climate is harmful, as all the perspiration is absorbed by the feet which thus grow tender. No socks were needed in the Transvaal as in India, but we thought that the feet must be protected against thorns, stones and the like. We therefore determined to learn to make sandals. There is at Mariannhill near Pinetown a monastery of German Catholic monks called the Trappists, where industries of this nature are carried on. Mr Kallenbach went there and acquired the art of making sandals. After he returned, he taught it to me and I in my turn to other workers. Thus several young men learnt how to manufacture sandals, and we commenced selling them to friends. I need scarcely say that many of my pupils easily surpassed me in the art. Another handicraft introduced was that of carpentry. Having founded a sort of village we needed all manner of things large and small from benches to boxes, and we made them all ourselves. The selfless carpenters already referred to helped us for several months. Mr Kallenbach was the head of the carpentry department, and as such every moment gave us the evidence of his mastery and exactitude.

A school was indispensable for the youngsters and the children. This was the most difficult of our tasks and we never achieved complete success in this matter till the very last. The burden of teaching work was largely borne by Mr Kallenbach and myself. The school could be held only after noon, when both of us were thoroughly exhausted by our morning labour, and so were our pupils. The teachers therefore would often be dozing as well as the taught. We would sprinkle water on the eyes, and by playing with the children try to pull them up and to pull up ourselves, but sometimes in vain. The body peremptorily demanded rest and would not take a denial. But this was only one and the least of our many difficulties. For the classes were conducted in spite of these dozings. What were we to teach pupils who spoke three languages, Gujarati, Tamil or Telugu, and how? I was anxious to make these languages the medium of instructions. I knew a little Tamil but no Telugu. What could one teacher do in these circumstances? I tried to use some of the young men as teachers, but the experiment was not altogether a success. Pragji's services were of course requisitioned. Some of the youngsters were very mischievous and lazy and were always on bad terms with their books. A teacher could not expect to make much headway with such pupils. Again we could not be regular in our teaching. Business sometimes took Mr Kallenbach as well as me to Johannesburg.

Religious teaching presented another tough problem. I would like Musalmans to read the Koran, and Parsis the Avesta. There was one Khoja child, whose father had laid upon me the responsibility of teaching him a small *pothi* of that sect. I collected books bearing on Islam and Zoroastrianism. I wrote out the fundamental doctrines of Hinduism according to my lights,—I forget now whether it was for my own children or for the Tolstoy Farmers. If this document was now in my possession, I should have inserted it here as a landmark in my spiritual progress. But I have thrown away or burnt many such things in my life. I desstroyed such papers as I felt it was not necessary to preserve them or as the scope of my activities was extended. I am not sorry for this, as to have preserved all of them would have been burdensome and expensive. I should have been compelled to keep cabinets and boxes, which would have been an eyesore to one who has taken the vow of poverty.

But this teaching experiment was not fruitless. The children were saved from the infection of intolerance, and learnt to view one another's religions and customs with a large-hearted charity. They learnt how to live together like blood-brothers. They imbibed the lessons of mutual service, courtesy and industry. And from what little I know about the later activities of some of the children on Tolstoy Farm, I am certain that the education which they received there has not been in vain. Even if imperfect, it was a thoughtful and religious experiment, and among the sweetest reminiscences of Tolstoy Farm, the reminiscences of this teaching experiment are no less sweet than the rest.

But another chapter must be devoted to these reminiscences.

CHAPTER XXXV

TOLSTOY FARM—III

In this chapter I propose to string together a number of Tolstoy Farm reminiscences which are rather disjointed and for which therefore I must crave the reader's indulgence.

A teacher hardly ever had to teach the kind of heterogeneous class that fell to my lot, containing as it did pupils of all ages and both the sexes, from boys and girls of about 7 years of age to young men of twenty and young girls 12 or 13 years old. Some of the boys were wild and mischievous.

What was I to teach this ill-assorted group? How was I to be all things to all pupils? Again in what language should I talk to all of them? The Tamil and Telugu children knew their own mother-tongue or English and a little

Dutch. I could speak to them only in English. I divided the class into two sections, the Gujarati section to be talked to in Gujarati and the rest in English. As the principal part of the teaching, I arranged to tell or read to them some interesting stories. I also proposed to bring them into close mutual contact and to lead them to cultivate a spirit of friendship and service. Then there was to be imparted some general knowledge of history and geography and in some cases of arithmetic. Writing was also taught, and so were some *bhajans* which formed part of our prayers, and to which therefore I tried to attract the Tamil children as well.

The boys and girls met freely. My experiment of co-education on Tolstoy Farm was the most fearless of its type. I dare not today allow, or train children to enjoy, the liberty which I had granted the Tolstoy Farm class. I have often felt that my mind then used to be more innocent than it is now, and that was due perhaps to my ignorance. Since then I have had bitter experiences, and have sometimes burnt my fingers badly. Persons whom I took to be thoroughly innocent have turned out corrupt. I have observed the roots of evil deep down in my own nature; and timidity has claimed me for its own.

I do not repent having made the experiment. My conscience bears witness that it did not do any harm. But as a child who has burnt himself with hot milk blows even into whey, my present attitude is one of extra caution.

A man cannot borrow faith or courage from others. The doubter is marked out for destruction, as the Gita puts it. My faith and courage were at their highest in Tolstoy Farm. I have been praying to God to permit me to re-attain that height, but the prayer has not yet been heard, for the number of such suppliants before the Great White Throne is legion. The only consolation is that God has as many ears as there are suppliants. I therefore repose full faith in Him and know that my prayer will be accepted when I have fitted myself for such grace.

This was my experiment. I sent the boys reputed to be mischievous and the innocent young girls to bathe in the same spot at the same time. I had fully explained the duty of self-restraint to the children, who were all familiar with my Satyagraha doctrine. I knew, and so did the children, that I loved them with a mother's love. The reader will remember the spring at some distance from the kitchen. Was it a folly to let the children meet there for bath and yet to expect them to be innocent? My eye always followed the girls as a mother's eye would follow a daughter. The time was fixed when all the boys and all the girls went together for a bath. There was an element of safety in the fact that they went in a body. Solitude was always avoided. Generally I also would be at the spring at the same time.

All of us slept in an open verandah. The boys and the girls would spread themselves around me. There was hardly a distance of three feet between any two beds. Some care was exercised in arranging the order of the beds, but any amount of such care would have been futile in the case of a wicked mind. I now see that God alone safeguarded the honour of these boys and girls. I made the experiment from a belief that boys and girls could thus live together without harm, and the parents with their boundless faith in me allowed me to make it.

One day one of the young men made fun of two girls, and the girls themselves or some child brought me the information. The news made me tremble. I made inquiries and found that the report was true. I remonstrated with the young men, but that was not enough. I wished the two girls to have some sign on their person as a warning to every young man that no evil eye might be cast upon them, and as a lesson to every girl that no one dare assail their purity. The passionate Ravana could not so much as touch Sita with evil intent while Rama was thousands of miles away. What mark should the girls bear so as to give them a sense of security and at the same time to sterilize the sinner's eye? This question kept me awake for the night. In the morning I gently suggested to the girls that they might let me cut off their fine long hair. On the Farm we shaved and cut the hair of one another, and we therefore kept scissors and clipping machines. At first the girls would not listen to me. I had already explained the situation to the elderly women who could not bear to think of my suggestion but yet quite understood my motive, and they had finally accorded their support to me. They were both of them noble girls. One of them is alas! now no more. She was very bright and intelligent. The other is living and the mistress of a household of her own. They came round after all, and at once the very hand that is narrating this incident set to cut off their hair. And afterwards I analysed and explained my procedure before my class, with excellent results. I never heard of a joke again. The girls in question did not lose in any case; goodness knows how much they gained. I hoped the young men still remember this incident and keep their eyes from sin.

Experiments such as I have placed on record are not meant for imitation. Any teacher who imitated them would be incurring grave risk. I have here taken note of them only to show how far a man can go in certain circumstances and to stress the purity of the Satyagraha struggle. This very puirty was a guarantee of its victory. Before launching on such experiments a teacher has to be both father and mother to his pupils and to be prepared for all eventualities whatever, and only the hardest penance can fit him to conduct them.

This act of mine was not without its effect on the entire life of the settlers on the Farm. As we had intended to cut down expenses to the barest minimum, we changed our dress also. In the cities the Indian men including the Satyagrahis put on European dress. Such elaborate clothing was not needed on the Farm. We had all become labourers and therefore put on labourers' dress but in the European style, *viz.* workingmen's trousers and shirts, which were imitated from prisoners' uniform. We all used cheap trousers and shirts which could be had ready-made out of coarse blue cloth. Most of the ladies were good hands at sewing and took charge of the tailoring department.

As for food we generally had rice, dal, vegetable and *rotlis* with porridge occasionally superadded. All this was served in a single dish which was not really a dish, but a kind of bowl such as is supplied to prisoners in jail. We had made wooden spoons on the Farm ourselves. There were three meals in the day. We had bread and homemade wheaten 'coffee'* at six o'clock in the morning, rice, *dal* and vegetable at eleven, and wheat pap and milk, or bread and 'coffee' at half past five in the evening. After the evening meal we had prayers at seven or half past seven. At prayers we sang *bhajans* and sometimes had readings from the *Ramayan* or books on Islam. The *bhajans* were in English, Hindi and Gujarati. Sometimes we had one *bhajan* [hymn] from each of the three languages, and sometimes only one. Every one retired at 9 o'clock.

Many observed the *Ekadashi* fast on the Farm. We were joined there by Shri P. K. Kotval who had much experience of fasting, and some of us followed him to keep the *chaturmas*. Ramzan also arrived in the meanwhile. There were Musalman youngsters among us, and we felt we must encourage them to keep the fasts. We arranged for them to have meals in the evening as well as in the early morning. Porridge etc. were prepared for them in the evening. There was no meat of course, nor did any one ask for it. To keep the Musalman friends company the rest of us had only one meal a day in the evening. As a rule we finished our evening meal before sunset; so the only difference was that the others finished their supper about when the Musalman boys commenced theirs. These boys were so courteous that they did not put any one to extra trouble although they were observing fasts, and the fact that the non-Muslim children supported them in the matter of fasting left a good impression on all. I do not remember that there ever was a quarrel, much less a split,

---

* 'A harmless and nutritious substitute for tea, coffee or cocoa can be prepared as follows. Even connoisseurs of coffee have failed to perceive any difference in taste between coffee and this substitute. Bake well-cleaned wheat on the fire, until it has turned quite red and begun to grow dark in colour. Then powder it like coffee. Take a spoonful of this powder in a cup and pour boiling water over it. Preferably keep it over the fire for a minute, and add milk and sugar to taste, but it can be taken without them also '— from the author's Gujarati booklet on health, Chapter V. *Indian Opinion*, XI-10, March 8, 1913. V. G. D.

between the Hindu and the Musalman boys on the score of religion. On the other hand I know that although staunch in their own beliefs, they all treated one another with respect and assisted one another in their respective religious observances.

Although we were living far from the amenities of city life, we did not keep even the commonest appliances against the possible attacks of illness. I had in those days as much faith in the nature cure of disease as I had in the innocence of children. I felt that there should not be disease as we lived a simple life, but if there was, I was confident of dealing with it. My booklet on health is a note-book of my experiments and of my living faith in those days. I was proud enough to believe that illness for me was out of the question. I held that all kinds of diseases could be cured by earth and water treatment, fasting or changes in diet. There was not a single case of illness on the Farm, in which we used drugs or called in a doctor. There was an old man from North India 70 years of age who suffered from asthma and cough, but whom I cured simply by changes in diet and water treatment. But I have now lost the courage, and in view of my two serious illnesses I feel that I have forfeited even the right, to make such experiments.

Gokhale arrived in South Africa while we were still living on the Farm. His tour must be described in another chapter, but I will place here on record a half sweet, half bitter reminiscence. The reader has now some idea of the sort of life we were leading. There was no cot on the Farm, but we borrowed one for Gokhale. There was no room where he could enjoy full privacy. For sitting accommodation we had nothing beyond the benches in our school. Even so, how could we resist the temptation of bringing Gokhale in spite of his delicate health to the Farm? And how could he help seeing it, either? I was foolish enough to imagine that Gokhale would be able to put up with a night's discomfort and to walk about a mile and a half from the station to the Farm. I had asked him beforehand, and he had agreed to everything without bestowing any thought upon it, thanks to his simplicity and overwhelming confidence in me. It rained that day, as fate would have it, and I was not in a position sunddenly to make any special arrangement. I have never forgotten the trouble to which I put Gokhale that day in my ignorant affection. The hardship was too much for him to bear and he caught a chill. We could not take him to the kitchen and dining-hall. He had been put up in Mr Kallenbach's room. His dinner would get cold while we brought it from the kitchen to his room. I prepared special soup, and Kotval special bread for him, but these could not be taken to him hot. We managed as best we could. Gokhale uttered not a syllable, but I understood from his face what a folly I had committed. When Gokhale came to know that all of us slept on the floor, he removed the cot which had been brought for him and had his own bed too spread on the floor. This whole night was a night of repentance for me. Gokhale had a rule in life which seemed to me a bad rule. He would not permit any one except a servant to wait upon him. He had no servant with him during this tour. Mr Kallenbach and I entreated him to let us massage his feet. But he would not let us even touch him, and half jocularly, half angrily said: 'You all seem to think that you have been born to suffer hardships and discomforts, and people like myself have been born to be pampered by you. You must suffer today the punishment for this extremism of yours. I will not let you even touch me. Do you think that you will go out to attend to nature's needs and at the same time keep a commode for me? I will bear any amount of hardship but I will humble your pride.' These words were to us like a thunderbolt, and deeply grieved Mr Kallenbach and me. The only consolation was, that Gokhale wore a smile on his face all the while. Krishna no doubts was often deeply offended by Arjuna, 'unknowing of His majesty and careless in the fondness of his love,' but he soon forgot such incidents. Gokhale remembered only our will to serve, though he did not accord us the high privilege of serving him. The deeply affectionate letter he wrote me from Mombasa is still imprinted upon my heart. Gokhale bore everything cheerfully, but till the last never accepted the service which it was in our power to render. He had to take the food etc., from our hands, but that he could not help.

The next morning he allowed no rest either to himself or to us. He corrected all his speeches which we proposed to publish in book form. When he had to write anything, he was in the habit of walking to and fro and thinking it out. He had to write a small letter and I thought that he would soon have done with it. But no. As I twitted him upon it, he read me a little homily: 'You do not know my ways of life. I will not do even the least little thing in a hurry. I will think about it and consider the central idea. I will next deliberate as to the language suited to the subject and then set to write. If every one did as I do, what a huge saving of time would there be? And the nation would be saved from the avalanche of half-baked ideas which now threatens to overwhelm her.'

As the reminiscences of Tolstoy Farm would be incomplete without an account of Gokhale's visit thereto, so would they be if I omitted to say something about the character and conduct of Mr Kallenbach. It was really a wonder how he lived on Tolstoy Farm among our people as if he were one of us. Gokhale was not the man to be attracted by ordinary things. But even he felt strongly drawn to the revolutionary change in Kallenbach's life. Kallenbach had been brought up in the lap of luxury and had never known what privation was. In fact, indulgence had been his religion. He had had his fill of all the pleasures of life, and he had never hesitated to secure for his comfort everything that money could buy.

It was no commonplace for such a man to live, move and have his being on Tolstoy Farm, and to become one with the Indian settlers. This was an agreeable surprise for the Indians. Some Europeans classed Kallenbach either as a fool or a lunatic, while others honoured him for his spirit of renunciation. Kallenbach never felt his renunciation to be painful. In fact he enjoyed it even more than he had enjoyed the pleasures of life before. He would be transported with rapture while describing the bliss of a simple life, and for a moment his hearers would be tempted to go in for it. He mixed so lovingly with the young as well as the old, that separation from him even for a short time left a clearly felt void in their lives. Mr Kallenbach was very fond of fruit trees and therefore he reserved gardening as his own portfolio. Every morning he would engage children as well as grown up people in tending the fruit trees. He would make them work hard, but he had such a cheerful temper and smiling face, that every one loved to work with him. Whenever a party of tourists left the Farm for Johannesburg at 2 a.m., Mr Kallenbach would always be one of them.

Mr Kallenbach and I had frequent talks on religion, which usually centred on fundamentals like non-violence or love, truth and the like. When I said that it was a sin to kill snakes and such other animals, Mr Kallenbach was shocked to hear it as well as my numerous other European friends. But in the end he admitted the truth of that principle in the abstract. At the very beginning of my intercourse with him, Mr Kallenbach had seen the propriety and the duty of carrying out in practice every principle of which he was convinced intellectually, and therefore he had been able to effect momentous changes in his life without a moment's hesitation. Now if it was improper to kill serpents and the like, we must cultivate their friendship, thought Mr Kallenbach. He therefore first collected books on snakes in order to identify different species of reptiles. He there read that not all snakes are poisonous and some of them actually serve as protectors of field-crops. He taught us all to recognize different kinds of snakes and at last tamed a huge cobra which was found on the Farm. Mr Kallenbach fed it every day with his own hands. I gently argued with him: 'Although you do all this in a friendly spirit, your friendliness may not be quite clear to the cobra, especially as your kindness is not unalloyed with fear. Neither you nor I have the courage to play with it if it was free, and what we should really cultivate is courage of that stamp. Therefore though there is friendliness, there is not love in this act of taming the cobra. Our behaviour should be such that the cobra can see through it. We see every day that all animals grasp at once whether the other party loves or fears them. Again you do not think the cobra to be venomous, and have imprisoned it in order to study its ways and habits. This is a kind of self-indulgence for which there should be no room in the case of real friendship.'

My argument appealed to Mr Kallenbach, but he could not bring himself all at once to release the cobra. I did not exercise any pressure upon him. I too was taking interest in the life of the cobra, and the children, of course, enjoyed it immensely. No one was allowed to harass the cobra, which however was casting about for some means of escape. Whether the door of the cage was inadvertently left open, or whether the cobra managed to open it, in a couple of days Mr Kallenbach found the cage empty as he one morning proceeded to call upon his friend. Mr Kallenbach was glad of it and so was I. But thanks to this taming experiment, snakes became a frequent subject of our talk. Mr Kallenbach brought to the Farm a poor and disabled German named Albrecht who was so humpbacked that he could not walk without supporting himself on a stick. Albrecht had boundless courage, and being an educated man, took deep interest in recondite problems. He too had become one with the Indian settlers and mixed freely with all. He began fearlessly to play with snakes. He would bring young snakes in his hand and let them play on his palm. If our stay on Tolstoy Farm had been further prolonged, goodness knows what would have been the upshot of Albrecht's adventures.

As a result of these experiments we did not fear snakes as much as we otherwise might have, but it must not be supposed that no one on the Farm feared serpents or that there was a total prohibition against killing them. To have a conviction that there is violence or sin in a certain course of conduct is one thing; to have the power of acting up to that conviction is quite another. A person who fears snakes and who is not ready to resign his own life cannot avoid killing snakes in case of emergency. I remember one such incident, which occurred on the Farm. The reader must already have seen that the Farm was pretty well infested with snakes. There was no human population on the Farm when we occupied it, and it had been in this deserted condition for some time. One day a snake was found in Mr Kallenbach's own room at such a place that it seemed impossible to drive it away or to catch it. One of the students saw it, and calling me there, asked me what was to be done. He wanted my permission to kill it. He could have killed it without such permission, but the settlers, whether students or others, would not generally take such a step without consulting me. I saw that it was my duty to permit the student to kill the snake, and I permitted him. Even as I am writing this, I do not feel that I did anything wrong in granting the permission. I had not the courage to seize the serpent with the hand or otherwise to remove the danger to the settlers, and I have not cultivated such courage to this day.

Needless to say, there was on the Farm an ebb and flow of Satyagrahis, some of whom would be expecting to go to prison while others had been released from it. Once it so happened that there arrived at the Farm two Satyagrahis who had been released by the Magistrate on personal recognizance and who had to attend the court the next day to receive the sentence. They were engrossed in talk, while time was up for the last train they must catch, and it was a question whether they would succeed in taking that train. They were both young men and good athletes. They ran for all that they were worth along with some of us who wanted to see them off. While still on the way, I heard the whistle of the train as it steamed into the station. When there was a second whistle indicating its departure, we had reached the precincts of the station. The young men increased their speed every moment, and I lagged behind them. The train started. Fortunately the station master saw them running up and stopped the moving train, thus enabling them to take it after all. I tendered my thanks to the station master when I reached the station. Two points emerge out of this incident; first, the eagerness of the Satyagrahis in seeking jail and in fulfilling their promises, and secondly, the sweet relations cultivated by the Satyagrahis with the local officers. If the young men had missed that train, they could not have attended the court the next day. No surety had been required of them, nor had they been asked to deposit any money with the court.

They had been released only on the word of gentlemen. The Satyagrahis had acquired such prestige that magistrates did not think it necessary to ask them for bail as they were courting jail. The young Satyagrahis therefore were deeply pained at the prospect of missing the train, and ran as swiftly as the wind. At the commencement of the struggle Satyagrahis were somewhat harassed by officials, and the jail authorities in some places were unduly severe. But as the movement advanced, we found that the bitterness of the officials was softened and in some cases even changed to sweetness. And where there was long continued intercourse with them, they even began to assist us like the station master I have referred to. The reader must not imagine that Satyagrahis bribed these officials in any shape or form in order to secure amenities from them. The Satyagrahis never thought of purchasing such irregular facilities. But where facilities were offered through courtesy, they were freely accepted, and the Satyagrahis had been enjoying such facilities in many places. If a station master is ill-disposed, he can harass passengers in a variety of ways, keeping himself all the while within the four corners of the rules and regulations. No complaint can be preferred against such harassment. On the other hand if the official is well disposed, he can grant many facilities without violating the rules. All such facilities we had been able to secure from the station master, Lawley, and that because of the courtesy, the patience and the capacity for self-suffering of the Satyagrahis.

It will not perhaps be amiss here to take note of an irrelevant incident. I have been fond for about the last thirty-five years of making experiments in dietetics from the religious, economic and hygienic standpoints. This predilection for food reform still persists. People around me would naturally be influenced by my experiments. Side by side with dietetics, I made experiments in treating diseases with natural curative agents only such as earth and water and without recourse to drugs. When I practised as a barrister, cordial relations were established with my clients so that we looked upon one another almost as members of the same family. The clients therefore made me a partner in their joys and sorrows. Some of them sought my advice being familiar with my experiments in nature cure. Stray patients of this class would sometimes arrive at Tolstoy Farm. One of these was Lutavan, and aged client who first came from North India as an indentured labourer. He was over seventy years old and suffered from chronic asthma and cough. He had given long trials to *vaidyas'* powders and doctors' mixtures. In those days I had boundless faith in the efficacy of my methods of curing disease, and therefore I agreed not indeed to treat him but to try my experiments upon him if he lived on the Farm and observed all my conditions. Lutavan complied with my conditions. One of these was that he should give up tobacco to which he was strongly addicted. I made him fast for 24 hours. At noon every day I commenced giving him a Kuhne bath in the sun, as the weather then was not extra warm. For food he had a little rice, some olive oil, honey, and along with honey, porridge and sweet oranges some times and at other times grapes and wheaten coffee. Salt and all condiments whatever were avoided. Lutavan slept in the same building as myself but in the inner apartment. For bed every one was given two blankets, one for spreading and the other for covering purposes, and a wooden pillow. A week passed. There was an accession of energy in Lutavan's body. His asthma and cough gave less trouble, but he had more fits at night than by day. I suspected he was smoking secretly, and I asked him if he did. Lutavan said he did not. A couple of days passed and as still there was no improvement, I determined to watch Lutavan secretly. Every one slept on the floor, and the place was full of snakes. Mr Kallenbach had therefore given me an electric torch and kept one himself. I always slept with this torch by my side. One night I resolved to lie in the bed awake. My bed was spread on the verandah just near the door, and Lutavan slept inside but also near the door. Lutavan coughed at midnight, lighted a cigarette and began to smoke. I slowly went up to his bed and switched on the torch. Lutavan understood everything and became nervous. He ceased smoking, stood up and touched my feet. 'I have done a great wrong,' he said. 'I will never smoke again henceforth. I have deceived you. Please excuse me.' So saying he almost began to sob. I consoled him and said that it was in his interest not to smoke. His cough should have been cured according to my calculations, and when I found that he was still suffering from it, I had suspected that he was smoking secretly. Lutavan gave up smoking. His asthma and cough grew less severe in two or three days, and in a month he was perfectly cured. He was now full of vigour and took his leave of us.

The station master's son, a child of two years, had an attack of typhoid. This gentleman too knew about my curative methods, and sought my advice. On the first day I gave the child no food at all, and from the second day onwards only half a banana well mashed with a spoonful of olive oil and a few drops of sweet orange juice. At night I applied a cold mud poultice to the child's abdomen, and in this case too my treatment was successful. It is possible that the doctor's diagnosis was wrong and it was not a case of typhoid.

I made many such experiments on the Farm, and I do not remember to have failed in even a single case. But today I would not venture to employ the same treatment. I would now shudder to have to give banana and olive oil in a case of typhoid. In 1918 I had an attack of dysentery myself and I failed to cure it. And I cannot say to this very day, whether it is due to my want of self-confidence or to the difference in climate that the same treatment which was effective in South Africa is not equally successful in India. But this I know that the home treatment of diseases and the simplicity of our life on Tolstoy Farm were responsible for a saving of at least two to three lakhs of public money. The settlers learned to look upon one another as members of the same family, the Satyagrahis secured a pure place of refuge, little scope was left for dishonesty or hypocrisy and the wheat was separated from the tares. The dietetic experiments thus far detailed were made from a hygienic standpoint, but I conducted a most important experiment upon myself which was purely spiritual in its nature.

I had pondered deeply and read widely over the question whether as vegetarians we had any right to take milk.

But when I was living on the Farm, some book or newspaper fell into my hands, in which I read about the inhuman treatment accorded to cows in Calcutta in order to extract the last drop of milk from them, and came across a description of the cruel and terrible process of *phuka*. I was once discussing with Mr Kallenbach the necessity for taking milk, and in course of the discussion, I told him about this horrible practice, pointed out several other spiritual advantages flowing from the rejection of milk, and observed that it was desirable to give up milk if it was possible. Mr Kallenbach with his usual spirit of a knight-errant was ready at once to launch upon the experiment of doing without milk, as he highly approved of my observations. The same day both he and I gave up milk, and in the end we came to restrict ourselves to a diet of fresh and dried fruit, having eschewed all cooked food as well. I may not here go into the later history of this experiment or tell of how it ended, but I may say this, that during five years of a purely fruitarian life I never felt weak, nor did I suffer from any disease. Again during the same period I possessed the fullest capacity for bodily labour, so much so that one day I walked 55 miles on foot, and 40 miles was an ordinary day's journey for me. I am firmly of opinion that this experiment yielded excellent spiritual results. It has always been a matter of regret for me that I was compelled somewhat to modify my fruitarian diet, and if I were free from my political preoccupations, even at this age of my life and at a risk to my body I would revert to it today further to explore its spiritual possibilities. The lack of spiritual insight in doctors and *vaidyas* has also been an obstacle in my path.

But I must now close this chapter of pleasant and important reminiscences. Such dangerous experiments could have their place only in a struggle of which self-purification was the very essence. Tolstoy Farm proved to be a centre of spiritual purification and penance for the final campaign. I have serious doubts as to whether the struggle could have been prosecuted for eight years, whether we could have secured larger funds, and whether the thousands of men who participated in the last phase of the struggle would have borne their share in it, if there had been no Tolstoy Farm. Tolstoy Farm was never placed in the limelight, yet an institution which deserved it attracted public sympathy to itself. The Indians saw that the Tolstoy Farmers were doing what they themselves were not prepared to do and what they looked upon in the light of hardship. This public confidence was a great asset to the movement when it was organized afresh on a large scale in 1913. One can never tell whether such assets give an account of themselves, and if yes, when. But I do not entertain and would ask the reader not to entertain, a shadow of a doubt that such latent assets do in God's good time become patent.

CHAPTER XXXVI

GOKHALE'S TOUR

Thus the Satyagrahis were pursuing the even tenor of their life on Tolstoy Farm, and preparing for whatever the future had in store for them. They did not know, nor did they care, when the struggle would end. They were only under one pledge, namely to refuse submission to the Black Act and to suffer whatever hardships were involved in such disobedience. For a fighter the fight itself is victory for he takes delight in it alone. And as it rests with him to prosecute the fight, he believes that victory or defeat, pleasure or pain, depends upon himself. There is no such word in his dictionary as pain or defeat. In the words of the Gita pleasure and pain, victory and defeat are the same to him.

Stray Satyagrahis now and then went to jail. But when there was no occasion for going to jail, any one who observed the external activities of the Farm could hardly believe that Satyagrahis were living there or that they were preparing for a struggle. When a sceptic happened to visit the Farm, if a friend he would pity us, and if a critic he would censure us. 'These fellows,' he would remark, 'have grown lazy and are therefore eating the bread of idleness in this secluded spot. They are sick of going to jail and are therefore enjoying themselves in this fruit garden away from the din and roar of cities.' How could it be explained to this critic that a Satyagrahi cannot go to jail by violating the moral law, that his very peacefulness and self-restraint constitute his preparation for 'war', and that the Satyagrahi, bestowing no thought on human help, relies upon God as his sole refuge? Finally there happened, or God brought to pass, events which no one had expected. Help also arrived which was equally unforeseen. The ordeal came all unexpected and in the end there was achieved a tangible victory which he who ran could read.

I had been requesting Gokhale and other leaders to go to South Africa and to study the condition of the Indian settlers on the spot. But I doubted whether any of them would really come over. Mr Ritch had been trying to have some Indian leader visit the sub-continent. But who would dare to go when the struggle was at a very low ebb? Gokhale was in England in 1911. He was a student of the struggle in South Africa. He had initiated debates in the Legislative Council of India and moved a resolution (February 25, 1910) in favour of prohibiting the recruitment of indentured labour for Natal, which was carried. I was in communication with him all along. He conferred with the Secretary of State for India and informed him of his intention to proceed to South Africa and acquaint himself with the facts of the case at first hand. The minister approved of Gokhale's mission. Gokhale wrote to me asking me to arrange a programme for a six weeks' tour and indicating the latest date when he must leave South Africa. We were simply overjoyed. No Indian leader had been to South Africa before or for that matter to any other place outside India where Indians had emigrated, with a view to examine their condition. We therefore realized the importance of the visit of a great leader like Gokhale and determined to accord him a reception which even princes might envy and to take him to the principal cities of South Africa. Satyagrahis and other Indians alike cheerfully set about making grand preparations of welcome. Europeans were also invited to join and did generally join the reception. We also resolved that public meetings should be held in Town Halls wherever possible and the Mayor of the place should generally occupy the chair if he consented to do so. We undertook to decorate the principal stations on the railway line and succeeded in securing the necessay permission in most cases. Such permission is not usually granted. But our grand preparations impressed the authorities, who evinced as much sympathy in the matter as they could. For instance, in Johannesburg alone the decorations at Park Station took us about a fortnight, including, as they did, a large ornamental arch of welcome designed by Mr Kallenbach.

In England itself Gokhale had a foretaste of what South Africa was like. The Secretary of State for India had informed the Union Government of Gokhale's high rank, his position in the empire etc. But who would think of booking his passage or reserving a good cabin for him? Gokhale had such delicate health that he needed a comfortable cabin where he could enjoy some privacy. The authorities of the Steamship Company roundly stated that there was no such cabin. I do not quite remember whether it was Gokhale or some friend of his who informed the India Office about this. A letter was addressed from the India Office to the directors of the Company and the best cabin was placed at Gokhale's disposal while none was available before. Good came out of this initial evil. The captain of the steamer received instructions to treat Gokhale well, and consequently he had a happy and peaceful voyage to South Africa. Gokhale was as jolly and humorous as he was serious. He participated in the various games and amusements on the steamer, and thus became very popular among his fellow passengers. The Union Government offered Gokhale their hospitality during his stay at Pretoria and placed the State railway saloon at his disposal. He consulted me on the point and then accepted the offer.

Gokhale landed at Cape Town on October 22, 1912. His health was very much more delicate than I had expected. He restricted himself to a particular diet, and he could not endure much fatigue. The programme I had framed was much too heavy for him, and I therefore cut it down as far as possible. Gokhale was ready to go through the whole programme as it originally stood if no modification was possible. I deeply repented of my folly in drawing up an onerous programme without consulting him. Some changes were made, but much had to be left as it was. I had not grasped the necessity of securing absolute privacy for Gokhale, and I had the greatest difficulty in securing it. Still I must in all humility state in the interests of truth that as I was fond of and proficient in waiting upon the sick and the elderly, as soon as I had realized my folly I revised all the arrangements so as to be able to give Gokhale great privacy and peace. I acted as his secretary throughout the tour. The volunteers, one of whom was Mr Kallenbach, were wide awake, and I do not think Gokhale underwent any discomfort or hardship for want of help. It was clear that we should have a great meeting in Cape Town. I have already written about the Schreiners. I requested Senator W. P. Schreiner, the head of that illustrious family, to take the chair on the occasion and he was good enough to consent. There was a big meeting attended by a large number of Indians and Europeans. Mr Schreiner welcomed Gokhale in well chosen words and expressed his sympathy with the Indians of South Africa. Gokhale made a speech, concise, full of sound judgment, firm but courteous, which pleased the Indians and fascinated the Europeans. In fact Gokhale won the hearts of the variegated people of South Africa on the very day that he set foot on South African soil.

From Cape Town Gokhale was to go to Johannesburg by a railway journey of two days. The Transvaal was the the field of battle. As we went from Cape Town, the first large frontier station of the Transvaal was Klerksdorp. As each of these places had a considerable population of Indians, Gokhale had to stop and attend a meeting at Klerksdorp, as well as at the intermediate stations of Potchefstroom and Krugersdorp, between Klerksdorp and Johannesburg. He therefore left Klerksdorp by a special train. The Mayors of these places presided at the meetings, and at none of the stations did the train halt longer than one or two hours. The train reached Johannesburg punctually to the miniute. On the platform there was a dais specially erected for the occasion and covered with rich carpets. Along with other Europeans there was present Mr Ellis the Mayor of Johannesburg who placed his car at Gokhale's disposal during his stay in the Golden City. An address was presented to Gokhale on the station itself. Addresses had of course been presented to him everywhere. The Johannesburg address was engraved on a solid heart-shaped plate of gold from the Rand mounted on Rhodesian teak. On the plate was a map of India and Ceylon and it was flanked on either side by two gold tablets, one bearing an illustration of the Taj Mahal and the other a characteristic Indian scene. Indian scenes were also beautifully carved on the woodwork. Introducing all present to Gokhale, reading the address, the reply, and receiving other addresses which were taken as read,—all this did not take more than twenty minutes. The address was short enough to be read in five minutes. Gokhale's reply did not occupy more than another five minutes. The volunteers maintained such excellent order, that there were no more persons on the platform than it was expected easily to accommodate. There was no noise. There was a huge crowd outside; yet no one was at all hampered in coming and going.

Gokhale was put up in a fine house belonging to Mr Kallenbach perched on a hill top five miles from Johannesburg. Gokhale liked the place immensely as the scenery there was pleasant, the atmosphere soothing, and the house though simple was full of art. A special office was hired in the city for Gokhale to receive all visitors, where there were three rooms, a private chamber for Gokhale, a drawing room, and a waiting room for visitors. Gokhale was taken to make private calls upon some distinguished men in the city. A private meeting of leading Europeans was organized so as to give Gokhale a thorough understanding of their standpoint. Besides this a banquet was held in Gokhale's honour to which were invited 400 persons including about 150 Europeans. Indians were admitted by tickets, costing a guinea each, an arrangement which enabled us to meet the expenses of the banquet. The menu was purely vegetarian and there were no wines. The cooking was attended to by volunteers. It is difficult to give an adequate idea of this here. Hindus and Musalmans in South Africa do not observe restrictions as to interdining. But the vegetarians do not take meat. Some of the Indians were Christians, with whom I was as intimate as with the rest. These Christians are mostly the descendants of indentured labourers and many of them make their living by serving in hotels as waiters. It was with the assistance of these latter that culinary arrangements could be made on such a large scale with about 15 items on the bill of fare. It was a novel and wonderful experience for the Europeans of South Africa to sit at dinner with so many Indians on the same table, to have a purely vegetarian menu and to do without wines altogether. For many of them all the three features were new while two features were new for all.

To this gathering Gokhale addressed his longest and most important speech in South Africa. In preparing this speech he subjected us to a very full examination. He declared that it had been his lifelong practice not to disregard the standpoint of local men and even to try to meet it as far as it was in his power, and therefore he asked me what I would like him to say from my own point of view. I was to put this on paper and undertake not to be offended even if he did not utilize a single word or idea from my draft, which should be neither too short nor too long, and yet which should not omit a single point of any consequence. I may say at once that Gokhale did not make any use of my language at all. Indeed I would never expect such a master of the English language as Gokhale was to take up my phraseology. I cannot even say that Gokhale adopted my ideas. But as he acknowledged the importance of my views, I took it for granted that he must have somehow incorporated my ideas into his utterances. Indeed Gokhale's train of thought was such, that one could never tell whether or not any room had there been allowed to one's own ideas. I listened to every speech made by Gokhale, but I do not remember a single occasion when I could have wished that he had not expressed a certain idea or had omitted a certain adjective. The clearness, firmness and urbanity of Gokhale's utterances flowed from his indefatigable labour and unswerving devotion to truth.

In Johannesburg we also had to hold a mass meeting of Indians only. I have always insisted on speaking either in the mother tongue or else in Hindustani, the *lingua franca* of India, and thanks to this insistence I have had much facility in establishing close relations with the Indians in South Africa. I was therefore anxious that Gokhale too should speak to the Indians in Hindustani. I was aware of Gokhale's views on the subject. Broken Hindi would not do for him, and therefore he would speak either in Marathi or in English. It seemed artificial to him to speak in Marathi in South Africa and even if he did speak in Marathi, his speech would have to be translated into Hindustani for the benefit of Gujarati and North Indian members of the audience. And that being so, where was the harm if he spoke in English? Fortunately for me, I had one argument which Gokhale would accept as conclusive in favour of his making a Marathi speech. There were many Konkani Musalmans as well as a few Maharashtra Hindus in Johannesburg, all of whom were eager to hear Gokhale speak in Marathi, and who had asked me to request Gokhale to speak in their mother tongue. I told Gokhale that these friends would be highly pleased if he spoke in Marathi and I would translate his Marathi into Hindustani. Gokhale burst into laughter and said, 'I have quite fathomed your knowledge of Hindustani, and accomplishment upon which you cannot exactly be congratulated. But now you propose to translate Marathi into Hindustani. May I know where you acquired such profound knowledge of Marathi?' I replied, 'What is true of my Hindustani is equally true of my Marathi. I cannot speak a single word of Marathi, but I am confident of gathering the purport of your Marathi speech on a subject with which I am familiar. In any case you will see that I do not misinterpret you to the people. There are others well versed in Marathi, who could act as your interpreters. But you will not perhaps approve of such arrangement. So please bear with me and do speak in Marathi. I too am desirous of hearing your Marathi speech in common with the Konkani friends.' 'You will always have your own way,' said Gokhale. 'And there is no help for me as I am here at your mercy.' So saying Gokhale fell in with my suggestion, and from this point onwards right up to Zanzibar he always spoke in Marathi at similar meetings and I served as translator by special appointment to him. I do not know if I was able to bring Gokhale round to the view, that rather than speak in perfect idiomatic English it was more desirable to speak as far as may be in the mother tongue and even in broken ungrammatical Hindi. But I do know that if only to please me he spoke in Marathi in South Africa. After he had made some speeches, I could see that he too was gratified by the results of the experiment. Gokhale by his conduct on many occasions in South Africa showed that there was merit in pleasing one's followers in cases not involving a question of principle.

CHAPTER XXXVII
GOKHALE'S TOUR (*Concluded*)

After Johannesburg Gokhale visited Natal and then proceeded to Pretoria, where he was put up by the Union Government at the Transvaal hotel. Here he was to meet the ministers of the Government, including General Botha and General Smuts. It was my usual practice to inform Gokhale of all engagements fixed for the day, early in the morning or on the previous evening if he so desired. The coming interview with the Union ministers was a most important affair. We came to the conclusion, that I should not go with Gokhale, nor indeed even offer to go. My presence would raise a sort of barrier between Gokhale and the ministers, who would be handicapped in speaking out without any reserve about what they considered to be the mistakes of the local Indians including my own. Then again they could not with an easy mind make any statement of future policy if they wished to make it. As for all these reasons Gokhale must go alone, it added largely to his burden of responsibility. What was to be done if Gokhale inadvertently committed some mistake of fact, or if he had nothing to say as regards some fact which had not been first brought to his notice, but which was first put to him by the ministers, or if he was called upon to accept some arrangement on behalf of the Indians in the absence of any one of their responsible leaders? But Gokhale resolved this difficulty at once. He asked me to prepare a summary historical statement of the condition of the Indians up to date, and also to put down in writing how far they were prepared to go. And Gokhale said that he would admit his ignorance if anything outside this 'brief' cropped up at the interview, and ceased to worry. It now only remained for me to prepare the statement and for him to read it. However it was impossible for me to narrate the vicissitudes of the Indians' history in four colonies ranging over a period of 18 years except by writing ten or twenty pages at the least, and there was hardly left any time for Gokhale to look over it. Again there would be many questions he would like to put us after reading the paper. But Gokhale had an infinite capacity for taking pains as he had an exceptionally sharp memory. He kept himself and others awake the whole night, posted himself fully on every point, and went over the whole ground again in order to make sure that he had rightly understood everything. He was at last satisfied. As for me I never had any fears.

Gokhale's interview with the ministers lasted for about two hours, and when he returned, he said, 'You must return to India in a year. Everything has been settled. The Black Act will be repealed. The racial bar will be removed from the emigration law. The £ 3 tax will be abolished.' 'I doubt it very much,' I replied. 'You do not know the ministers as I do. Being an optimist myself, I love your optimism, but having suffered frequent disappointments, I am not as hopeful in the matter as you are. But I have no fears either. It is enough for me that you have obtained this undertaking from the ministers. It is my duty to fight it out only where it is necessary and to demonstrate that ours is a righteous struggle. The promise given to you will serve as a proof of the justice of our demands and will redouble our fighting spirit if it comes to fighting after all. But I do not think I can return to India in a year and before many more Indians have gone to jail.'

Gokhale said: 'What I have told you is bound to come to pass. General Botha promised me that the Black Act would be repealed and the £ 3 tax abolished. You must return to India within twelve months, and I will not have any of your excuses.'

During his visit to Natal Gokhale came in contact with many Europeans in Durban, Maritzburg and other places. He also saw the diamond mines in Kimberley, where as well as at Durban public dinners were arranged by the reception committees, and attended by many Europeans. Thus having achieved a conquest of Indian as well as European hearts, Gokhale left South Africa on November 17, 1912. At his wish Mr Kallenbach and I accompanied him as far as Zanzibar. On the steamer we had arranged to have suitable food for him. On his way back to India he was given an ovation at Delagoa Bay, Inhambane, Zanzibar and other ports.

On the steamer our talks were confined to India or to the duty we owed to the motherland. Every word of Gokhale glowed with his tender feeling, truthfulness and patriotism. I observed that even in the games which he played on board the steamer Gokhale had a patriotic motive rather than the mere desire to amuse himself, and excellence was his aim there too.

On the steamer we had ample time to talk to our heart's content. In these conversations Gokhale prepared me for India. He analysed for me the characters of all the leaders in India and his analysis was so accurate, that I have hardly perceived any difference between Gokhale's estimate and my own personal experience of them.

There are many sacred reminiscences of mine relating to Gokhale's tour in South Africa which could be set down here. But I must reluctantly check my pen as they are not relevant to a history of Satyagraha. The parting at Zanzibar was deeply painful to Kallenbach and me, but remembering that the most intimate relations of mortal men must come to an end at last, we somehow reconciled ourselves, and hoped that Gokhale's prophecy would come true and both of us would be able to go to India in a year's time. But that was not to be.

However Gokhale's visit to South Africa stiffened our resolution, and the implications and the importance of his tour were better understood when the struggle was renewed in an active form. If Gokhale had not come over to South Africa, if he had not seen the Union ministers, the abolition of the £ 3 tax could not have been made a plank in our platform.

If the Satyagraha struggle had closed with the repeal of the Black Act, a fresh fight would have been necessary against the £ 3 tax, and not only would the Indians have come in for endless trouble, but it was doubtful whether they would have been ready so soon for a new and arduous campaign. It was incumbent upon the free Indians to have the tax abolished. All constitutional remedies to that end had been applied but in vain. The tax was being paid ever since 1895. But when a wrong, no matter how flagrant, has continued for a long period of time, people get habituated to it, and it becomes difficult to rouse them to a sense of their duty to resist it, and no less difficult to convince the world that it is a wrong at all. The undertaking given to Gokhale cleared the way for the Satyagrahis. The Government must repeal the tax in terms of their promise, and if they did not, their breach of pledge would be a most cogent reason for continuing the struggle. And this was exactly what happened. Not only did the Government not abolish the tax within a year, but they declared in so many words that it could not be removed at all.

Gokhale's tour thus not only helped us to make the £ 3 tax one of the targets of our Satyagraha, but it led to his being recognized as a special authority on the South African question. His views on South Africa now carried greater weight, thanks to his personal knowledge of the Indians in South Africa, and he understood himself and could explain to India what steps the mother country ought to adopt. When the struggle was resumed, India rendered munificent help to the Satyagraha funds and Lord Hardinge heartened the Satyagrahis by expressing his 'deep and burning' sympathy for them (December 1913). Messrs Andrews and Pearson came to South Africa from India. All this would have been impossible without Gokhale's mission.

The breach of the ministers' pledge and its consequences will be the subject of the next chapter.

CHAPTER XXXVIII
BREACH OF PLEDGE

In prosecuting the Satyagraha struggle the Indians were very careful not to take a single step not warranted by their principles, and they always remembered that they should not take any illegitimate advantage over the Government. For instance, as the Black Act was restricted in its application to Indians in the Transvaal, only the Transvaal Indians were admitted as recruits in the struggle. Not only was there no attempt made to obtain recruits from Natal, the Cape Colony etc., but offers from outside the Transvaal were politely refused. The struggle also was limited to a repeal of the Act in question. This limitation was understood neither by the Europeans nor by Indians. In the early stages the Indians were every now and then asking for other grievances besides the Black Act to be covered by the struggle. I patiently explained to them that such extension would be a violation of the truth, which could not be so much as thought of in a movement professing to abide by truth and truth alone. In a pure fight the fighters would never go beyond the objective fixed when the fight began even if they received an accession to their strength in course of the fighting, and on the other hand they could not give up their objective if they found their strength dwindling away. This twofold principle was fully observed in South Africa. The strength of the community, upon which we counted in determining our goal at the commencement of the struggle, did not answer our expectations as we have already seen, and yet the handful of Satyagrahis who remained stuck to their posts. Fighting thus single-handed in the face of odds was comparatively easy, but it was more difficult, and called for the exercise of greater self-restraint, not to enlarge one's objective when one had received large reinforcements. Such temptations often faced us in South Africa, but I can emphatically declare that we did not succumb to them in any single case. And therefore I have often said that a Satyagrahi has a single objective from which he cannot recede and beyond which he cannot advance, which can in fact be neither augmented nor abridged. The world learns to apply to a man the standards which he applies to himself. When the Government saw, that the Satyagrahis claimed to follow these fine principles, they began to judge the conduct of the Satyagrahis in the light of those principles, although they themselves were apparently not bound by any principle whatever, and several times charged the Satyagrahis with a violation of their principles. Even a child can see that if fresh anti-Indian legislation was enacted after the Black Act, it must be included in the Satyagraha programme. And yet when fresh restrictions were imposed on Indian immigration and necessitated an extension of our programme, the Government levelled against us the totally undeserved charge of raising fresh issues. If new restraints were placed on Indian newcomers, we must have the right to recruit them for the movement, and hence Sorabji and others entered the Transvaal, as we have already seen. Government could not tolerate this at all, but I had no difficulty in persuading impartial people about the propriety of the step. Another such occasion arose after Gokhale's departure. Gokhale supposed that the £ 3 tax would be taken off in a year and the necessary legislation would be introduced in the next ensuing session of the Union Parliament. Instead of this, General Smuts from his seat in the House of Assembly said that as the Europeans in Natal objected to the repeal of the tax, the Union Government were unable to pass legislation directing its removal, which however was not the case. The members from Natal by themselves could do nothing in a body upon which the four Colonies were represented. Again General Smuts ought to have brought forward the necessary Bill in the Assembly on behalf of the Cabinet and then left the measure to its fate. But he did nothing of the kind, and provided us with the welcome opportunity of including the despicable impost as a cause of 'war.' There were two reasons for this. First, if in course of the struggle the Government made a promise and then went back upon it, the programme would naturally be extended so as to embrace such repudiation as well, and secondly, the breach of a promise, made to such a representative of India as Gokhale was, was not only a personal insult to him but also to the whole of India, and as such could not be taken lying down. If there had been only one reason, namely the first by itself, the Satyagrahis, in case they felt themselves unequal to the task, could have been excused if they did not offer Satyagraha against the £ 3 tax. But it was impossible to pocket an insult offered to the mother country, and therefore we felt the Satyagrahis were bound to include the £ 3 tax in their programme, and when this tax thus fell within the scope of the struggle, the indentured Indians had an opportunity of participating in it. The reader must note that thus far this class had been kept out of the fray. This new orientation of our policy increased our burden of responsibility on the one hand, and on the other opened up a fresh field of recruitment for our 'army.'

Thus far Satyagraha had not been so much as mentioned among the indentured labourers; still less had they been educated to take part in it. Being illiterate, they could not read *Indian Opinion* or other newspapers. Yet I found that these poor folk were keen observers of the struggle and understood the movement, while some of them regretted their inability to join it. But when the Union ministers broke their pledged word, and repeal of the £ 3 tax was also included in our programme, I was not at all aware as to which of them would participate in the struggle.

wrote to Gokhale about the breach of pledge, and he was deeply pained to hear of it. I asked him not to be anxious and assured him that we would fight unto death and wring a repeal of the tax out of the unwilling hands of the Transvaal Government. The idea, however, of my returning to India in a year had to be abandoned, and it was impossible to say when I would be able to go. Gokhale was nothing if not a man of figures. He asked me to let him know the maximum and the minimum strength of our army of peace, along with the names of the fighters. As far as I can now remember, I sent 65 or 66 names as the highest and 16 as the lowest number, and also informed Gokhale that I would not expect monetary assistance from India for such small numbers. I besought him to have no fears and not to put an undue strain upon his physical resources. I had learnt from newspapers and otherwise that after Gokhale returned to Bombay from South Africa, charges of weakness etc. had been laid at his door. I therefore wished that Gokhale should not try to raise any funds for us in India. But this was his stern answer: 'We in India have some idea of our duty even as you understand your obligations in South Africa. We will not permit you to tell us what is or is not proper for us to do. I only desired to know the position in South Africa, but did not seek your advice as to what we may do.' I grasped Gokhale's meaning, and never afterwards said or wrote a word on the subject. In the same letter he gave me consolation and caution. He was afraid in view of the breach of pledge that it would be a long protracted struggle, and he doubted how long a handful of men could continue to give battle to the insolent brute force of the Union Government. In South Africa we set about making our preparations. There could be no sitting at ease in the ensuing campaign. It was realized that we would be imprisoned for long terms It was decided to close Tolstoy Farm. Some families returned to their homes upon the release of the breadwinners. The rest mostly belonged to Phoenix, which therefore was pitched upon as the future base of operations for the Satyagrahis. Another reason for preferring Phoenix was, that if the indentured labourers joined the struggle against the £ 3 tax, it would be more convenient to meet them from a place in Natal.

While preparations were still being made for resuming the struggle, a fresh grievance came into being, which afforded an opportunity even to women to do their bit in the struggle. Some brave women had already offered to participate, and when Satyagrahis went to jail for hawking without a licence, their wives had expressed a desire to follow suit. But we did not then think it proper to send women to jail in a foreign land. There seemed to be no adequate reason for sending them into the firing line, and I for my part could not summon courage enough to take them to the front. Another argument was, that it would be derogatory to our manhood if we sacrificed our women in resisting a law which was directed only against men. But an event now happened, which involved a special affront to women, and which therefore left no doubt in our minds as to the propriety of sacrificing them.

CHAPTER XXXIX

WHEN MARRIAGE IS NOT A MARRIAGE

As if unseen by any one God was preparing the ingredients for the Indians' victory and demonstrating still more clearly the injustice of the Europeans in South Africa, an event happened which none had expected. Many married men came to South Africa from India, while some Indians contracted a marriage in South Africa itself. There is no law for the registration of ordinary marriages in India, and the religious ceremony suffices to confer validity upon them. The same custom ought to apply to Indians in South Africa as well and although Indians had settled in South Africa for the last forty years, the validity of marriages solemnized according to the rites of the various religions of India had never been called in question. But at this time there was a case in which Mr Justice Searle of the Cape Supreme Court gave judgment on March 14, 1913 to the effect that all marriages were outside the pale of legal marriages in South Africa with the exception of such as were celebrated according to Christian rites and registered by the Registrar of Marriages. This terrible judgment thus nullified in South Africa at a stroke of the pen all marriages celebrated according to the Hindu, Musalman and Zoroastrian rites. The many married Indian women in South Africa in terms of this judgment ceased to rank as the wives of their husbands and were degraded to the rank of concubines, while their progeny were deprived of their right to inherit the parent's property. This was an insufferable situation for women no less than men, and the Indians in South Africa were deeply agitated.

According to my usual practice I wrote to the Government, asking them whether they agreed to the Searle judgment and whether, if the judge was right in interpreting it, they would amend the law so as to recognize the validity of Indian marriages consecrated according to the religious customs of the parties and recognized as legal in India. The Government were not then in a mood to listen and could not see their way to comply with my request.

The Satyagraha Association held a meeting to consider whether they should appeal against the Searle judgment, and came to the conclusion that no appeal was possible on a question of this nature. If there was to be an appeal, it must be preferred by Government, or if they so desired, by the Indians provided that the Government openly sided with them through their Attorney General. To appeal when these conditions were not satisfied would be in a way tantamount to tolerating the invalidation of Indian marriages. Satyagraha would have to be resorted to, even if such an appeal was made and if it was rejected. In these circumstances therefore it seemed best not to prefer any appeal against this unspeakable insult.

A crisis now arrived, when there could not be any waiting for an auspicious day or hour. Patience was impossible in the face of this insult offered to our womanhood. We decided to offer stubborn Satyagraha irrespective of the number of fighters. Not only could the women now be not prevented from joining the struggle, but we decided even to invite them to come into line along with the men. We first invited the sisters who had lived on Tolstoy Farm. I found that they were only too glad to enter the struggle.

WHEN MARRIAGE IS NOT A MARRIAGE

I gave them an idea of the risks incidental to such participation. I explained to them that they would have to put up with restraints in the matter of food, dress and personal movements. I warned them that they might be given hard work in jail, made to wash clothes and even subjected to insult by the warders. But these sisters were all brave and feared none of these things. One of them was pregnant while six of them had young babies in arms. But one and all were eager to join and I simply could not come in their way. These sisters were with one exception all Tamilians. Here are their names:

1. Mrs Thambi Naidoo, 2. Mrs N. Pillay, 3. Mrs K. Murugasa Pillay, 4. Mrs A. Perumal Naidoo, 5. Mrs P. K. Naidoo, 6. Mrs K. Chinnaswami Pillay, 7. Mrs N. S. Pillay, 8. Mrs R. A. Mudalingam, 9. Mrs Bhavani Dayal, 10. Miss Minachi Pillay, 11. Miss Baikum Murugasa Pillay.

It is easy to get into prison by committing a crime but it is difficult to get in by being innocent. As the criminal seeks to escape arrest, the police pursue and arrest him. But they lay their hands upon the innocent man who courts arrest of his own free will only when they cannot help it. The first attempts of these sisters were not crowned with success. They entered the Transvaal at Vereeniging without permits, but they were not arrested. They took to hawking without a licence, but still the police ignored them. It now became a problem with the women how they should get arrested. There were not many men ready to go to jail and those who were ready could not easily have their wish.

We now decided to take a step which we had reserved till the last, and which in the event fully answered our expectations. I had contemplated sacrificing all the settlers in Phoenix at a critical period. That was to be my final offering to the God of Truth. The settlers at Phoenix were mostly my close co-workers and relations. The idea was to send all of them to jail with the exception of a few who would be required for the conduct of *Indian Opinion* and of children below sixteen. This was the maximum of sacrifice open to me in the circumstances. This sixteen stalwarts to whom I had referred in writing to Gokhale were among the pioneers of the Phoenix settlement. It was proposed that these friends should cross over into the Transvaal and as they crossed over, get arrested for entering the country without permits. We were afraid that Government would not arrest them if we made a previous announcement of our intention, and therefore we guarded it as a secret except from a couple of friends. When the pioneers entered the Transvaal, the police officer would ask them their names and addresses, and it was part of the programme not to supply this information as there was an apprehension that if their identity was disclosed, the police would come to know that they were my relations and therefore would not arrest them. Refusal to give name and address to an officer was also held to be a separate offence. While the Phoenix group entered the Transvaal, the sisters who had courted arrest in the Transvaal in vain were to enter Natal. As it was an offence to enter the Transvaal from Natal without a permit it was equally an offence to enter Natal from the Transvaal. If the sisters were arrested upon entering Natal, well and good. But if they were not arrested, it was arranged that they should proceed to and post themselves at Newcastle, the great coal-mining centre in Natal, and advise the indentured Indian labourers there to go on strike. The mother tongue of the sisters was Tamil, and they could speak a little Hindustani besides. The majority of labourers on the coal mines hailed from Madras State and spoke Tamil or Telugu, though there were many from North India as well. If the labourers struck in response to the sisters' appeal, Government was bound to arrest them along with the labourers, who would thereby probably be fired with still greater enthusiasm. This was the strategy I thought out and unfolded before the Transvaal sisters.

I went to Phoenix, and talked to the settlers about my plans. First of all I held a consultation with the sisters living there. I knew that the step of sending women to jail was fraught with serious risk. Most of the sisters in Phoenix spoke Gujarati. They had not had the training or experience of the Transvaal sisters. Moreover, most of them were related to me, and might think of going to jail

WHEN MARRIAGE IS NOT A MARRIAGE 255

only on account of my influence with them. If afterwards they flinched at the time of actual trial or could not stand the jail, they might be led to apologize, thus not only giving me a deep shock but also causing serious damage to the movement. I decided not to broach the subject to my wife, as she could not say no to any proposal I made, and if she said yes, I would not know what value to attach to her assent, and as I knew that in a serious matter like this the husband should leave the wife to take what step she liked on her own initiative, and should not be offended at all even if she did not take any step whatever. I talked to the other sisters who readily fell in with my proposal and expressed their readiness to go to jail. They assured me that they would complete their term in jail, come what might. My wife overheard my conversation with the sisters, and addressing me, said, "I am sorry that you are not telling me about this. What defect is there in me which disqualifies me for jail? I also wish to take the path to which you are inviting the others." "You know I am the last person to cause you pain," I replied. "There is no question of my distrust in you. I would be only too glad if you went to jail, but it should not appear at all as if you went at my instance. In matters like this every one should act relying solely upon one's own strength and courage. If I asked you, you might be inclined to go just for the sake of complying with my request. And then if you began to tremble in the law court or were terrified by hardships in jail, I could not find fault with you, but how would it stand with me? How could I then harbour you or look the world in the face? It is fears like these which have prevented me from asking you too to court jail." "You may have nothing to do with me," she said, "if being unable to stand jail I secure my release by an apology. If you can endure hardships and so can my boys, why cannot I? I am bound to join the struggle." "Then I am bound to admit you to it," said I. "You know my conditions and you know my temperament. Even now reconsider the matter if you like, and if after mature thought you deliberately come to the conclusion not to join the movement, you are free to withdraw. And you must understand that there is nothing to be ashamed of in changing your decision even now."

"I have nothing to think about, I am fully determined," she said.

I suggested to the other settlers also that each should take his or her decision independently of all others. Again and again, and in a variety of ways I pressed this condition on their attention that none should fall away whether the struggle was short or long, whether the Phoenix settlement flourished or faded, and whether he or she kept good health or fell ill in jail. All were ready. The only member of the party from outside Phoenix was Rustomji Jivanji Ghorkhodu, from whom these conferences could not be concealed, and Kakaji, as he was affectionately called, was not the man to lag behind on an occasion like the present. He had already been to jail, but he insisted upon paying it another visit. The 'invading' party was composed of the following members:

1. Mrs Kasturbai Gandhi, 2. Mrs Jayakunvar Manilal Doctor, 3. Mrs Kashi Chhaganlal Gandhi, 4. Mrs Santok Maganlal Gandhi, 5. Parsi Rustomji Jivanji Ghorkhodu, 6. Chhaganlal Khushalchand Gandhi, 7. Ravjibhai Manibhai Patel, 8. Maganbhai Haribhai Patel, 9. Solomon Royeppen, 10. Raju Govindu, 11. Ramdas Mohandas Gandhi, 12. Shivpujan Badari, 13. V. Govindarajulu, 14. Kuppuswami Moonlight Mudaliar, 15. Gokuldas Hansraj, and 16. Revashankar Ratansi Sodha.

The sequel must be taken up in a fresh chapter.

CHAPTER XL
WOMEN IN JAIL

These 'invaders' were to go to jail for crossing the border and entering the Transvaal without permits. The reader who has seen the list of their names will have observed, that if some of them were disclosed beforehand, the police might not perhaps arrest the persons bearing them. Such in fact had been the case with me. I was arrested twice or thrice but after this the police ceased to meddle with me at the border. No one was informed of this party having started and the news was of course withheld from the papers. Moreover the party had been instructed not to give their names even to the police and to state that they would disclose their identity in court.

The police were familiar with cases of this nature. After the Indians got into the habit of courting arrest, they would often not give their names just for the fun of the thing, and the police therefore did not notice anything strange about the behaviour of the Phoenix party, which was arrested accordingly. They were then tried and sentenced to three months' imprisonment with hard labour (September 23, 1913).

The sisters who had been disappointed in the Transvaal now entered Natal but were not arrested for entering the country without permits. They therefore proceeded to Newcastle and set about their work according to the plans previously settled. Their influence spread like wildfire. The pathetic story of the wrongs heaped up by the £ 3 tax touched the labourers to the quick, and they went on strike. I received the news by wire and was as much perplexed as I was pleased. What was I to do? I was not prepared for this marvellous awakening. I had neither men nor the money which would enable me to cope with the work before me. But I visualized my duty very clearly. I must go to Newcastle and do what I could. I left at once to go there.

Government could not now any longer leave the brave Transvaal sisters free to pursue their activities. They too were sentenced to imprisonment for the same term—three months—and were kept in the same prison as the Phoenix party (October 21, 1913).

These events stirred the heart of the Indians not only in South Africa but also in the motherland to its very depths. Sir Pherozeshah had been so far indifferent. In 1901 he had strongly advised me not to go to South Africa. He held that nothing could be done for Indian emigrants beyond the seas so long as India had not achieved her own freedom, and he was little impressed with the Satyagraha movement in its initial stages. But women in jail pleaded with him as nothing else could. As he himself put it in his Bombay Town Hall speech, his blood boiled at the thought of these women lying in jails herded with ordinary criminals and India could not sleep over the matter any longer.

The women's bravery was beyond words. They were all kept in Maritzburg jail, where they were considerably harassed. Their food was of the worst quality and they were given laundry work as their task. No food was permitted to be given them from outside nearly till the end of their term. One sister was under a religious vow to restrict herself to a particular diet. After great difficulty the jail authorities allowed her that diet, but the food supplied was unfit for human consumption. The sister badly needed olive oil. She did not get it at first, and when she got it, it was old and rancid. She offered to get it at her own expense but was told that jail was no hotel, and she must take what food was given her. When this sister was released she was a mere skeleton and her life was saved only by a great effort.

Another returned from jail with a fatal fever to which she succumbed within a few days of her release (February 22, 1914). How can I forget her? Valliamma R. Munuswami Mudaliar was a young girl of Johannesburg only sixteen years of age. She was confined to bed when I saw her. As she was a tall girl, her emaciated body was a terrible thing to behold.

"Valliamma, you do not repent of your having gone to jail?" I asked.

"Repent? I am even now ready to go to jail again if I am arrested," said Valliamma.

"But what if it results in your death?" I pursued.

"I do not mind it. Who would not love to die for one's motherland?" was the reply.

Within a few days after this conversation Valliamma was no more with us in the flesh, but she left us the heritage of an immortal name. Condolence meetings were held at various places, and the Indians resolved to erect 'Valliamma Hall', to commemorate the supreme sacrifice of this daughter of India. Unfortunately the resolution has not still been translated into action. There were many difficulties. The community was torn by internal dissensions; the principal workers left one after another. But whether or not a hall is built in stone and mortar, Valliamma's service is imperishable. She built her temple of service with her own hands, and her glorious image has a niche even now reserved for it in many a heart. And the name of Valliamma will live in the history of South African Satyagraha as long as India lives.

It was an absolutely pure sacrifice that was offered by these sisters, who were innocent of legal technicalities, and many of whom had no idea of country, their patriotism being based only upon faith. Some of them were illiterate and could not read the papers. But they knew that a mortal blow was being aimed at the Indians' honour, and their going to jail was a cry of agony and prayer offered from the bottom of their heart, was in fact the purest of all sacrifices. Such heart prayer is always acceptable to God. Sacrifice is fruitful only to the extent that it is pure. God hungers after devotion in man. He is glad to accept the widow's mite offered with devotion, that is to say, without a selfish motive, and rewards it a hundredfold. The unsophisticated Sudama offered a handful of rice, but the small offering put an end to many years' want and starvation. The imprisonment of many might have been fruitless but the devoted sacrifice of a single pure soul could never go in vain. None can tell whose sacrifice in South

Africa was acceptable to God, and hence bore fruit. But we do know that Valliamma's sacrifice bore fruit and so did the sacrifice of the other sisters.

Souls without number spent themselves in the past, are spending themselves in the present and will spend themselves in the future in the service of country and humanity, and that is in the fitness of things as no one knows who is pure. But Satyagrahis may rest assured, that even if there is only one among them who is pure as crystal, his sacrifice suffices to achieve the end in view. The world rests upon the bedrock of *satya* or truth. *Asatya* meaning untruth also means non-existent, and *satya* or truth also means that which *is*. If untruth does not so much as exist, its victory is out of the question. And truth being that which *is* can never be destroyed. This is the doctrine of Satyagraha in a nutshell.

CHAPTER XLI
A STREAM OF LABOURERS

The women's imprisonment worked like a charm upon the labourers on the mines near Newcastle who downed their tools and entered the city in succeeding batches. As soon as I received the news, I left Phoenix for Newcastle.

These labourers have no houses of their own. The mine-owners erect houses for them, set up lights upon their roads, and supply them with water, with the result that the labourers are reduced to a state of utter dependence. And as Tulsidas put it, a dependent cannot hope for happiness even in a dream.

The strikers brought quite a host of complaints to me. Some said the mine-owners had stopped their lights or their water, while others stated that they had thrown away the strikers' household chattels from their quarters. Saiyad Ibrahim, a Pathan, showed his back to me and said, "Look here, how severely they have thrashed me. I have let the rascals go for your sake, as such are your orders. I am a Pathan, and Pathans never take but give a beating."

"Well done, brother," I replied. "I look upon such conduct alone as pure bravery. We will win through people of your type."

I thus congratulated him, but thought to myself that the strike could not continue if many received the same treatment as the Pathan did. Leaving the question of flogging aside, there was not much room for complaint if the collieries cut off the lights, the water supply and other amenities enjoyed by the strikers. But whether or not complaint was justified, the strikers could not hold on in the circumstances, and I must find a way out of the difficulty, or else it was very much to be preferred that they should own themselves to be defeated and return to work at once rather than that they should resume work after a period of weary waiting. But defeatist counsel was not in my line. I therefore suggested that the only possible course was for the labourers to leave their masters' quarters, to fare forth in fact like pilgrims.

The labourers were not to be counted by tens but by hundreds. And their number might easily swell into thousands. How was I to house and feed this ever growing multitude? I would not appeal to India for monetary help. The river of gold which later on flowed from the motherland had not yet started on its course. Indian traders were mortally afraid and not at all ready to help me publicly, as they had trading relations with the coal-owners and other Europeans. Whenever I went to Newcastle, I used to stop with them. But this time, as I would place them in an awkward position, I resolved to put up at another place.

As I have already stated, the Transvaal sisters were most of them Tamilians. They had taken up their quarters in Newcastle with Mr D. Lazarus, a middle-class Christian Tamilian, who owned a small plot of land and a house consisting of two or three rooms. I also decided to put up with this family, who received me with open arms. The poor have no fears. My host belonged to a family of indentured labourers, and hence he .. or his relations would be liable to pay the £ 3 tax. No wonder he and his people would be familiar with the woes of indentured labourers and would therefore deeply sympathize with them. It has never been easy for friends to harbour me under their roof, but to receive me now was tantamount to inviting financial ruin upon one's head or perhaps even to facing imprisonment. Very few well-to-do traders would like to place themselves in a like predicament. I realized their limitations as well as my own, and therefore remained at a respectable distance from them. Poor Lazarus would sacrifice some wages if it came to that. He would be willingly cast into prison, but how could he tolerate the wrongs heaped upon indentured labourers still poorer than himself? Lazarus saw that the Transvaal sisters who had been his guests went to the indentured labourers' succour and suffered imprisonment in the act of doing so. He realized that he owed a debt of duty to the labourers too and therefore gave me shelter at his place. He not only sheltered me but he devoted his all to the cause. My stopping there converted his house into a caravanserai. All sorts and conditions of men would come and go and the premises at all times would present the appearance of an ocean of heads. The kitchen fire would know no rest day and night. Mrs Lazarus would drudge like a slave all day long, and yet her face as well as her husband's would always be lit up with a smile as with perpetual sunshine.

But Lazarus could not feed hundreds of labourers. I suggested to the labourers, that they should take it that their strike was to last for all time and leave the quarters provided by their masters. They must sell such of their goods as could find a purchaser. The rest they must leave in their quarters. The coal-owners would not touch their belongings, but if with a view to wreak further revenge upon them they threw them away on the streets, the labourers must take that risk as well. When they came to me, they should bring nothing with them except their wearing apparel and blankets. I promised to live and have my meals with them so long as the strike lasted and so long as they were outside jail. They could sustain their strike and win a victory if and only if they came out on these conditions. Those who could not summon courage enough to take this line of action should return to work. None should despise or harass those who thus resumed their work. None of the labourers demurred to my conditions. From the very day that I made this announcement, there was a continuous stream of pilgrims who 'retired from the household life to the houseless one' along with their wives and children with bundles of clothes upon their heads.

I had no means of housing them; the sky was the only roof over their heads. Luckily for us the weather was favourable, there being neither rain nor cold. I was confident that the trader class would not fail to feed us. The traders of Newcastle supplied cooking pots and bags of rice and *dal*. Other places also showered rice, *dal*, vegetables, condiments and other things upon us. The contributions exceeded my expectations. Not all were ready to go to jail, but all felt for the cause, and all were willing to bring their quota to the movement to the best of their ability. Those who could not give anything served as volunteer workers. Well-known and intelligent volunteers were required to look after these obscure and uneducated men, and they were forthcoming. They rendered priceless help, and many of them were also arrested. Thus every one did what he could, and smoothed our path.

There was a huge concourse of men, which was continuously receiving accessions. It was a dangerous if not an impossible task to keep them in one place and look after them while they had no employment. They were generally ignorant of the laws of sanitation. Some of them had been to jail for criminal offences such as murder, theft or adulttery. But I did not consider myself fit to sit in judgment over the morality of the strikers. It would have been silly for me to attempt at distinguishing between the goats and the sheep. My business was only to conduct the strike, which could not be mixed up with any other reforming activity. I was indeed bound to see that the rules of morality were observed in the camp, but it was not for me to inquire into the antecedents of each striker. There were bound to be crimes if such a heterogeneous multitude was pinned down to one place without any work to do. The wonder was that the few days that we stopped here like that passed without any incident. All were quiet as if they had thoroughly grasped the gravity of the situation.

I thought out a solution of my problem. I must take this 'army' to the Transvaal and see them safely deposited in jail like the Phoenix party. The army should be divided into small batches, each of which should cross the border separately. But I dropped this last idea as soon as it was formed as it would have taken too long a time in its execution, and the successive imprisonment of small batches would not produce the normal effect of a mass movement.

The strength of the 'army' was about five thousand. I had not the money to pay the railway fare for such a large number of persons, and therefore they could not all be taken by rail. And if they were taken by rail, I would be without the means of putting their morale to the test. The Transvaal border is 36 miles from Newcastle. The border villages of Natal and the Transvaal are Charlestown and Volksrust respectively. I finally decided to march on foot. I consulted the labourers who had their wives and children with them and some of whom therefore hesitated to agree to my proposal. I had no alternative except to harden my heart, and declared that those who wished were free to return to the mines. But none of them would avail themselves of this liberty. We decided that those who were disabled in their limbs should be sent by rail, and all able-bodied persons announced their readiness to go to Charlestown on foot. The march was to be accomplished in two days. In the end every one was glad that the move was made. The labourers realized that it would be some relief to poor Lazarus and his family. The Europeans in Newcastle anticipated an outbreak of plague, and were anxious to take all manner of steps in order to prevent it. By making a move we restored to them their peace of mind and also saved ourselves from the irksome measures to which they would have subjected us.

While preparations for the march were on foot, I received an invitation to meet the coal-owners and I went to Durban. This conference and the events subsequent thereto will be considered in the next chapter.

CHAPTER XLII
THE CONFERENCE AND AFTER

At their invitation I saw the mine-owners in Durban. I observed that they were somewhat impressed by the strike, but I did not expect anything big to come out of the conference. The humility of a Satyagrahi however knows no bounds. He does not let slip a single opportunity for settlement, and he does not mind if any one therefore looks upon him as timid. The man who has faith in him and the strength which flows from faith, does not care if he is looked down upon by others. He relies solely upon his internal strength. He is therefore courteous to all, and thus cultivates and enlists world opinion in favour of his own cause.

I therefore welcomed the coal-owners' invitation and when I met them, I saw that the atmosphere was surcharged with the heat and passion of the moment. Instead of hearing me explain the situation, their representative proceeded to cross-examine me. I gave him suitable answers.

'It is in your hands to bring the strike to an end,' I said.

'We are not officials,' was the reply.

'You can do a deal though you are not officials,' I said. 'You can fight the labourers' battle for them. If you ask the Government to take off the £3 tax, I do not think they will refuse to repeal it. You can also educate European opinion on the question.'

'But what has the £3 tax to do with the strike? If the labourers have any grievance against the coal-owners, you approach them for redress in due form.'

'I do not see that the labourers have any other weapon except a strike in their hands. The £3 tax too has been imposed in the interest of the mine-owners who want the labourers to work for them but do not wish that they should work as free men. If therefore the labourers strike work in order to secure a repeal of the £3 tax, I do not see that it involves any impropriety or injustice to the mine-owners.'

'You will not then advise the labourers to return to work?'

'I am sorry I can't.'

'Do you know what will be the consequences?'

'I know, I have a full sense of my responsibility.'

'Yes, indeed. You have nothing to lose. But will you compensate the misguided labourers for the damage you will cause them?'

'The labourers have gone on strike after due deliberation, and with a full consciousness of the losses which would accrue to them. I cannot conceive a greater loss to a man than the loss of his self-respect, and it is a matter of deep satisfaction to me that the labourers have realized this fundamental principle.'

And so on. I cannot now remember the whole of the conversation. I have put down in brief the points which I do remember. I saw that the mine-owners understood the weakness of their case, for they had already put themselves in communication with the Government.

During my journey to Durban and back I saw that the strike and the peaceful behaviour of the strikers had produced an excellent impression upon the railway guards and others. I travelled in third class as usual, but even there the guard and other officers would surround me, make diligent inquiries and wish me success. They would provide me with various minor facilities. I scrupulously maintained the spotless purity of my relations with them. I did not hold out any inducement to them for a single amenity. I was delighted if they were courteous of their own free will, but no attempt was made to purchase courtesy. These officers were astonished to find that poor, illiterate and ignorant labourers made such a splendid display of firmness. Firmness and courage are qualities which are bound to leave their impress even upon the adversary.

I returned to Newcastle. Labourers were still pouring in from all directions. I clearly explained the whole situation to the 'army.' I said they were still free to return to work if they wished. I told them about the threats held out by the coal-owners, and pictured before them the risks of the future. I pointed out that no one could tell them when the struggle would end. I described to the men the hardships of jail, and yet they would not flinch. They fearlessly replied, that they would never be down-hearted so long as I was fighting by their side, and they asked me not to be anxious about them as they were inured to hardships.

It was now only left for us to march. The labourers were informed one evening that they were to commence the march early next morning (October 28, 1913), and the rules to be observed on the march were read to them. It was no joke to control a multitude of five or six thousand men. I had no idea of the exact number, nor did I know their names or places of residence. I was merely content with as many of them as chose to remain. I could not afford to give anything on the road beyond a daily ration of one pound and a half of bread and an ounce of sugar to each 'soldier.' I planned to get something more from the Indian traders on the way. But if I failed they must rest content with bread and sugar. My experience of the Boer War and the Zulu 'rebellion' stood me in good stead on the present occasion. None of the 'invaders' was to keep with him any more clothes than necessary. None was to touch any one's property on the way. They were to bear it patiently if any official or non-official European met them and abused or even flogged them. They were to allow themselves to be arrested if the police offered to arrest them. The march must continue even if I was arrested. All these points were explained to the men and I also announced the names of those who should successively lead the 'army' in my place.

The men understood the instructions issued to them, and our caravan safely reached Charlestown where the traders rendered us great help. They gave us the use of their houses, and permitted us to make our cooking arrangements on the grounds of the mosque. The ration supplied on the march would be exhausted when camp was reached and therefore we were in need of cooking pots, which were cheerfully supplied by the traders. We together. Animal passion knows no shame. As soon as the cases occurred, I arrived on the scene. The guilty parties were abashed and they were segregated. But who can say how many such cases occurred which never came to my knowledge? It is no use dwelling any further upon this topic, which I have brought in in order to show that everything was not in perfect order and that even when some one did go wrong there was no exhibition of insolence. On many similar occasions I have seen how well-behaved people become in a good atmosphere even when they are originally semi-barbarous and not over-observant of the dictates of morality, and it is more essential and profitable to realize this truth.

CHAPTER XLIII

CROSSING THE BORDER

We have now arrived at the beginning of November 1913. But before we proceed, it will be well to take note of two events. Bai Fatma Mehtab of Durban could no longer be at peace when the Tamilian sisters received sentences of imprisonment in Newcastle. She therefore left for Volksrust to court arrest along with her mother Hanifabai and seven years old son. Mother and daughter were arrested but the Government declined to arrest the boy. Fatma Bai was called upon to give her finger impressions at the charge office but she fearlessly refused to submit to the indignity. Eventually she and her mother were sent to prison for three months (October 13, 1913).

The labourers' strike was in full swing at this time. Men as well as women were on the move between the mining district and Charlestown. Of these, there were two women with their little ones one of whom died of exposure on the march. The other fell from the arms of its mother while she was crossing a spruit and was drowned. But the brave mothers refused to be dejected and continued their march. One of them said, 'We must not pine for the dead who will not come back to us for all our sorrow. It is the living for whom we must work.' I have often among the poor come across such instances of quiet heroism, sterling faith and saving knowledge.

The men and women in Charlestown held to their difficult post of duty in such a stoical spirit. For it was no mission of peace that took us to that border village. If any one wanted peace, he had to search for it within. Outwardly the words 'there is no peace here' were placarded everywhere, as it were. But it is in the midst of such storm that a devotee like Mirabai takes the cup of poison to her lips with cheerful equanimity, that Socrates quietly embraces death in his dark and solitary cell and initiates his friends and us into the mysterious doctrine that he who seeks peace must look for it within himself.

With such ineffable peace brooding over them the Satyagrahis were living in their camp, careless of what the morrow would bring.

I wrote to the Government, that we did not propose to enter the Transvaal with a view to domicile, but as an effective protest against the minister's breach of pledge and as a pure demonstration of our distress at the loss of our self-respect. Government would be relieving us of all anxiety if they were good enough to arrest us where we then were, that is in Charlestown. But if they did not arrest us, and if any of us surreptitiously entered the Transvaal, the responsibility would not be ours. There was no secrecy about our movement. None of us had a personal axe to grind. We would not like it if any of us secretly entered the Transvaal. But we could not hold ourselves responsible for the acts of any as we had to deal with thousands of unknown men and as we could not command any other sanction but that of love. Finally I assured the Government that if they repealed the £3 tax, the strike would be called off and the indentured labourers would return to work, as we would not ask them to join the general struggle directed against the rest of our grievances.

The position therefore was quite uncertain, and there was no knowing when the Government would arrest us. But at a crisis like this we could not await the reply of the Government for a number of days, but only for one or two returns of the post. We therefore decided to leave Charlestown and enter the Transvaal at once if the Government did not put us under arrest. If we were not arrested on the way, the 'army of peace' was to march twenty to twenty-four miles a day for eight days together, with a view to reach Tolstoy Farm, and to stop there till the struggle was over and in the meanwhile to maintain themselves by working the Farm. Mr Kallenbach had made all the necessary arrangements. The idea was to construct mud huts with the help of the pilgrims themselves. So long as the huts were under construction, the old and the infirm should be accommodated in small tents, the able-bodied camping in the open. The only difficulty was, that the rains were now about to set in, and every one must have a shelter over his head while it rained. But Mr Kallenbach was courageously confident of solving it somehow or other.

We also made other preparations for the march. The good Dr Briscoe improvised a small medical chest for us, and gave us some instruments which even a layman like myself could handle. The chest was to be carried by hand as there was to be no conveyance with the pilgrims. We therefore carried with us the least possible quantity of medicines, which would not enable us to treat even a hundred persons at the same time. But that did not matter as we proposed to encamp every day near some village, where we hoped to get the drugs of which we ran short, and as we were not taking with us any of the patients or disabled persons whom we had arranged to leave in the villages *en route*.

Bread and sugar constituted our sole ration, but how was a supply of bread to be ensured on the eight days' march? The bread must be distributed to the pilgrims every day and we could not hold any of it in stock. The only solution of this problem was, that some one should supply us with bread at each stage. But who would be our provider? There were no Indian bakers at all. Again there could not be found a baker in each of the villages, which usually depended upon the cities for their supply of bread. The bread therefore must be supplied by some baker and sent by rail to the appointed station. Volksrust was about double the size of Charlestown, and a large European bakery there willingly contracted to supply bread at each place. The baker did not take advantage of our awkward plight to charge us higher than the market rates and supplied bread made of excellent flour. He sent it in time by rail, and the railway officials, also Europeans, not only honestly delivered it to us, but they took good care of it in transit and gave us some special facilities. They knew that we harboured no enmity in our hearts, intended no harm to any living soul and sought redress only through self-suffering. The atmosphere around us was thus purified and continued to be pure. The feeling of love which is dormant though present in all mankind was roused into activity. Every one realized that we are all brothers whether we are ourselves Christians, Jews, Hindus, Musalmans or anything else.

When all the preparations for the march were completed, I made one more effort to achieve a settlement. I had already sent letters and telegrams. I now decided to 'phone even at the risk of my overtures being answered by an insult. From Charlestown I 'phoned to General Smuts in Pretoria. I called his secretary and said: 'Tell General Smuts that I am fully prepared for the march. The Europeans in Volksrust are excited and perhaps likely to violate even the safety of our lives. They have certainly held out such a threat. I am sure that even the General would not wish any such untoward event to happen. If he promises to abolish the £3 tax, I will stop the march, as I will not break the law merely for the sake of breaking it but I am driven to it by inexorable necessity. Will not the General accede to such a small request?' I received this reply within half a minute: 'General Smuts will have nothing to do with you. You may do just as you please.' With this the message closed.

I had fully expected this result, though I was not prepared for the curtness of the reply. I hoped for a civil answer, as my political relations with the General since the organization of Satyagraha had now subsisted for six years. But as I would not be elated by his courtesy, I did not weaken in the face of his incivility. The strait and narrow path I had to tread was clear before me. The next day (November 6, 1913) at the appointed stroke of the hour 6-30) we offered prayers and commenced the march in the name of God. The pilgrim band was composed of 2,037 men, 127 women and 57 children.

CHAPTER XLIV

THE GREAT MARCH

The caravan of pilgrims thus started punctually at the appointed hour. There is a small spruit one mile from Charlestown, and as soon as one crosses it, one has entered Volksrust or the Transvaal. A small patrol of mounted policemen was on duty at the border gate. I went up to them, leaving instructions with the 'army' to cross over when I signalled to them. But while I was still talking with the police, the pilgrims made a sudden rush and crossed the border. The police surrounded them, but the surging multitude was not easy of control. The police had no intention of arresting us. I pacified the pilgrims and got them to arrange themselves in regular rows. Everything was in order in a few minutes and the march into the Transvaal began.

Two days before this the Europeans of Volksrust held a meeting where they offered all manner of threats to the Indians. Some said that they would shoot the Indians if they entered the Transvaal. Mr Kallenbach attended this meeting to reason with the Europeans who were however not prepared to listen to him. Indeed some of them even stood up to assault him. Mr Kallenbach is an athlete, having received physical training at the hands of Sandow, and it was not easy to frighten him. One European challenged him to a dual. Mr Kallenbach replied, 'As I have accepted the religion of peace, I may not accept the challenge. Let him who will come and do his worst with me. But I will continue to claim a hearing at this meeting. You have publicly invited all Europeans to attend, and I am here to inform you that not all Europeans are ready as you are to lay violent hands upon innocent men. There is one European who would like to inform you that the charges you level at the Indians are false. The Indians do not want what you imagine them to do. The Indians are not out to challenge your position as rulers. They do not wish to fight with you or to fill the country. They only seek justice pure and simple. They propose to enter the Transvaal not with a view to settle there, but only as an effective demonstration against the unjust tax which is levied upon them. They are brave men. They will not injure you in person or in property, they will not fight with you, but enter the Transvaal they will, even in the face of your gunfire. They are not the men to beat a retreat from the fear of your bullets or your spears. They propose to melt, and I know they will melt, your hearts by self-suffering. This is all I have to say. I have had my say and I believe that I have thus rendered you a service. Beware and save yourselves from perpetrating a wrong.' With these words Mr Kallenbach resumed his seat. The audience was rather abashed. The pugilist who had invited Mr Kallenbach to single combat became his friend.

We had heard about this meeting and were prepared for any mischief by the Europeans in Volksrust. It was possible that the large number of policemen massed at the border was intended as a check upon them. However that may be, our procession passed through the place in peace. I do not remember that any European attempted even a jest. All were out to witness this novel sight, while there was even a friendly twinkle in the eyes of some of them.

On the first day we were to stop for the night at Palmford about eight miles from Volksrust, and we reached the place at about five p. m. The pilgrims took their ration of bread and sugar, and spread themselves in the open air. Some were talking while others were singing *bhajans*. Some of the women were thoroughly exhausted by the march. They had dared to carry their children in their arms, but it was impossible for them to proceed further. I therefore, according to my previous warning, kept them as lodgers with a good Indian shopkeeper who promised to send them to Tolstoy Farm if we were permitted to go there, and to their homes if we were arrested.

As the night advanced, all noises ceased and I too was preparing to retire when I heard a tread. I saw a European coming lantern in hand. I understood what it meant, but had no preparations to make. The police officer said,

'I have a warrant of arrest for you. I want to arrest you.'

'When?' I asked.

'Immediately.'

'Where will you take me?'

'To the adjoining railway station now, and to Volksrust when we get a train for it.'

'I will go with you without informing any one, but I will leave some instructions with one of my co-workers.'

'You may do so.'

I roused P. K. Naidoo who was sleeping near me. I informed him about my arrest and asked him not to awake the pilgrims before morning. At daybreak they must regularly resume the march. The march would commence before sunrise, and when it was time for them to halt and get their rations, he must break to them the news of my arrest. He might inform any one who inquired about me in the interval. If the pilgrims were arrested, they must allow themselves to be arrested. Otherwise they must continue the march according to the programme. Naidoo had no fears at all. I also told him what was to be done in case he was arrested. Mr Kallenbach too was in Volksrust at the time.

I went with the police officer, and we took the train for Volksrust the next morning. I appeared before the Court in Volksrust, but the Public Prosecutor himself asked for a remand until the 14th as he was not ready with the evidence. The case was postponed accordingly. I applied for bail as I had over 2,000 men, 122 women and 50 children in my charge whom I should like to take on to their destination within the period of postponement. The Public Prosecutor opposed my application. But the Magistrate was helpless in the matter, as every prisoner not charged with a capital offence is in law entitled to be allowed to give bail for his appearance, and I could not be deprived of that right. He therefore released me on bail of £ 50. Mr Kallenbach had a car ready for me, and he took me at once to rejoin the 'invaders.' The special reporter of *The Transvaal Leader* wanted to go with us. We took him in the car, and he published at the time a vivid description of the case, the journey, and the meeting with the pilgrims, who received me with enthusiasm and were transported with joy. Mr Kallenbach at once returned to Volksrust, as he had to look after the Indians stopping at Charlestown as well as fresh arrivals there.

We continued the march, but it did not suit the Government to leave me in a state of freedom. I was therefore re-arrested at Standerton on the 8th. Standerton is comparatively a bigger place. There was something rather strange about the manner of my arrest here. I was distributing bread to the pilgrims. The Indian storekeepers at Standerton presented us with some tins of marmalade, and the distribution therefore took more time than usual. Meanwhile the Magistrate came and stood by my side. He waited till the distribution of rations was over, and then called me aside. I knew the gentleman, who, I thought, perhaps wanted to talk with me. He laughed and said,

'You are my prisoner.'

'It would seem I have received promotion in rank,' I said, 'as magistrates take the trouble to arrest me instead of mere police officials. But you will try me just now.'

'Go with me,' replied the Magistrate, 'the Courts are still in session.'

I asked the pilgrims to continue their march, and then left with the Magistrate. As soon as I reached the Court room, I found that some of my co-workers had also been arrested. There were five of them there, P. K. Naidoo, Biharilal Maharaj, Ramnarayan Sinha, Raghu Narasu and Rahimkhan.

I was at once brought before the Court and applied for remand and bail on the same grounds as in Volksrust. Here too the application was strongly opposed by the Public Prosecutor and here too I was released on my own recognizance of £ 50 and the case was remanded till the 21st. The Indian traders had kept a carriage ready for me and I rejoined the pilgrims again when they had hardly proceeded three miles further. The pilgrims thought, and I thought too, that we might now perhaps reach Tolstoy Farm. But that was not to be. It was no small thing however that the invaders got accustomed to my being arrested. The five co-workers remained in jail.

CHAPTER XLV

ALL IN PRISON

We were now near Johannesburg. The reader will remember that the whole pilgrimage had been divided into eight stages. Thus far we had accomplished our marches exactly according to programme and we now had four days' march in front of us. But if our spirits rose from day to day, Government too got more and more anxious as to how they should deal with the Indian invasion. They would be charged with weakness and want of tact if they arrested us after we had reached our destination. If we were to be arrested, we must be arrested before we reached the promised land.

Government saw that my arrest did not dishearten or frighten the pilgrims, nor did it lead them to break the peace. If they took to rioting, Government would have an excellent opportunity of converting them into food for gunpowder. Our firmness was very distressing to General Smuts coupled as it was with peacefulness, and he even said as much. How long can you harass a peaceful man? How can you kill the voluntarily dead? There is no zest in killing one who welcomes death and therefore soldiers are keen upon seizing the enemy alive. If the mouse did not flee before the cat, the cat would be driven to seek another prey. If all lambs voluntarily lay with the lion, the lion would be compelled to give up feasting upon lambs. Great hunters would give up lion hunting if the lion took to non-resistance. Our victory was implicit in our combination of the two qualities of non-violence and determination.

Gokhale desired by cable that Polak should go to India and help him in placing the facts of the situation before the Indian and Imperial Governments. Polak's temperament was such that he would make himself useful wherever he went. He would be totally absorbed in whatever task he undertook. We were therefore preparing to send him to India. I wrote to him that he could go. But he would not leave without meeting me in person and taking full instructions from me. He therefore offered to come and see me during our march. I wired to him, saying that he might come if he wished though he would be in so doing running the risk of arrest. Fighters never hesitate to incur necessary risks. It was a cardinal principle of the movement that every one should be ready for arrest if Government extended their attentions to him, and should make all straightforward and moral efforts to get arrested until he overcame the reluctance of Government to lay hands upon him. Polak therefore preferred to come even at the risk of being arrested.

Mr Polak joined us on the 9th at Teakworth between Standerton and Greylingstad. We were in the midst of our consultation and had nearly done with it. It was about 3 o'clock in the afternoon. Polak and I were walking at the head of the whole body of pilgrims. Some of the co-workers were listening to our conversation. Polak was to take the evening train for Durban. But God does not always permit man to carry out his plans. Rama had to retire to the forest on the very day that was fixed for his coronation. While we were thus engaged in talking, a Cape cart came and stopped before us and from it alighted Mr Chamney, the Principal Immigration Officer of the Transvaal and a police officer. They took me somewhat aside and one of them said, 'I arrest you.'

I was thus arrested thrice in four days.

'What about the marchers?' I asked.

'We shall see to that,' was the answer.

I said nothing further. I asked Polak to assume charge of and go with the pilgrims. The police officer permitted me only to inform the marchers of my arrest. As I proceeded to ask them to keep the peace etc., the officer interrupted me and said,

'You are now a prisoner and cannot make any speeches.'

I understood my position, but it was needless. As soon as he stopped me speaking, the officer ordered the driver to drive the cart away at full speed. In a moment the pilgrims passed out of my sight.

The officer knew that for the time being I was master of the situation, for trusting to our non-violence, he was alone in this desolate veldt confronted by two thousand Indians. He also knew that I would have surrendered to him even if he had sent me a summons in writing. Such being the case, it was hardly necessary to remind me that I was a prisoner. And the advice which I would have given the pilgrims would have served the Government's purpose no less than our own. But how could an officer forego an opportunity of exercising his brief authority? I must say, however, that many officers understood us better than this gentleman. They knew that not only had arrest no terrors for us but on the other hand we hailed it as the gateway of liberty. They therefore allowed us all legitimate freedom and thankfully sought our aid in conveniently and expeditiously effecting arrests. The reader will come across apposite cases of both the kinds in these pages.

I was taken to Greylingstad, and from Greylingstad via Balfour to Heidelberg where I passed the night.

The pilgrims with Polak as leader resumed their march and halted for the night at Greylingstad where they were met by Sheth Ahmad Muhammad Kachhalia and Sheth Amad Bhayat who had come to know that arrangements were complete for arresting the whole body of marchers. Polak therefore thought that when his responsibility ceased in respect of the pilgrims upon their arrest, he could reach Durban even if a day later and take the steamer for India after all. But God had willed otherwise. At about 9 o'clock in the morning on the 10th the pilgrims reached Balfour where three special trains were drawn up at the station to take them and deport them to Natal. The pilgrims were there rather obstinate. They asked for me to be called and promised to be arrested and to board the trains if I advised them to that effect. This was a wrong attitude. And the whole game must be spoiled and the movement must receive a set-back unless it was given up. Why should the pilgrims want me for going to jail? It would ill become soldiers to claim to elect their commanders or to insist upon their obeying only one of them. Mr Chamney approached Mr Polak and Kachhalia Sheth to help him in arresting them. These friends encountered difficulty in explaining the situation to the marchers. They told them that jail was the pilgrims' goal and they should therefore apperciate the Government's action when they were ready to arrest them. Only thus could the Satyagrahis show their quality and bring their struggle to a triumphant end. They must realize that no other procedure could have my approval. The pilgrims were brought round and all entrained peacefully.

I, on my part, was again hauled up before the Magistrate. I knew nothing of what transpired after I was separated from the pilgrims. I asked for a remand once again. I said that a remand had been granted by two courts, and that we had not now much to go to reach our destination. I therefore requested that either the Government should arrest the pilgrims or else I should be permitted to see them safe in Tolstoy Farm. The Magistrate did not comply with my request, but promised to forward it at once to the Government. This time I was arrested on a warrant from Dundee where I was to be prosecuted on the principal charge of inducing indentured labourers to leave the province of Natal. I was therefore taken to Dundee by rail the same day.

Mr Polak was not only not arrested at Balfour but he was even thanked for the assistance he had rendered to the authorities. Mr Chamney even said that the Government had no intention of arresting him. But these were Mr Chamney's own views or the views of the Government in so far as they were known to that officer. Government in fact would be changing their mind every now and then. And finally they reached the decision that Mr Polak should not be allowed to sail for India and should be arrested along with Mr Kallenbach who was working most energetically on behalf of the Indians. Mr Polak therefore was arrested in Charlestown whilst waiting for the corridor train. Mr Kallenbach was also arrested and both these friends were confined in Volksrust jail.

I was tried in Dundee on the 11th and sentenced to nine months' imprisonment with hard labour. I had still to take my second trial at Volksrust on the charge of aiding and abetting prohibited persons to enter the Transvaal. From Dundee I was therefore taken on the 13th to Volksrust where I was glad to meet Kallenbach and Polak in the jail.

I appeared before the Volksrust court on the 14th. The beauty of it was that the charge was proved against me only by witnesses furnished by myself at Kromdraai. The police could have secured witnesses but with difficulty. They had therefore sought my aid in the matter. The courts here would not convict a prisoner merely upon his pleading guilty.

This was arranged as regards me, but who would testify against Mr Kallenbach and Mr Polak? It was impossible to convict them in the absence of evidence, and it was also difficult at once to secure witnesses against them. Mr Kallenbach intended to plead guilty as he wished to be with the pilgrims. But Mr Polak was bound for India, and was not deliberately courting jail at this moment. After a joint consultation therefore we three resolved that we should say neither yes nor no in case we were asked whether Mr Polak was guilty of the offence with which he was charged.

I provided the evidence for the Crown against Mr Kallenbach and I appeared as witness against Mr Polak. We did not wish that the cases should be protracted, and we therefore did our best to see that each case was disposed of within a day. The proceedings against me were completed on the 14th, against Kallenbach on the 15th and and against Polak on the 17th, and the Magistrate passed sentences of three months' imprisonment on all three of us. We now thought we could live together in Volksrust jail

ALL IN PRISON

for these three months. But the Government could not afford to allow it.

Meanwhile, we passed a few happy days in Volksrust jail, where new prisoners came every day and brought us news of what was happening outside. Among these Satyagrahi prisoners there was one old man named Harbatsinh who was about 75 years of age. Harbatsinh was not working on the mines. He had completed his indenture years ago and he was not therefore a striker. The Indians grew far more enthusiastic after my arrest, and many of them got arrested by crossing over from Natal into the Transvaal. Harbatsinh was one of these enthusiasts.

'Why are you in jail?' I asked Harbatsinh. 'I have not invited old men like yourself to court jail.'

'How could I help it,' replied Harbatsinh, 'when you, your wife and even your boys went to jail for our sake?'

'But you will not be able to endure the hardships of jail life. I would advise you to leave jail. Shall I arrange for your release?'

'No, please. I will never leave jail. I must die one of these days, and how happy should I be to die in jail!'

It was not for me to try to shake such determination which would not have been shaken even if I had tried. My head bent in reverence before this illiterate sage. Harbatsinh had his wish and he died in Durban jail on January 5, 1914. His body was with great honour cremated according to Hindu rites in the presence of hundreds of Indians. There was not one but there were many like Harbatsinh in the Satyagraha struggle. But the great good fortune of dying in jail was reserved for him alone and hence he becomes entitled to honourable mention in the history of Satyagraha in South Africa.

Government would not like that men should thus be attracted to jail, nor did they appreciate the fact that prisoners upon their release should carry my messages outside. They therefore decided to separate Kallenbach, Polak and me, send us away from Volksrust, and take me in particular to a place where no Indian could go and see me. I was sent accordingly to the jail in Bloemfontein, the capital of Orangia, where there were not more than 50 Indians, all of them serving as waiters in hotels. I was the only Indian prisoner there, the rest being Europeans and Negroes. I was not troubled at this isolation but hailed it as a blessing. There was no need now for me to keep my eyes or ears open, and I was glad that a novel experience was in store for me. Again, I never had had time for study for years together, particularly since 1893, and the prospect of uninterrupted study for a year filled me with joy.

I reached Bloemfontein jail where I had as much solitude as I could wish. There were many discomforts but they were all bearable, and I will not inflict a description of them upon the reader. But I must state that the medical officer of the jail became my friend. The jailer could think only of his own powers while the doctor was anxious to maintain the prisoners in their rights. In those days I was purely a fruitarian. I took neither milk nor *ghi* nor food grains. I lived upon a diet of bananas, tomatoes, raw groundnuts, limes and olive oil. It meant starvation for me if the supply of any one of these things was bad in quality. The doctor was therefore very careful in ordering them out, and he added almonds, walnuts and Brazil nuts to my diet. He inspected everything indented for me in person. There was not sufficient ventilation in the cell which was assigned to me. The doctor tried his best to have the cell doors kept open but in vain. The jailer threatened to resign if the doors were kept open. He was not a bad man, but he had been moving in a single rut from which he could not deviate. He had to deal with refractory prisoners, and if he discriminated in favour of a mild prisoner like myself, he would run the real risk of the turbulent prisoners getting the upper hand of him. I fully understood the jailer's standpoint, and in the disputes between the doctor and the jailer in respect of me, my sympathies were always with the jailer who was an experienced, straightforward man, seeing the way clear before him.

Mr Kallenbach was taken to Pretoria jail and Mr Polak to Germiston jail.

But the Government might have saved all this trouble. They were like Mrs Partington trying to stem the rising tide of the ocean broom in hand. The Indian labourers of Natal were wide awake, and no power on earth could hold them in check.

CHAPTER XLVI

THE TEST

The jeweller rubs gold on the touchstone. If he is not still satisfied as to its purity, he puts it into the fire and hammers it so that the dross if any is removed and only pure gold remains. The Indians in South Africa passed through a similar test. They were hammered, and passed through fire and had the hall-mark attached to them only when they emerged unscathed through all the stages of examination.

The pilgrims were taken on special trains not for a picnic but for baptism through fire. On the way the Government did not care to arrange even to feed them and when they reached Natal, they were prosecuted and sent to jail straightaway. We expected and even desired as much. But the Government would have to incur additional expenditure and would appear to have played into the Indians' hands if they kept thousands of labourers in prison. And the coal mines would close down in the interval. If such a state of things lasted for any length of time, the Government would be compelled to repeal the £ 3 tax. They therefore struck out a new plan. Surrounding them with wire netting, the Government proclaimed the mine compounds as outstations to the Dundee and Newcastle jails and appointed the mineowners' European staffs as the warders. In this way they forced the labourers underground against their will and the mines began to work once more. There is this difference between the status of a servant and that of a slave, that if a servant leaves his post, only a civil suit can be filed against him, whereas the slave who leaves his master can be brought back to work by main force. The labourers therefore were now reduced to slavery pure and simple.

But that was not enough. The labourers were brave men, and they flatly declined to work on the mines with the result that they were brutally whipped. The insolent men dressed in a brief authority over them kicked and abused them and heaped upon them other wrongs which have never been placed on record. But the poor labourers patiently put up with all their tribulations. Cablegrams regarding these outrages were sent to India addressed to Gokhale who would inquire in his turn if he did not even for a day receive a fully detailed message. Gokhale broadcast the news from his sickbed, as he was seriously ill at the time. In spite of his illness, however, he insisted upon attending to the South African business himself and was at it at night no less than by day. Eventually all India was deeply stirred, and the South African question became the burning topic of the day.

It was then (December 1913) that Lord Hardinge in Madras made his famous speech which created a stir in South Africa as well as in England. The Viceroy may not publicly criticize other members of the Empire, but Lord Hardinge not only passed severe criticism upon the Union Government, but he also whole-heartedly defended the action of the Satyagrahis and supported their civil disobedience of unjust and invidious legislation. The conduct of Lord Hardinge came in for some adverse comment in England, but even then he did not repent but on the other hand asserted the perfect propriety of the step he had been driven to adopt. Lord Hardinge's firmness created a good impression all round.

Let us leave for the moment these brave but unhappy labourers confined to their mines, and consider the situation in other parts of Natal. The mines were situated in the north-west of Natal, but the largest number of Indian labourers was to be found employed on the north and the south coasts. I was fairly intimate with the labourers on the north coast, that is, in and about Phoenix, Verulam, Tongaat etc., many of whom served with me in the Boer

THE TEST

War. I had not met the labourers on the south coast from Durban to Isipingo and Umzinto at such close quarters, and I had but few co-workers in those parts. But the news of the strike and the arrest spread everywhere at lightning speed, and thousands of labourers unexpectedly and spontaneously came out on the south as well as on the north coast. Some of them sold their household chattels from an impression that it would be a long drawn out struggle and they could not expect to be fed by others. When I went to jail, I had warned my co-workers against allowing any more labourers to go on strike. I hoped that a victory could be achieved only with the help of the miners. If all the labourers,—there were about sixty thousand of them all told,—were called out it would be difficult to maintain them. We had not the means of taking so many on the march; we had neither the men to control them nor the money to feed them. Moreover, with such a large body of men it would be impossible to prevent a breach of the peace.

But when the floodgates are opened, there is no checking the universal deluge. The labourers everywhere struck work of their own accord, and volunteers also posted themselves in the various places to look after them.

Government now adopted a policy of blood and iron. They prevented the labourers from striking by sheer force. Mounted military policemen chased the strikers and brought them back to their work. The slightest disturbance on the part of the labourers was answered by rifle fire. A body of strikers resisted the attempt to take them back to work. Some of them even threw stones. Fire was opened upon them, wounding many and killing some. But the labourers refused to be cowed down. The volunteers prevented a strike near Verulam with great difficulty. But all the labourers did not return to work. Some hid themselves for fear and did not go back.

One incident deserves to be placed on record. Many labourers came out in Verulam and would not return in spite of all the efforts of the authorities. General Lukin was present on the scene with his soldiers and was about to order his men to open fire. Brave Sorabji, son of the late Parsi Rustomji then hardly 18 years of age, had reached here from Durban. He seized the reins of the General's horse and exclaimed, 'You must not order firing. I undertake to induce my people peacefully to return to work.' General Lukin was charmed with the young man's courage and gave him time to try his method of love. Sorabji reasoned with the labourers who came round and returned to their work. Thus a number of murders were prevented by the presence of mind, valour and loving kindness of one young man.

The reader must observe that this firing and the treatment accorded by the Government to the strikers on the coast were quite illegal. There was an appearance of legality about the Government's procedure in respect of the miners who were arrested not for going on strike but for entering the Transvaal without proper credentials. On the north and the south coast however the very act of striking work was treated as an offence not in virtue of any law but of the authority of the Government. Authority takes the place of law in the last resort. There is a maxim in English law that the king can do no wrong. The convenience of the powers that be is the law in the final analysis. This objection is applicable to all governments alike. And as a matter of fact it is not always objectionable thus to lay the ordinary law on the shelf. Sometimes adherence to ordinary law is itself open to objection. When the authority charged with and pledged to the public good is threatened with destruction by the restraints imposed upon it, it is entitled in its discretion to disregard such restraints. But occasions of such a nature must always be rare. If the authority is in the habit of frequently exceeding the limits set upon it, it cannot be beneficial to the commonweal. In the case under consideration the authority had no reason whatever to act arbitrarily. The labourer has enjoyed the right to strike from times immemorial. The Government had sufficient material before them to know that the strikers were not bent upon mischief. At the most the strike was to result only in the repeal of the £ 3 tax. Only peaceful methods can be properly adopted against men of peace. Again the authority in South Africa was not pledged to the public good but existed for the exclusive benefit of the Europeans, being generally hostile to the Indians. And therefore the breach of all restraints on the part of such a partisan authority could never be proper or excusable.

Thus in my view there was here a sheer abuse of authority, which could never achieve the ends which it proposed to itself. There is sometimes a momentary success, but a permanent solution cannot be reached by such questionable methods. In South Africa the very £ 3 tax for bolstering up which the Government perpetrated all these outrages had to be abolished within six months of the firing. Pain is often thus the precursor of pleasure. The pain of the Indians in South Africa made itself heard everywhere. Indeed, I believe, that as every part has its place in a machine, every feature has its place in a movement of men, and as a machine is clogged by rust, dirt and the like, so is a movement hampered by a number of factors. We are merely the instruments of the Almighty Will and are therefore often ignorant of what helps us forward and what acts as an impediment. We must thus rest satisfied with a knowledge only of the means, and if these are pure, we can fearlessly leave the end to take care of itself.

I observed in this struggle, that its end drew nearer as the distress of the fighters became more intense, and as the innocence of the distressed grew clearer. I also saw that in such a pure, unarmed and non-violent struggle, the very kind of material required for its prosecution, be it men, money or munitions, is forthcoming at the right moment. Many volunteers rendered spontaneous help, whom I do not know even to this day. Such workers are generally selfless and put in a sort of invisible service even in spite of themselves. No one takes note of them, no one awards them a certificate of merit. Some of them do not even know that their nameless but priceless unremembered acts of love do not escape the sleepless vigilance of the recording angel.

The Indians of South Africa successfully passed the test to which they were subjected. They entered the fire and emerged out of it unscathed. The beginning of the end of the struggle must be detailed in a separate chapter.

CHAPTER XLVII

THE BEGINNING OF THE END

The reader has seen that the Indians exerted as much quiet strength as they could and more than could be expected of them. He has also seen that the very large majority of these passive resisters were poor downtrodden men of whom no hope could possibly be entertained. He will recall too, that all the responsible workers of the Phoenix settlement with the exception of two or three were now in jail. Of the workers outside Phoenix the late Sheth Ahmad Muhammad Kachhalia was still at large, and so were Mr West, Miss West and Maganlal Gandhi in Phoenix. Kachhalia Sheth exercised general supervision. Miss Schlesin kept all the Transvaal accounts and looked after the Indians who crossed the border. Mr West was in charge of the English section of *Indian Opinion* and of the cable correspondence with Gokhale. At a time like the present, when the situation assumed a new aspect every moment, correspondence by post was out of the question. Cablegrams had to be despatched, no shorter in length than letters, and the delicate responsibility regarding them was shouldered by Mr West.

Like Newcastle in the mine area, Phoenix now became the centre of the strikers on the north coast, and was visited by hundreds of them who came there to seek advice as well as shelter. It therefore naturally attracted the attention of the Government, and the angry looks of the Europeans thereabouts. It became somewhat risky to live in Phoenix, and yet even children there accomplished dangerous tasks with courage. West was arrested in the meanwhile, though as a matter of fact there was no reason for arresting him. Our understanding was, that West and Maganlal Gandhi should not only not try to be arrested, but on the other hand should, as far as possible, avoid any occasion for arrest. West had not therefore allowed any ground to arise for the Government to arrest him. But the Government could scarcely be expected to consult the convenience of the Satyagrahis, nor did they need to wait for some occasion to arise for arresting any one whose freedom jarred upon their nerves. The authority's very desire to take a step amply suffices as a reason for adopting it. As soon as the news of the arrest of West was cabled to Gokhale, he initiated the policy of sending out able men from India. When a meeting was held in Lahore in support of the Satyagrahis of South Africa, Mr C. F. Andrews gave away in their interest all the money in his possession, and ever since then Gokhale had had his eye upon him. No sooner, therefore, did he hear about West's arrest, than he inquired of Andrews by wire if he was ready to proceed to South Africa at once. Andrews replied in the affirmative. His beloved friend Pearson also got ready to go the same moment, and the two friends left India for South Africa by the first available steamer.

But the struggle was now about to close. The Union Government had not the power to keep thousands of innocent men in jail. The Viceroy would not tolerate it, and all the world was waiting to see what General Smuts would do. The Union Government now did what all governments similarly situated generally do. No inquiry was really needed. The wrong perpetrated was well known on all hands, and every one realized that it must be redressed. General Smuts too saw that there had been injustice which called for remedy, but he was in the same predicament as a snake which has taken a rat in its mouth but can neither gulp it down nor cast it out. He must do justice, but he had lost the power of doing justice, as he had given the Europeans in South Africa to understand, that he would not repeal the £3 tax nor carry out any other reform. And now he felt compelled to abolish the tax as well as to undertake other remedial legislation. States amenable to public opinion get out of such awkward positions by appointing a commission which conducts only a nominal inquiry, as its recommendations are a foregone conclusion. It is a general practice that the recommendations of such a commission should be accepted by the state, and therefore under the guise of carrying out the recommendations, governments give the justice which they have first refused. General Smuts appointed a commission of three members, with which the Indians pledged themselves to have nothing to do so long as certain demands of theirs in respect of the commission were not granted by the Government. One of these demands was, that the Satyagrahi prisoners should be released, and another that the Indians should be represented on the commission by at least one member. To a certain extent the first demand was accepted by the commission itself which recommended to the Government 'with a view to enabling the enquiry to be made as thorough as possible' that Mr Kallenbach, Mr Polak and I should be released unconditionally. The Government accepted this recommendation and released all three of us simultaneously (December 18, 1913) after an imprisonment of hardly six weeks. West who had been arrested was also released as Government had no case against him.

All these events transpired before the arrival of Andrews and Pearson whom I was thus able to welcome as they landed at Durban. They were agreeably surprised to see me, as they knew nothing of the events which happened during their voyage. This was my first meeting with these noble Englishmen.

All three of us were disappointed upon our release. We knew nothing of the events outside. The news of the commission came to us as a surprise, but we saw that we could not co-operate with the commission in any shape or form. We felt that the Indians should be certainly allowed to nominate at least one representative on the commission. We three, therefore, upon reaching Durban, addressed a letter to General Smuts on December 21, 1913 to this effect:

'We welcome the appointment of the commission, but we strongly object to the inclusion in it of Messrs Esselen and Wylie. We have nothing against them personally. They are well-known and able citizens. But as both of them have often expressed their dislike for the Indians, there is likelihood of their doing injustice without being conscious of it. Man cannot change his temperament all at once. It is against the laws of nature to suppose, that these gentlemen will suddenly become different from what they are. However we do not ask for their removal from the commission. We only suggest that some impartial men should be appointed in addition to them, and in this connection we would mention Sir James Rose Innes and the Hon. Mr W. P. Schreiner, both of them well-known men noted for their sense of justice. Secondly, we request that all the Satyagrahi prisoners should be released. If this is not done, it would be difficult for us to remain outside jail. There is no reason now for keeping the Satyagrahis in jail any longer. Thirdly, if we tender evidence before the commission, we should be allowed to go to the mines and factories where the indentured labourers are at work. If these requests are not complied with, we are sorry that we shall have to explore fresh avenues for going to jail.'

General Smuts declined to appoint any more members on the commission, and stated that the commission was appointed not for the sake of any party but merely for the satisfaction of the Government. Upon receiving this reply on December 24, we had no alternative but to prepare to go to jail. We therefore published a notification to the Indians that a party of Indians courting jail would commence their march from Durban on January 1, 1914.

But there was one sentence in General Smuts' reply, which prompted me to write to him again, and it was this: 'We have appointed an impartial and judicial commission, and if while appointing it, we have not consulted the Indians, neither have we consulted the coal-owners or the sugar-planters.' I wrote privately to the General, requesting to see him and place some facts before him if the Government were out to do justice. General Smuts granted my request for an interview, and the march was postponed for a few days accordingly.

When Gokhale heard that a fresh march was under contemplation, he sent a long cablegram, saying that such a step on our part would land Lord Hardinge and himself in an awkward position and strongly advising us to give up the march, and assist the commission by tendering evidence before it.

We were on the horns of a dilemma. The Indians were pledged to a boycott of the commission if its *personnel* was not enlarged to their satisfaction. Lord Hardinge might be displeased, Gokhale might be pained, but how could we go back upon our pledged word? Mr Andrews suggested to us the considerations of Gokhale's feelings, his delicate health and the shock which our decision was calculated to impart to him. But in fact these considerations were never absent from my mind. The leaders held a conference and finally reached the decision that the boycott must stand at any cost if more members were not co-opted to the commission. We therefore sent a long cablegram to Gokhale, at an expense of about a hundred pounds. Andrews too concurred with the gist of our message which was to the following effect:

'We realize how you are pained, and would like to follow your advice at considerable sacrifice. Lord Hardinge has rendered priceless aid, which we wish we would continue to receive till the end. But we are anxious that you should understand our position. It is a question of thousands of men having taken a pledge to which no exception can be taken. Our entire struggle has been built upon a foundation of pledges. Many of us would have fallen back today had it not been for the compelling force of our pledges. All moral bonds would be relaxed at once if thousands of men once proved false to their plighted word. The pledge was taken after full and mature deliberation, and there is nothing immoral about it. The community has an unquestionable right to pledge itself to boycott. We wish that even you should advise that a pledge of this nature should not be broken but be observed inviolate by all, come what might. Please show this cable to Lord Hardinge. We wish you might not be placed in a false position. We have commenced this struggle with God as our witness and His help as our sole support. We desire and bespeak the assistance of elders as well as big men,

THE BEGINNING OF THE END 295

and are glad when we get it. But whether or not such assistance is forthcoming, we are humbly of opinion that pledges must ever be scrupulously kept. We desire your support and your blessing in such observance.'

This cable, when it reached Gokhale, had an adverse effect upon his health, but he continued to help us with unabated or even greater zeal than before. He wired to Lord Hardinge on the matter but not only did he not throw us overboard, but he on the other hand defended our standpoint. Lord Hardinge too remained unmoved.

I went to Pretoria with Andrews. Just at this time there was a great strike of the European employees of the Union railways, which made the position of the Government extremely delicate. I was called upon to commence the Indian march at such a fortunate juncture. But I declared that the Indians could not thus assist the railway strikers, as they were not out to harass the Government, their struggle being entirely different and differently conceived. Even if we undertook the march, we would begin it at some other time when the railway trouble had ended. This decision of ours created a deep impression, and was cabled to England by Reuter. Lord Ampthill cabled his congratulations from England. English friends in South Africa too appreciated our decision. One of the secretaries of General Smuts jocularly said: 'I do not like your people, and do not care to assist them at all. But what am I to do? You help us in our days of need. How can we lay hands upon you? I often wish you took to violence like the English strikers, and then we would know at once how to dispose of you. But you will not injure even the enemy. You desire victory by self-suffering alone and never transgress your self-imposed limits of courtesy and chivalry. And that is what reduces us to sheer helplessness.' General Smuts also gave expression to similar sentiments.

I need scarcely suggest to the reader that this was not the first incident of chivalrous consideration for others being shown by the Satyagrahis. When the Indian labourers on the north coast went on strike, the planters at Mount Edgecombe would have been put to great losses if all the cane that had been cut was not brought to the mill and crushed. Twelve hundred Indians therefore returned to work solely with a view to finish this part of the work, and joined their compatriots only when it was finished. Again when the Indian employees of the Durban Municipality struck work, those who were engaged in the sanitary services of the borough or as attendants upon the patients in hospitals were sent back, and they willingly returned to their duties. If the sanitary services were dislocated, and if there was no one to attend upon the patients in hospitals, there might be an outbreak of disease in the city and the sick would be deprived of medical aid, and no Satyagrahi would wish for such consequences to ensue. Employees of this description were therefore exempted from the strike. In every step that he takes, the Satyagrahi is bound to consider the position of his adversary.

I could see that the numerous cases of such chivalry left their invisible yet potent impress everywhere, enhanced the prestige of the Indians, and prepared a suitable atmosphere for a settlement.

CHAPTER XLVIII

THE PROVISIONAL SETTLEMENT

The atmosphere was thus becoming favourable for a settlement. Sir Benjamin Robertson, who had been sent by Lord Hardinge in a special steamer, was to arrive about the same time that Mr Andrews and I went to Pretoria. But we did not wait for him and set out as we had to reach Pretoria on the day fixed by General Smuts. There was no reason indeed to await his arrival, as the final result could only be commensurate with our strength.

Mr Andrews and I reached Pretoria. But I alone was to interview General Smuts. The General was preoccupied with the railway strike, which was so serious in nature, that the Union Government had declared martial law. The European workmen not only demanded higher wages, but aimed at taking the reins of government into their hands. My first interview with the General was very short, but I saw that he today did not ride the same high horse as he did before, when the Great March began. At that time the General would not so much as talk with me. The threat of Satyagraha was the same then as it was now. Yet he had declined to enter into negotiations. But now he was ready to confer with me.

The Indians had demanded that a member should be co-opted to the commission to represent Indian interests. But on this point General Smuts would not give in. 'That cannot be done,' said he, 'as it would be derogatory to the Government's prestige, and I would be unable to carry out the desired reforms. You must understand that Mr Esselen is our man, and would fall in with, not oppose, the Government's wishes as regards reform. Colonel Wylie is a man of position in Natal and might even be considered anti-Indian. If therefore even he agrees to a repeal of the £3 tax, the Government will have an easy task before them. Our troubles are manyfold; we have not a moment to spare and therefore wish to set the Indian question at rest. We have decided to grant your demands, but for this we must have a recommendation from the commission. I understand your position too. You have solemnly declared that you will not lead evidence before it so long as there is no representative of the Indians sitting on the commission. I do not mind if you do not tender evidence, but you should not organize any active propaganda to prevent any one who wishes to give evidence from doing so, and should suspend Satyagraha in the interval. I believe that by so doing you will be serving your own interests as well as giving me a respite. As you will not tender evidence, you will not be able to prove your allegations as regards ill-treatment accorded to the Indian strikers. But that is for you to think over.'

Such were the suggestions of General Smuts, which on the whole I was inclined to receive favourably. We had made many complaints about ill-treatment of strikers by soldiers and warders, but the difficulty was that we were precluded by a boycott of the commission from proving our allegations. There was a difference of opinion among the Indians on this point. Some held that the charges levelled by the Indians against the soldiers must be proved, and therefore suggested that if the evidence could not be placed before the commission, we must challenge libel proceedings by publishing the authentic evidence in our possession. I disagreed with these friends. There was little likelihood of the commission giving a decision unfavourable to the Government. Challenging libel proceedings would land the community in endless trouble, and the net result would be the barren satisfaction of having proved the charges of ill-treatment. As a barrister, I was well aware of the difficulties of proving the truth of statements giving rise to libel proceedings. But my weightiest argument was, that the Satyagrahi is out to suffer. Even before Satyagraha was started, the Satyagrahis knew that they would have to suffer even unto death, and they were ready to undergo such suffering. Such being the case, there was no sense in proving now that they did suffer. A spirit of revenge being alien to Satyagraha, it was best for a Satyagrahi to hold his peace when he encountered extraordinary difficulties in proving the fact of his suffering. A Satyagrahi fights only for essentials. The essential thing was that the obnoxious laws should be repealed or suitably amended, and when this was fairly within his grasp, he need not bother himself with other things. Again a Satyagrahi's silence would at the time of settlement stand him in good stead in his resistance to unjust laws. With such arguments I was able to win over most of these friends who differed from me, and we decided to drop the idea of proving our allegations of ill-treatment.

CHAPTER XLIX
LETTERS EXCHANGED

Correspondence passed between General Smuts and myself, placing on record the agreement arrived at as the result of a number of interviews. My letter dated January 21, 1914 may be thus summarized:

'We have conscientious scruples with regard to leading evidence before the commission as constituted at present. You appreciate these scruples and regard them as honourable, but are unable to alter your decision. As, however, you have accepted the principle of consultation with the Indians, I will advise my countrymen not to hamper the labours of the commission by any active propaganda, and not to render the position of the Government difficult by reviving passive resistance, pending the result of the commission and the introduction of legislation during the forthcoming session. It will further be possible for us to assist Sir Benjamin Robertson who has been deputed by the Viceroy.

'As to our allegations of ill-treatment during the progress of the Indian strike in Natal, the avenue of proving them through the commission is closed to us by our solemn declaration to have nothing to do with it. As Satyagrahis we endeavour to avoid, as far as possible, any resentment of personal wrongs. But in order that our silence may not be mistaken, may I ask you to recognize our motive and reciprocate by not leading evidence of a negative character before the commission on the allegations in question?

'Suspension of Satyagraha, moreover, carries with it a prayer for the release of Satyagrahi prisoners.

'It might not be out of place here to recapitulate the points on which relief has been sought:

1. Repeal of the £3 tax;

2. Legalization of the marriages celebrated according to the rite of Hinduism, Islam, etc.;

3. The entry of educated Indians;

4. Alteration in the assurance as regards the Orange Free State;

5. An assurance that the existing laws especially affecting Indians will be administered justly, with due regard to vested rights.

'If you view my submission with favour, I shall be prepared to advise my countrymen in accordance with the tenor of this letter.'

General Smuts' reply of the same date was to this effect:

'I regret but understand your inability to appear before the commission. I also recognize the motive which makes you unwillling to revive old sores by courting libel proceedings before another tribunal. The Government repudiates the charges of harsh action against the Indian strikers. But as you will not lead evidence in support of those allegations, it would be futile for the Government to lead rebutting evidence in vindication of the conduct of its officers. As regards the release of Satyagrahi prisoners, the Government had already issued the necessary orders before your letter arrived. In regard to the grievances summarized at the end of your letter, the Government will await the recommendations of the commission before any action is taken.'

Mr Andrews and I had had frequent interviews with General Smuts before these letters were exchanged. But meanwhile Sir Benjamin Robertson too arrived at Pretoria. Sir Benjamin was looked upon as a popular official, and he brought a letter of recommendation from Gokhale, but I observed that he was not entirely free from the usual weakness of the English official. He had no sooner come than he began to create factions among the Indians and to bully the Satyagrahis. My first meeting with him in Pretoria did not prepossess me in his favour. I told him about the telegrams I had received informing me of his bullying procedure. I dealt with him, as indeed with every one else, in a frank and straightforward manner, and we therefore became friends. But I have often seen that officials are apt to bully those who will tamely submit to them, and will be correct with those who are correct themselves and will not be cowed down.

We thus reached a provisional agreement, and Satyagraha was suspended for the last time. Many English friends were glad of this, and promised their assistance in the final settlement. It was rather difficult to get the Indians to endorse this agreement. No one would wish that enthusiasm which had arisen should be allowed to subside. Again whoever would trust General Smuts? Some reminded me of the fiasco in 1908, and said, 'General Smuts once played us false, often charged you with forcing fresh issues, and subjected the community to endless suffering. And yet what a pity that you have not learnt the necessary lesson of declining to trust him! This man will betray you once again, and you will again propose to revive Satyagraha. But who will then listen to you? Is it possible that men should every now and then go to jail, and be ready to be faced with failure each time? With a man like General Smuts settlement is possible only if he actually delivers the goods. It is no use having his assurances. How can we any further trust a man who pledges his word and then breaks it?'

I knew that such arguments would be brought forward, and was not therefore surprised when they were. No matter how often a Satyagrahi is betrayed, he will repose his trust in the adversary so long as there are not cogent grounds for distrust. Pain to a Satyagrahi is the same as pleasure. He will not therefore be misled by the mere fear of suffering into groundless distrust. On the other hand, relying as he does upon his own strength, he will not mind being betrayed by the adversary, will continue to trust in spite of frequent betrayals, and will believe that he thereby strengthens the forces of truth and brings victory nearer. Meetings were therefore held in various places, and I was able at last to persuade the Indians to approve of the terms of the agreement. The Indians now came to a better understanding of the spirit of Satyagraha. Mr Andrews was the mediator and the witness in the present agreement, and then there was Sir Benjamin Robertson as representing the Government of India. There was therefore the least possible likelihood of the agreement being subsequently repudiated. If I had obstinately refused to accept the agreement, it would have become a count of indictment against the Indians, and the victory which was achieved in the next six months would have been beset with various obstacles. The author of the Sanskrit saying, 'Forgiveness is an ornament to the brave', drew upon his rich experience of Satyagrahis never giving any one the least opportunity of finding fault with them. Distrust is a sign of weakness and Satyagraha implies the banishment of all weakness and therefore of distrust, which is clearly out of place when the adversary is not to be destroyed but to be won over.

When the agreement was thus endorsed by the Indians, we had only to wait for the next session of the Union Parliament. Meanwhile the commission set to work. Only a very few witnesses appeared before it on behalf of the Indians, furnishing striking evidence of the great hold which the Satyagrahis had acquired over the community. Sir Benjamin Robertson tried to induce many to tender evidence but failed except in the case of a few who were strongly opposed to Satyagraha. The boycott of the commission did not produce any bad effect. Its work was shortened and its report was published at once. The commission strongly criticized the Indians for withholding their assistance and dismissed the charges of misbehaviour against the soldiers, but recommended compliance without delay with all the demands of the Indian community, such as for instance the repeal of the £3 tax and the validation of Indian marriages, and the grant of some trifling concessions in addition. Thus the report of the commission was favourable to the Indians as predicted by General Smuts. Mr Andrews left for England and Sir Benjamin Robertson for India. We had received an assurance that the requisite legislation would be undertaken with a view to implement the recommendations of the commission. What this legislation was and how it was brought forward will be considered in the next chapter.

CHAPTER L

THE END OF THE STRUGGLE

Within a short time of the issue of the report, the Government published in the official Gazette of the Union the Indians Relief Bill which was to effect a settlement of their long-standing dispute with the Indians; and I went at once to Cape Town where the Union Parliament sits. The Bill contained 9 sections and would take up only two columns of a paper like *Young India*. One part of it dealt with the question of Indian marriages and validated in South Africa the marriages which were held legal in India, except that if a man had more wives than one, only one of them would at any time be recognized as his legal wife in South Africa. The second part abolished the annual licence of £3 to be taken out by every indentured Indian labourer who failed to return to India and settled in the country as a free man on the completion of his indenture. The third part provided that the domicile certificates issued by the Government to Indians in Natal and bearing the thumb-impression of the holder of the permit should be recognized as conclusive evidence of the right of the holder to enter the Union as soon as his identity was established. There was a long and pleasant debate over the bill in the Union Parliament.

Administrative matters which did not come under the Indians Relief Bill were settled by correspondence between General Smuts and me, as for example, safeguarding the educated Indians' right of entry into the Cape Colony, allowing 'specially exempted' educated Indians to enter South Africa, the status of educated Indians who had entered South Africa within the last three years, and permitting existing plural wives to join their husbands in South Africa. After dealing with all these points, General Smuts, in his letter of June 30, 1914, added:

'With regard to the administration of existing laws, it has always been and will continue to be the desire of the

Government to see that they are administered in a just manner and with due regard to vested rights.'

I replied to the above letter to this effect:

'I beg to acknowledge receipt of your letter of even date. I feel deeply grateful for the patience and courtesy which you showed during our discussions.

'The passing of the Indians Relief Bill and this correspondence finally closed the Satyagraha struggle which commenced in the Septemper of 1906 and which to the Indian community cost much physical suffering and pecuniary loss and to the Government much anxious thought and consideration.

'As you are aware, some of my countrymen have wished me to go further. They are dissatisfied that the Trade Licence laws of the different provinces, the Transvaal Gold Law, the Transvaal Townships Act, the Transvaal Law 3 of 1885 have not been altered so as to give them full rights of residence, trade and ownership of land. Some of them are dissatisfied that full inter-provincial migration is not permitted, and some are dissatisfied that on the marriage question the Relief Bill goes no further than it does. They have asked me that all the above matters might be included in the Satyagraha struggle. I have been unable to comply with their wishes. Whilst, therefore, they have not been included in the programme of Satyagraha, it will not be denied that some day or other these matters will require further and sympathetic consideration by the Government. Complete satisfaction cannot be expected until full civic rights have been conceded to the resident Indian population.

'I have told my countrymen that they will have to exercise patience, and by all honourable means at their disposal educate public opinion so as to enable the Government of the day to go further than the present correspondence does. I shall hope when the Europeans of South Africa fully appreciate the fact that now the importation of indentured labour from India is prohibited, and the Immigrants Regulation Act of last year has in practice all but stopped further free Indian immigration, and that my countrymen do not entertain any political ambition, they, the Europeans, will see the justice and indeed the necessity of my countrymen being granted the rights I have just referred to.

Meanwhile, if the generous spirit that the Government have applied to the treatment of the problem during the past few months continues to be applied, as promised in your letter, in the administration of the existing laws, I am quite certain that the Indian community throughout the Union will be able to enjoy some measure of peace and never be a source of trouble to the Government.'

CONCLUSION

Thus the great Satyagraha struggle closed after eight years, and it appeared that the Indians in South Africa were now at peace. On July 18, 1914, I sailed for England, to meet Gokhale, on my way back to India, with mixed feelings of pleasure and regret,—pleasure because I was returning home after many years and eagerly looked forward to serving the country under Gokhale's guidance, regret because it was a great wrench for me to leave South Africa, where I had passed twenty-one years of my life sharing to the full in the sweets and bitters of human experience, and where I had realized my vocation in life.

When one considers the painful contrast between the happy ending of the Satyagraha struggle and the present condition of the Indians in South Africa, one feels for a moment as if all this suffering had gone for nothing, or is inclined to question the efficacy of Satyagraha as a solvent of the problems of mankind. Let us here consider this point for a little while. There is a law of nature that a thing can be retained by the same means by which it has been acquired. A thing acquired by violence can be retained by violence alone, while one acquired by truth can be retained only by truth. The Indians in South Africa, therefore, can ensure their safety today if they can wield the weapon of Satyagraha. There are no such miraculous properties in Satyagraha, that a thing acquired by truth could be retained even when truth was given up. It would not be desirable even if it was possible. If therefore the position of Indians in South Africa has now suffered deterioration, that argues the absence of Satyagrahis among them. There is no question here of finding fault with the present generation of South African Indians, but of merely stating the facts of the case. Individuals or bodies of individuals cannot borrow from others qualities which they themselves do not possess. The Satyagrahi veterans passed away one after another. Sorabji, Kachhalia, Thambi Naidoo, Parsi Rustomji and others are no more, and there are very few now

CONCLUSION

who passed through the fire of Satyagraha. The few that remain are still in the fighting line, and I have not a shadow of a doubt that they will be the saviours of the community on the day of its trial if the light of Satyagraha is burning bright within them.

Finally, the reader of these pages has seen that had it not been for this great struggle and for the untold sufferings which many Indians invited upon their devoted heads, the Indians today would have been hounded out of South Africa. Nay, the victory achieved by Indians in South Africa more or less served as a shield for Indian emigrants in other parts of the British Empire, who, if they are suppressed, will be suppressed thanks to the absence of Satyagraha among themselves, and to India's inability to protect them, and not because of any flaw in the weapon of Satyagraha. I will consider myself amply repaid if I have in these pages demonstrated with some success that Satyagraha is a priceless and matchless weapon, and that those who wield it are strangers to disappointment or defeat.

INDEX

ABDUL GANI, 95
Abdul Kadar Bavazir=Imam Saheb *q.v.*
Abdulla Haji Adam Jhaveri, Sheth, 39
Abdul Rahman, Doctor, 12
Abubakar Amad, Sheth, 21, 30
Accounts, the importance of keeping proper, 114-15
Adajania, Sorabji Shapurji, 192 ff.
Adam, Sheth Haji, 40
Adamji Miyankhan, 45
Agreements, golden rule for interpreting, 17
Ahmedabad, Satyagraha of the millhands in, xiii
Aiyar, Sir Subramanya, 48
Albrecht, 230
Alexander, Mrs, helps to save the author from being lynched, 54-55
Alexander, Police Superintendent, contrives to save the author from mob fury, 54 ff., 170
Ali, 124
Ali, H.O., 110 ff.
Allahabad, 46
Amad Bhayat, Sheth, 280
Ampthill, Lord, 209 ff., 295
Anandacharulu, P., 48
Andrews, C.F., 163, 247, 291-92, 294, 295, 296, 300, 302

Asiatic Department created, 77 ff., 79 ff.
Asiatic Law Amendment Ordinance, 90 ff.
Asiatic Registration Act, 117 ff.
Avesta, the, 220

BADARI SHIVPUJAN, 256
Badruddin Tyabji, 46
Bagasra, xii
Balfour, 280-81
Banerji, Surendranath, 48
Basutos, the, 7
Beauty, false notions of, 8
Bechuanas, the, 7
Bhagavata, the, 9
Bhandarkar, Professor, 47 ff.
Bhavani Dayal, Mrs, 253
Bhownuggree, Sir Muncherjee, 61 ff., 110 ff.
Bible, the, 10
Biharilal Maharaj, 277
Bloemfontein, 4, 167
Bloemfontein jail, 283
Boers, the, 13; compel 'natives' to till land for them, 13; come into conflict with the English and 'trek' into the interior, 13; love their own language, 14-5; their large farms, 14; love of liberty, 14; their women equally brave, 14, 15; their religion, 15

INDEX

Boer War, the, 13, 62 ff.; Indian ambulance corps in, 69 ff.
Bombay, xii, 45, 48, 75
Booth, Dr, 70
Boston tea party, 187
Botha, General, 14, 16 ff., 101, 121 ff., 144, 168, 209 ff., 243, 245
Briscoe, Dr, 269, 272
Buller, General, 71

CALCUTTA, 45, 48, 235
Campbell-Bannerman, Sir Henry, 16, 18
Cape Colony, the, 5, 12, 18, 23, 33; Indian grievances in, 33 ff.
Cape of Good Hope, 5
Cape Town, 5, 6, 7, 12, 33, 239
Cartwright, Albert, 142 ff., 167, 181
Chamberlain, 57 ff., 63, 75, 76
Chamney, 155 ff., 279, 281
Champaran, Satyagraha in, xii, xiii, 78
Charlestown, 264, 267 ff., 270 ff.,
Chelmsford, Lord, xii
Chesney, 46
Christ, 11, 15, 106, 159
Christopher, A., 268-69
Clifford, Dr, 104
Clothes, the philosophy of, 9
'Colour Bar' in legislation, 27, 81 ff.
Co-education on Tolstoy Farm, 221 ff.
Constitution of the Union of South Africa, how framed, 17 ff.

Courland, s.s., 48 ff.
Crewe, Lord, 208
Cronje, General, 13, 74
Cullinan, the, the world's largest diamond, 4
Curtis, Lionel, 87, 89, 101
Curzon, Lord, 73

DADA ABDULLA, Indian firm in Durban, 37-39, 48 ff.
Dadabhai Naoroji, 60 ff., 110 ff.
Dadibarjor, Dr, 55
Daily Mail, the, 187
Daily Star, the, 142
Damania, N., 216
Daud Muhammad, Sheth, 170, 197 ff.
Deccan Sabha, 46 ff.
Defence of India Act, 87
Delagoa Bay, 4, 35, 164
Deportation to India, Satyagrahis punished with, 202 ff.
Desai, Pragji Khandubhai, 197, 217, 220
De Wet, General, 14
Dharma-yuddha, xiv
Dick, Miss, 164
Diepkloof prison, hunger strike in, 206
Doctor, Mrs, J.M., 256
Doke, Miss Olive, 157
Doke, Rev. J., 131, 154 ff., 165, 167
Doukhobors of Russia, 106
Drew, Rev. Dewdney, 167
Drugless healing on Tolstoy Farm, 226 ff., 232 ff.
Duncan, 101
Dundee, 281-82

Durban, 4, 6, 7, 38-39, 50 ff., 131, 161, 163, 169 ff., 264 ff.; the author mobbed in, 54

EDWARD, KING, 15
Elgin, Lord, 26, 110 ff., 112; his crooked policy, 115 ff.
Ellis, 240
Emigration Act, the Indian, xii
Empire, the British, 18
English, the, in South Africa 13; defeated by the Dutch at Majuba, 13; in Natal, 19
Escombe, Harry, 20, 41, 50, 69
Esselen, 292, 297
Europeans' argument for excluding Indians from South Africa, 83-84
European traders, their relations with Negroes, 22-23

FARRAR, SIR GEORGE, 113
Food on Tolstoy Farm, 224-25
Fourth Resolution, the famous, 95
Friend, the, 167

GANDHI, C. K., 256
Gandhi, Harilal Mohandas, 197
Gandhi, Maganlal Khushalchand, 102, 163, 291
Gandhi, Mrs Kasturba, 255-56
Gandhi, Mrs K.C., 256
Gandhi, Mrs S.M., 256
Gandhi, Mohandas Karamchand, the author, leaves India for South Africa in Dada Abdulla's case, 37; lands in Durban, 38; is pushed out of the train at Maritzburg and insulted in other ways, 38-39; but sees the case through, 39; admitted as advocate of the Supreme Court of Natal, 41; helps to found the Natal Indian Congress, 41 ff.; and the Natal Indian Educational Association, 43; returns to India, 44; writes pamphlet on condition of Indians in South Africa, 46; meets Lokamanya, 46; and Gokhale, 47; addresses meetings in Poona and Madras, 47-48; recalled to South Africa, 48; mobbed in Durban, 53-54; but declines to prosecute assailants, 58 ff.; serves upon the ambulance corps in the Boer War, 69; returns to India and starts practice in Bombay, but is called to South Africa again, 75; opens an attorney's office in Johannesburg, 79; joins the Indian Stretcher-bearer Corps in the Zulu 'rebellion', 90 ff.; his speech adumbrating Satyagraha, 97 ff.; serves on deputation to England, 110; starts *Indian Opinion* and founds Phoenix Settlement, 131 ff.; gets two months' imprisonment, 137 ff.; his experiences in Johannesburg jail, 138 ff.; comes to terms with the Government on behalf of the Indians, 142 ff.; but is opposed and assaul-

INDEX

ted, 148 ff.; nursed by the Dokes, 154 ff.; his attempt to cast out fear, 171; charged with cunning, 189; in prison again, 201; goes to England on a second deputation, 207 ff.; writes *Hind Swaraj*, 211; his experiment of co-education, 222 ff.; experiments in drugless healing, 225 ff., 232 ff.; rejection of milk, 234-35; insistence upon speaking in the mother tongue, 242; requests Gokale to speak in Marathi, 242-43; meets the mine-owners in connection with Indian labourers' strike, 265 ff.; goes with the strikers to Charlestown, 267 ff.; and with them crosses over into the Transvaal, 270 ff.; gets nine months' imprisonment at Dundee, 282; and three months' at Volksrust, 282; released after six weeks, 292; meets General Smuts, 296 ff.; negotiates provisional agreement, 299 ff.; his letter to General Smuts marking the end of the Satyagraha struggle, 303 ff.; leaves South Africa for England en route to India, 306

Gandhi, R. M., 256
Germiston, 103, 128
Ghelani, M. M., 201
Ghorkhodu Rustomji Jivanji = Parsi Rustomji *q. v.*
Gibson, J.C., 154
Gita, the Bhagavad, 222

Godfrey, George, 77
Gokhale, Gopal Krishna, 34, 46; the author meets, 47, 74, 163, 194; his visit to Tolstoy Farm, 226; tour in South Africa, 237 ff., 248 ff., 253, 279, 286, 291, 300, 306
Gokuldas, H., 256
Govindarajulu, V., 256
Greylingstad, 279-80
Griffin, Sir Lepel, 110
Gujarat, xiii, 21
Gujarati, 43, 91, 95, 122, 131-32, 220, 222, 225, 254

HABIB, SHETH HAJI, 95 ff., 101, 208 ff.
Harbatsinh, 283
Hardinge, Lord, 247, 286, 294, 295, 296
Heidelberg, 280
Henry on finger prints, 93
Hertzog, General, 14, 208
Hind Swaraj (Indian Home Rule), 211, 212
Hindi, 95, 131, 225
Hindu, the, 48
Hobhouse, Miss, 167
Hosken, 103 ff., 122 ff., 166, 181
Hunger strike in jail, 206
Hunter, Sir W. W., 20, 61 ff., 110
Husen Daud, 198

IMAM SAHEB, 200
Indentured Indian labour, stopping of, xii
India, Government of, 19 ff.
Indian Ambulance Corps in the Boer War, 69

Indian immigration restricted in Natal, 28-29

Indian labourers reach Natal, 19-20; their condition bordering on slavery, 20, 21; Europeans' agitation against them, 24; poll-tax imposed upon them upon expiry of indenture, 26; strike work, 257, 260 ff.; march into the Transvaal, 267 ff.; sent back to Natal and cruelly compelled to work, 285 ff.; but secure a repeal of the poll-tax in the end, 303

Indian Opinion, 90, 91, 101, 102, 131, 134, 163, 165 ff., 169, 171, 181, 182, 211, 214, 249, 253, 290

Indian settlers, their hardships in Natal, 24 ff.; in the Transvaal, 29 ff.; in Orangia, 32, 33; in the Cape Colony, 33 ff.; divided among themselves, 35-36; their resistance to an attempt to disfranchise them in Natal, 40; form ambulance corps in the Boer War, 69 ff.; undergo voluntary registration, 88; and get the Asiatic Ordinance as reward, 89 ff.; raise a Stretcher-bearer Corps in the Zulu 'rebellion', 90 ff.; declare Satyagraha against the Asiatic Act, 95 ff.; send a deputation to England, 108 ff.; inaugurate a fresh body for Satyagraha struggle, 119; send 150 of their number to jail, 141; reach with General Smuts a settlement, 142 ff.; which is repudiated, 173 ff.; send an ultimatum to the Transvaal Government, 182 ff.; make a bonfire of registration certificates, 185 ff.; charged with forcing fresh issue, 188 ff., send a second deputation to England, 207 ff. etc.

Indians, 'free', 21-22

Indians Relief Bill, 303

Indian Stretcher-bearer Corps in the Zulu 'rebellion', 90 ff.

Indian traders enter South Africa, 21; their relations with Negroes, 22 ff.; disfranchised in Natal, 27; restrictions imposed upon them, 28

Iyengar, Bhashyam, 48

JAIL, JOHANNESBURG, author's experiences in, 138 ff.; clothing in, 138, 139; diet in 140 ff.

Jail, Pretoria, 201

Jail, Volksrust, 201, 283

Jameson, Dr, his raid on Johannesburg, 62

Java, 12

Johannesburg, 3, 4, 18, 62 ff., 79, 89, 90, 91, 103, 121, 138, 142, 145, 164, 169, 185, 194 ff., 214, 218, 239 ff.

John King of Portugal, 5

Joshi, H. I., 91

Juhu, xiv, xv

KACHHALIA, A.M., 123 ff., 137, 159, 165, 176 ff., 194, 280, 290

Kallenbach, H., 164 ff., 214, 215, 216, 219 ff., 227-31,

235, 239 ff., 245-46, 268, 272, 275-76, 277, 282-83, 284, 292
Kashmir, 3
Kenilworth Castle, s.s., 208
Kheda, Satyagraha in, xiii
Khilafat wrong, Satyagraha against, xiii
Kildonan Castle, s.s., 211
Kitchener, Lord, 15, 17, 74, 167
Kitchin, Herbert, 131, 166
Klerksdorp, 239
Kohinoor, the, 4
Koran, the, 20
Kotval, P.K., 225, 227
Kruger, President, 14, 30-31, 63
Krugersdorp, 239

LADYSMITH, 65, 71, 72 ff.
Landsdowne, Lord, 30, 75
Laughton, F.A., 50
Lawley, 214, 232
Lawley, Sir Arthur, 79
Lazarus, D., 261-62, 264
Locations, Indians segregated in, 32
Lukin, General, 288
Lutavan, 233

MADANJIT VYAVAHARIK, 161 ff.
Madeira, 112, 115, 117
Madras, 41, 48, 204, 286
Madras Standard, the, 48
Majuba Hill, 13
Malays, the, 12, 33
Marathi, Gokhale requested to speak in, 242-43
Mariannhill, Trappist monastery at, 219

Maritzburg = Pietermartizburg *q. v.*
Mauritius, 21, 136
Meat excluded from Tolstoy Farm, 215-16
Medh, S.B., 91, 197
Mehta, Dr. Pranjivan Jagjivan, 193
Mehta, Sir Pherozeshah Merwanji, 46, 258
Mehtab, Bai Fatma, 270
Merriman, 34, 208
Milk, the propriety of rejecting, 235
Milner, Lord, 16 ff., 64, 65, 79, 80, 82, 87, 142, 167
Mir Alam, 154 ff., 172, 187
Mirabai, 271
Molteno, Miss, 168
Molteno, Sir John, 34
Moodaley, Jack, 171
Morley, Lord, 29, 110, 208
Moses, 15
Motilal, the Vadhvan worker, xi
Mudaliar, K. M., 256
Mudaliar, Valliamma, 258-59
Mudalingam, Mrs, R.A., 253

NADERI, s.s. 48 ff.
Nagappan, Swami, 205 ff.
Naidoo, Mrs A. P., 253
Naidoo, Mrs P. K., 253
Naidoo, Mrs Thambi, 253
Naidoo, P. K., 204, 268, 276-77
Naidoo, Thambi, 136, 137, 144, 154, 217
Nanabhai Haridas, Mr Justice, 51
Narayanswami, 206

Natal, 4, 5, 18, 19 ff.; Indians' grievances in, 24 ff., 34, 48, 49, 81; *passim*

Natal Indian Congress, the, founded, 42 ff.

Natal Indian Educational Association founded, 43

Natal Mercury, the 39-40

Natesan, G.A., 204

Navajivan, 47

Nawabkhan, 142

Nazar, M. H., 51, 62, 74, 131

Negroes, the, of South Africa, 7; their physique, 7-8; huts, 8; clothing, 9; food innocent of spices or condiments, 9-10; languages, 10; religion, 10; truthfulness, 10; timidity, 10-11; 'civilization' leads them into vice and disease, 11-12, 19; their relations with Indian and European traders, 22

Newcastle, 254, 257, 260, 266, 269

Norton, Mr, 48

ORANGE FREE STATE= Orangia, *q. v.*

Orangia, 4, 13, 23; Indian grievances in, 32 ff.

Orloff, the, 4

PALMFORD, 275

Parbhusingh, an Indian, assigned most responsible work at the siege of Ladysmith, 73

Parsi Rustomji, 52 ff., 170, 197, 204, 256

Passive Resistance, phrase first used to denote the Indian struggle but since given up, 102; distinguished from Satyagraha, 103

Patel, M. H., 256

Patel, R. M., 256

Peace Preservation Ordinance, 87

Pearson, Willie, 163, 247, 292

Permanent funds, the impropriety of managing public bodies with, 120

Petit, Mrs Jaiji, xii

Phillips, Rev. Charles, 167

Phoenix, 90, 91, 131, 163, 169, ff, 200, 214, 250, 253, 286, 290

Phuka, the cruel practice of, 235

Pietermartizburg, 4; author pushed out of the train at, 38, 39

Pietermaritzburg jail, 258

Pillai Parameshvaran, 48

Pillay, Miss B. M., 253

Pillay, Miss Minachi, 253

Pillay, Mrs K.C., 253

Pillay, Mrs K. Murugasa, 253

Pillay, Mrs N., 253

Pillay, Mrs N. S., 253

Pioneer, the, 46

Polak, H. S. L., 131, 163, 279 ff., 292 ff.

Poll-tax on Indian labourers, 26

Poona, 46 ff.

Porbandar, 21, 37, 48

Portugal, 5

Portuguese, the, 4

Potchefstroom, 239

INDEX

Pretoria, 4, 37, 39 ff., 75 ff., 120, 121, 137, 145, 199, 238, 243 ff., 295, 296

Pretoria News, the 167

Progression, law of, applicable to all righteous movements, 190-92

Punjab wrong, the Satyagraha against, xiii

QUINN, LEUNG, 135, 144

RAGHU NARASU, 277
Rahimkhan, 277
Rajendraprasad, Babu, xii
Rajkot, xii
Raju Govindu, 256
Rama Sundara, Pandit, 128
Ramzan on Tolstoy Farm, 225
Ranade, Mahadev Govind, 46
Redmond, 111
Reuter sends exaggerated summary of the author's speeches to South Africa, 48
Rickshaw, the author spared the shame of a—ride, 53
Ripon, Lord, 27, 40, 43
Ritch, L. W., 111, 112, 115, 163, 237
Roberts, Lord, 13
Robertson, Sir Benjamin, 296, 299, 300, 301, 302
Rose Inns, Sir James, 293
Roosevelt, President, 85
Rowlatt Act, the, xiii, Satyagraha against, xiii
Royeppen, Joseph, 200, 217
Royeppen, Solomon, 256
Rule, the golden, for the interpretation of agreements, 17

SAIYAD IBRAHIM, 260,
Sandals made on Tolstoy Farm, 219-20
Sanitary arrangements on Tolstoy Farm, 218-19
Sarvajanik Sabha, 46 ff.
Satyagraha, advent of, 95 ff; implications of, xiv, 16, 86-87, 172-73, 191-92, 260, 278; invention of the term, 102; distinguished from passive resistance, 103; fresh association organized for, 119 ff.
Satyagraha in India in respect of Viramgam customs, xi, xii; as regards the stopping of indentured labour, xii; in Champaran, xii, xiii; by the mill-hands in Ahmedabad, xiii; in Kheda, xiii; against the Rowlatt Act, xiii; against Khilafat and Punjab wrongs, xiii, xiv; for Swaraj, xiii, xiv
Satyagrahis keen upon keeping promises, 231; their chivalry, 294-96
Saunders, 48
Saurashtra, xii, 21, 37
Savage, Dr, 90
Schlesin, Miss Sonja, 164 ff., 268, 290
Schreiner, Olive, 34, 168 ff.
Schreiner, W.P., 34, 239, 293
Searle, Mr Justice, 251 ff.
Selborne, Lord, 30, 75, 79
Servants, no domestic—on Tolstoy Farm, 215
Shelat, U.M., 91
Shukadeva, 9
Sinha, Ramnarayan, 277

Smuts, General, 14, 16, 83, 121 ff., 142 ff.; his breach of faith (?), 173 ff., 189 ff., 208 ff., 243, 248, 273, 278, 291 ff.
Snakes on Tolstoy Farm, 230 ff.
Socrates, 271
Sodha, Ratansi Mulji, 197
Sodha, Revashankar R., 256
Solomon, Sir Richard, 115 ff.
Sorabji Rustomji, 288
South Africa, climate, 3; geography, 4 ff.; cereals, fruits etc., 5, 6; cattle, 5; landscape 6; rivers, 6 ff.; agriculture, 6; seasons and rainfall, 7; the Negroes of, 7 ff.; area and population, 7 ff.; the Dutch in, 12 ff.; the Malays in, 12; Indians in, 19 ff.
Standerton, 279
Stead, W.T., 16, 167
Stent, Vere, 167
Subramanyam, G., 48
Subramanyam, Indian labourer, assaulted by his master, 49
Surat, 21
Swaraj, the fight for, xiii, xiv
Swazis, the, 7
Symonds, 113

TAAL, THE BOER LANGUAGE, 13
Table Mountain, 6
Tagore, Maharaja J.M., 48
Taib Haji Khanmamad, Indian firm in Pretoria, 37
Tamil, 95, 131, 220, 221, 254
Tata, Sir Ratanji, 212

Teaching children on Tolstoy Farm, 220
Teakworth, 209
Telugu, 95, 220, 221, 254
Testament, the New, 15
Testament, the Old, 15, 31
Theatre, Empire (Johannesburg), Indians declare Satyagraha at meeting in, 95 ff.
Thwaites, Dr, 156
Tibet, 3
Tilak, Lokamanya, 47 ff.
Tolstoy, 106, 173
Tolstoy Farm, 124, 212 ff., 272
Transvaal, the, gold and diamond mines in, 4, 13, 23; Indian grievances in, 29 ff., 35, 74; *passim*
Transvaal Immigrants Restriction Act, 188
Transvaal Leader, the, 142, 277
Tulsidas, 260

UNION, THE, OF SOUTH AFRICA, 17

VADHVAN, xi
Vereeniging, the Peace of, 16, 17, 253
Vernon, Police Superintendent, 144, 196
Verulam, 286, 287
Victoria, Queen, 13
Vihari, 217
Viramgam customs cordon, Satyagraha as regards, xi, xii, xiv
Volksrust, 195, 199, 264, 270, 273 ff., 282

WASHINGTON, BOOKER T., 85
Weakness, the duty of judging —charitably, 130, 206
Wedderburn, Sir W., 60 ff., 111
West, Albert, 160, 290, 291
West, Miss Ada, 162, 290
White, General, 71
Wylie, Col., 292, 297

YAJNIK, INDULAL, xiv
Yeravda Jail, xiv
Young India, 47
Yusuf Mian, 121, 145, 154, 177, 187

ZANZIBAR, 164, 243, 245
Zulu 'rebellion', Indian stretcher-bearers in, 90
Zulus, the, 7 ff., 19

INDEX

WASHINGTON, BOOKER T., 85
Weakness, the duty of judging —charitably, 130, 206
Wedderburn, Sir W., 60 ff., 111
West, Albert, 160, 290, 291
West, Miss Ada, 162, 290
White, General, 71
Wylie, Col., 292, 297

YAJNIK, INDULAL, xiv
Yeravda Jail, xiv
Young India, 47
Yusuf Mian, 121, 145, 154, 177, 187

ZANZIBAR, 164, 243, 245
Zulu 'rebellion', Indian stretcher-bearers in, 90
Zulus, the, 7 ff., 19